ANTHONY WOODVILLE

‘Speak my name so that I may live again.’

Ancient Egyptian epitaph

ANTHONY WOODVILLE

SOPHISTICATE OR SCHEMER?

DANIELLE BURTON

AMBERLEY

First published 2024

Amberley Publishing
The Hill, Stroud
Gloucestershire, GL5 4EP

www.amberley-books.com

ISBN 978 1 3981 1469 2 (hardback)
ISBN 978 1 3981 1470 8 (ebook)

British Library Cataloguing in Publication Data.
A catalogue record for this book is available from the British Library.

1 2 3 4 5 6 7 8 9 10

Typesetting by SJmagic DESIGN SERVICES, India.
Printed in the UK.

CONTENTS

Acknowledgements 7

Preface 10

List of Illustrations 12

Introduction 14

1 The Woodville Family and Their Connections 20

2 After the Royal Wedding 35

3 Marriages and an Illegitimate Child 55

4 Military Career 74

5 Tournament Champion 92

6 Connections with Burgundy 101

7 Man of Letters and Patron of William Caxton 112

8 Governor of the Household of Edward, Prince of Wales 129

9 Piety 142

10 Stony Stratford and Execution 148

11 Legacy 169

Appendix 1: Anthony Woodville's will 176

Appendix 2: Final poem 181

Appendix 3: List of lordships and manors 183

Appendix 4: Extract from *On the Recovery of the Throne by Edward IV* 188

Appendix 5: Members of the council of Edward, Prince of Wales 191

Endnotes 193

Bibliography 227

Index 248

ACKNOWLEDGEMENTS

There have been many people along the way who have offered me encouragement, support and guidance in writing this book. I would like to give a special thank you to the following for all of their help and support.

I would first like to offer my thanks to Amberley Publishing for allowing me to write my first book on the topic I love the most. A special thanks go to Connor Stait and Nikki Embery for their help.

I would not have been able to complete this book without the help and support of my family. I apologise for the amount of time it has taken up. I would especially like to thank my Dad for being my proofreader and my Mum for always being a good sounding board for discussions and ideas. I would also like to thank them, as well as my sister Louise, for our stay at Ludlow Castle. It was very special to be in one of the only places left standing that has a connection to Anthony. And it was well worth it for taking some of the photographs needed for this book. A big thank you to my other sister, Tracy, brother-in-law, Sean, and nieces, Lara and Emma, who were under orders to take photographs for me on their visit to Carisbrooke Castle.

There are many friends who have also listened to my ideas along the way. A special mention to Paige and Kyle for being so supportive throughout, as well as buying me a special author's pen. I would like to say thank you to the many Twitter followers who have helped find sources for me, as well as offering a lot of encouragement. I am incredibly grateful for that. Special thanks go to Laura Adkins for her help with images of Pontefract Castle and Amy McElroy for her patience in teaching me how to format the notes.

Kevin Wilson and Alan Archer, volunteers at Pontefract and Sandal Castles, have been particularly helpful in their discussions of Anthony Woodville's execution. I thank them for their insider knowledge and support throughout the whole writing process.

I want to give a very special thanks and acknowledgement to my lecturers at the University of Derby. You all helped me gain the confidence I needed to get this done. I would like to give a mention to Dr Cath Feely, who has been a particular help and support through the years. Your kindness will never be forgotten.

Thank you to all of my colleagues at the Derbyshire Record Office. Your enthusiasm for this project has always meant a lot. I cannot mention my colleagues without giving special credit to Neil, who is a very dear friend as well as a colleague. He has been a godsend in terms of translating and understanding some of the primary source material, especially from Latin.

The staff at the National Archives at Kew, as well the archives in the Isle of Wight and Norfolk have been very helpful in providing primary source material at a time when travelling to see them has been a particular challenge, through Covid and personal injury. Likewise, the staff at the University of Nottingham's Hallward Library have been a great help.

Another person who deserves special mention is Graham Turner. As an artist who specialises in historical warfare, including the Wars of the Roses, and a former jouster himself, he has been especially helpful in giving insight into the Smithfield Tournament and what it would have looked like. We have had some very interesting discussions.

Thanks also to the Richard III Society, of which I have been a member for nearly two decades now. The chairman, Matt Lewis, has been very helpful and supportive whenever I have had queries.

A big thank you to Amanda Geary for her very lovely photos of the church at Grafton Regis frequented by the Woodville family. Thanks also to Anne Ayres, secretary of the Notts & Derby group I have attended for as long as I have been a Richard III Society member, for her help with the subtitle of this book.

If I have left anyone out at all, then please accept my apologies.

PREFACE

This book began with a visit to Pontefract Castle. At the time all I knew of Anthony Woodville was his execution at Pontefract, along with his nephew Richard Grey and Thomas Vaughan, who were all members of the household of the Prince of Wales, on the orders of the future Richard III. As a self-confessed Ricardian, this information has always confused me. How could two men who were friendly with each other due to their familial connection to Edward IV have ended their relationship in such a way? This is what started my research into the life of Anthony Woodville, as well as watching the BBC series *The White Queen* (2013), in which Anthony was portrayed as a loyal family man, even if he was rather sullen.

At Pontefract Castle, I asked the staff questions about where he would have been held and under what sort of conditions. To my disappointment, Anthony Woodville was virtually unknown to them, for the site's interpretation mostly dealt with Richard II's death there. While I understand the fate of a deposed king was probably more important than Anthony's execution, I was still surprised. How could a brother of a queen and a man executed on the orders of one of England's most well-known kings be forgotten?

On that visit to Pontefract Castle, I made a vow to myself to discover more about Anthony, this intriguing forgotten man, in the hope of bringing his story to others. That journey started in 2015, the summer after I started my history degree at the University of Derby. Since then, my research on Anthony Woodville has uncovered a man who fits the modern conception of a medieval knight: a man of chivalry who participated in battles and tournaments, honoured women of the court and even had literary talent. In many ways, I saw similarities to Heath Ledger in *A Knight's Tale*, minus the peasant background.

I have visited the very few places that are connected to Anthony in some way, and I believe that it is this paucity of sites linking us to the man that has caused history to leave him behind. Hopefully, this book will redress some of this neglect and allow for further study of the life and times of Anthony Woodville, Earl Rivers and Baron Scales.

LIST OF ILLUSTRATIONS

1. 'Engraving of Earl Rivers Presenting His Book and Caxton, His Printer, to Edward IV'. (Yale Center for British Art)
2. Engraving of Queen Elizabeth Woodville. (British Library)
3. St Mary the Virgin Church, Grafton Regis, Northamptonshire. (Courtesy of Amanda Geary)
4. Stained glass window of Edward IV at St Laurence's, Ludlow. (Author's collection)
5. Plan of the Battle of Towton. (British Library)
6. Gateway of Carisbrooke Castle, Isle of Wight. (Courtesy of Lara Green)
7. Stained glass window depicting Richard, Duke of York, at St Laurence's, Ludlow. (Author's collection)
8. Engraving of St Mary Overy. (British Library)
9. The manor house at Middleton. (Author's collection)
10. Later engraving of King's Lynn. (British Library)
11. The White Tower at the Tower of London. (Author's collection)
12. William Caxton showing the work of his printing press to King Edward IV. (British Library)
13. Stained glass window of Edward V at St Laurence's, Ludlow. (Author's collection)

14. Ludlow Castle. (Author's collection)
15. The chapel at Ludlow Castle. (Author's collection)
16. St Laurence's Church at Ludlow. (Author's collection)
17. Denbigh Castle. (Author's collection)
18. Later engraving of Santiago de Compostela. (British Library)
19. Engraving of Richard III. (British Library)
20. Pontefract Castle. (Courtesy of Laura Adkins)

INTRODUCTION

Since the body of Richard III was found in 2012, there has been a resurgence of interest in the period known as the Wars of the Roses. This turbulent period has been seen as the last bloody flowering of the medieval age. While there is no doubt that there were violent clashes between the First Battle of St Albans in 1455 and the Battle of Stoke in 1487, J. R. Lander for one has suggested that there has been some overemphasis on conflict in the public perception of the period. He has shown that between the two battles there was only a dozen weeks' worth of fighting in the thirty-two years between them.[1] In fact, compared with Continental Europe, England enjoyed a period of relative peace. The war was fought in the names of the Houses of York and Lancaster, but these are not terms that would necessarily have been employed at the time; they are later inventions used to describe the infighting between the royal cousins, hence the conflict's other name, 'the Cousins' War'.

The role Anthony Woodville, second Earl Rivers, played in culture and society during the period of the late fifteenth century known as the Wars of the Roses has always been overshadowed by the life of his much more famous sister, Queen Elizabeth Woodville. The standing he gained from his sister's marriage to Edward IV is usually all that is noted; but Anthony was a champion jouster who knew how to create a spectacle on the tournament field, most notably at Smithfield against the Bastard of Burgundy. He was also the most influential of printing pioneer William Caxton's patrons in England, having translated many of the first books to be printed by him in Westminster. Knowing Woodville's connections with Burgundy, where Caxton first printed books, it is quite possible that Anthony was the one to initiate Caxton's move to England.

Yet, Anthony's importance in the creation of late fifteenth-century culture has been overlooked. While he has been an elusive figure due to gaps in the contemporary sources concerning his life, he deserves more credit than he has previously been given. Even so, there is still enough to reveal him. What has been left behind about Anthony is sufficient for us to judge his character and examine his activities, which helped shape English culture in the later fifteenth century.

The Woodville family are often viewed as grasping and power hungry. This is true of some of the family members, particularly Thomas Grey, Marquess of Dorset, who was the eldest son of Anthony's sister Elizabeth by her first marriage to John Grey. However, Anthony, while of course benefitting from the advancement of his sister to the status of queen, notably avoided meddling wherever possible. His interests in piety, tutoring Edward, the Prince of Wales, jousting, and translating books let him play a background role in the Wars of the Roses.

While Anthony Woodville may have been a secondary figure in political terms, it is clear that he had a significant part in transforming English culture, especially through his patronage of William Caxton, as well as his tutelage of Edward, Prince of Wales, who resided at Ludlow Castle for around ten years. According to Dominic Mancini, an Italian visitor who stayed in England between late summer 1482 and July 1483, Anthony Woodville was 'always considered a kind, serious, and just man' who was 'tested by every vicissitude of life'.[2] It was for this reason that he had been entrusted with 'the care and direction' of the prince.[3] Further to Mancini's description of Anthony, he purposefully contrasts his character with that of other Woodvilles, who were 'detested by the nobles'.[4] There is a certain amount of truth in this, for unlike some other family members Anthony preferred to stay away from court life, favouring more academic and religious pursuits.

As a foreign visitor who did not venture out of London, Mancini would have had to rely on a London-centric viewpoint. He does not relay his sources, but it is entirely possible that he would have heard gossip that was either second- or third-hand. As London had a favourable opinion of Anthony Woodville, thanks to his brave defence of the city during an attack by Lancastrian rebels led by the Bastard of Fauconberg, his appraisal reflects the Londoners' favourable judgement.[5] It is perhaps for this reason that Mancini separated Anthony from his family, who were seen as the cause of friction among the nobility thanks to Elizabeth Woodville's marriage to Edward IV.

Thomas More, in his *History of Richard III*, written at some point between 1510 and 1518, describes Anthony Woodville in a similar way. Anthony was a 'right honourable man', who was chosen to look after the Prince of Wales because he was 'valiaunte of hande as politike in counsayle', meaning that not only was he a man of military skill, but he gave good and trustworthy instruction.[6] These abilities must have been demonstrated to Anthony's brother-in-law, Edward IV, who entrusted not only his eldest son but the future king to the care of Earl Rivers.

William Caxton had many personal connections with Anthony Woodville, both on a professional and personal level. Anthony was his friend, patron and translator. In his prologue to Anthony's translation of *The Cordyale*, a religious text, Caxton describes Anthony's life as one full of 'great labours', that he was always someone who was 'vertuously occupied'.[7] While it is easy to dismiss Caxton as biased due to Anthony's patronage, Caxton was not averse to criticism when it came to Anthony's translations. In the first book to be printed in England with a date and place of publication, printed by Caxton and translated by Woodville, *The Dictes and Sayings*, Caxton openly derides Woodville for his removal of misogynistic language from his version of the text.[8]

However favourably the majority of sources appear to show Anthony Woodville, that does not mean that he was universally liked. There were some, such as the Earl of Warwick, known as the Kingmaker, and Lord Hastings, who had reason to dislike him. Warwick in particular had a well-known hatred of the Woodville family after Elizabeth, the eldest sister of Anthony, married Edward IV secretly, which undid his work towards a French alliance. In Warwick's eyes, the whole family came from a lesser gentry background, save for Jacquetta, Anthony's mother, who had previously been married to John, Duke of Bedford, prior to her love match with Richard Woodville. They were reaching too far above themselves, he thought. In a rebellion fuelled by Warwick – one from which he cleverly tried to distance himself – 'favourites of the king' were cited as one of the reasons for the uprising.[9] They were seen as being undeserving of their position and were seeking to abuse it. Sometimes Anthony's name was included as one of these deceitful advisors surrounding Edward IV.[10] However, most of these statements were purposefully sweeping, so were often general comments made about the Woodville family, without naming individuals.

In the eighteenth century, writer and antiquarian Horace Walpole, the son of Britain's first Prime Minister Robert Walpole, was well-known for his interest in the medieval, not just as an antiquarian but also by association with the architecture of his home, Strawberry Hill, one of the first buildings to be built in what we now know as the Gothic Revival style. While this could appear to suggest that Walpole was something of an amateur, the opposite is in fact true. Walpole has been commended as one of the first writers to reassess the reputation of Richard III beyond so-called Tudor propaganda. He highly commended Anthony Woodville in his *Catalogue of Royal and Noble Authors*. He described Woodville as being 'as gallant as his luxurious brother-in-law [Edward IV], without his weaknesses'.[11] He found him to be full of chivalric purpose, not only in a military capacity but also in terms of learning and piety.

While this description may appear whimsical, it is in keeping with Walpole's writing style in both his personal and professional capacities and in fact, there is a lot of truth to be found in his description of Woodville. Woodville certainly was a man of far-ranging capabilities and there is no denying that he was a distinctive figure during the Wars of the Roses, one very different to most of his contemporaries. Walpole was right in his description of a fifteenth-century knight who was keen to reflect the values of the tournament circuit and of courtesy associated with chivalry. Woodville lived during the last days of chivalry, and perhaps he was striving to keep these ideals alive.

Not only was Woodville involved in chivalric pursuits, he was also a bibliophile, a man interested in acquiring knowledge, which manifested itself in his being a patron and translator for Caxton. Alongside these more academic aspects, he also had proven himself militarily. Not only had he been a tournament champion but he had participated in some of the biggest battles of the Wars of the Roses, such as Towton and Barnet, and had also successfully defended London against Lancastrian rebels, for which he was greatly admired by the citizens of the capital.

Woodville was also known for his piety. He had a hermit-like persona at times, including wearing a hair shirt at tournaments – as well as at his execution at Pontefract on 25 June 1483. This shirt was given to Our Lady of Doncaster, a Carmelite friary. He visited many pilgrimage sites during his lifetime, both in England and across Europe. While a religious mindset was part of life during the late fifteenth century, perhaps where Woodville differed was in his deep reflection upon it. He seriously considered going on crusade, for which Edward IV denounced him as a coward who would abandon his king during his time of need.[12]

Despite Anthony Woodville generally being perceived in a positive way during his own lifetime, historians since have not all been as kind to him. Lynda Pidgeon suggests that while his pious devotion was genuine, the literature he produced was no different from that produced at the same time by others.[13] It is true that it may not have been too different from other texts produced during Anthony's lifetime, but that does not necessarily throw doubt on Anthony's personal motivations when translating texts for Caxton. All have either a religious, moral or chivalric theme to them, which fits with the interests he had in life. Pidgeon also sees Anthony's will as an indication of a darker side. She suggests that he 'seems to have had little feeling' for his illegitimate and only child, Margaret, because she had little mention in his will.[14] But as a will is a legal document, and Anthony's was written in haste after he discovered that he was to be executed, he would have been unsure as to how many, if any, of his requests would be acted upon. Margaret was also already married and so looked after. Her husband, Robert Poyntz, was mentioned as an executor, which suggests she was not entirely forgotten.[15]

In a similar vein, Michael Hicks has suggested that Anthony was 'meticulous, predatory and ruthless'.[16] It is true that Anthony did investigate whether he could gain from forfeited estates belonging to Lady Roos and Warwick, but it is also true that he was struggling to maintain his lifestyle as an earl, for he had inherited little from his own father.[17]

In her book on the Woodville family, in contrast, Susan Higginbotham has rightly suggested that Anthony 'may not have been the cold and chilly creature his detractors have depicted him as'.[18] In fact, he was a man who was more than just the brother-in-law of the king. He was able successfully to cross the boundaries of tournament champion, diplomat, governor of the Prince of Wales, landowner, pilgrim, literary and religious patron, and translator.

It would appear that the real Anthony Woodville was more than this 'cold and chilly' manipulator passed down to us by some historians. In fact, contemporary chronicles do not seem to portray him as such a man. In reality, he was just as multifaceted as any of us.

I

THE WOODVILLE FAMILY AND THEIR CONNECTIONS

The Woodvilles were a lesser gentry family with their lands centred around Grafton Regis in Northamptonshire. They were notable, if only on a local level within that county. They possessed land in five counties and had held local offices since the mid-fourteenth century.[1] While most attention to the family has naturally come from the marriage of Richard Woodville and Jacquetta of Luxembourg, it is imperative to consider the family further back than that to understand the opposition to their match.

Richard Woodville's father, also called Richard, was the first to have connections to the royal family, despite never being knighted. He was the younger son of John Woodville and his second wife, Isabel. This meant his older half-brother, Thomas, was set to inherit the family estates. Richard did own small amounts of land in his own right, but these were in Kent, a long way from the family's main lands around Grafton Regis. When Thomas died in 1435, the senior male line came to an end, meaning that his heirs were his full-blood sisters.[2] However, Richard did inherit Grafton and the Hundred of Cleyley.[3] While this inheritance provided Richard with more land, it did not necessarily improve his social standing. This meant, in the words of M. A. Hicks, that Richard had 'to build his fortune more or less from scratch'.[4] He managed this through his involvement in the Hundred Years War, which also greatly improved his social circle.

In 1415 and 1417, Richard Woodville held French commands in the service of Henry V, and by 1418 he was granted seigniories of confiscated French lands in Preaux and Dangu. Following this, it didn't take Richard long to gain promotion. By 1420, he had become an esquire of the body of Henry V and seneschal of Normandy. With the death of Henry V in 1422, there was a possibility that things could have gone wrong, but the Duke of Bedford, who became Regent of France upon the king's death, retained Richard in his employ, either because he had shown competence or because it was simply easier to keep things as they were; maybe it was a little of both. Richard was again promoted, to the role of chamberlain to Bedford, and was rewarded with more confiscated French lands.[5] In June 1429, he was made Lieutenant of Calais.

For someone who was born a second son, with little chance of a large inheritance, Richard had come a long way. However, the promotions he gained did not come without difficulties. In 1428, Richard Beauchamp, Earl of Warwick, accused Woodville, John Lewis (also known as Lewis John), warden of the mint in London and Calais, and Richard Bokeland, treasurer of Calais, of depriving him of the captaincy of Calais. While the truth behind this accusation has been lost over time, it is clear that around the time of Warwick's removal from the captaincy of Calais he was put in charge of the education of the young King Henry VI, meaning he would have had to have stayed in England.[6] Whatever the truth behind it, the matter was certainly serious enough for the men to take this matter to the Duke of Bedford, asking him to talk to Warwick on their behalf, which he did. Bedford asked Warwick to forgive and forget the matter, diplomatically choosing to remain silent on whether he believed the allegations made by

Warwick to be true or not. Perhaps his private actions indicate what he thought, as the men stayed in their positions.

Despite interventions from Bedford, Bokeland continued to be out of favour with Warwick. Bokeland himself explains this in a letter to an unknown friend: 'For cause and principal of his offense and hevy lordeshipp to me wardes, like as he doeth to my cousin Wydvyle and to Lowis John, but principally to me.'[7] Bokeland felt especially aggrieved because in an explanation to Warwick, Woodville had laid the blame on Bokeland and Lewis, exonerating himself. Perhaps Woodville had behaved in this way as he knew Bedford trusted him, but this came at the expense of Bokeland's reputation. If Lewis had an opinion on the matter, no documentation of it survives.

The dispute with Warwick was something that would come back to haunt the Woodvilles in future decades. The feud would continue between the family and Beauchamp's son-in-law, Richard Neville, who would inherit the title of Earl of Warwick. In the meantime, Woodville's reputation was not dinted. Instead, he quietly retired from his military life in France to become Sheriff of Northamptonshire in 1438, dying in either 1441 or 1442, just prior to the birth of a grandson, Anthony Woodville.[8]

Anthony Woodville was born sometime between 1442 and 1444. As with many nobles and gentry of the time, his exact birth date is not recorded. There are no precise dates of birth for Anthony or his thirteen siblings, but we know that twelve survived into adulthood while two died in infancy. There has been some debate as to whether Anthony or his more famous sister, Elizabeth Woodville, the future queen of Edward IV, was the eldest sibling. Elizabeth's birth date is thought to have been sometime in 1437, based upon a painting by an unknown hand that is thought to depict Elizabeth. This portrait, labelled as 'Elizabeth Woodville, 1463', indicates that her age in the image is twenty-six, thus indicating that date of birth.[9] However, the label could easily be wrong. It is quite possible that there was a misunderstanding with the time Elizabeth became Edward IV's queen. A note by Richard Glover, Somerset Herald, references the Woodville children:

> Richard Erle Ryvers and Jacquett Duchesse of Bedford hath yssue Anthony Erle Ryvers, Richard, Elizabeth first wedded to Sir John Grey, after to Kinge Edward the fourth, Lowys, Richard Erle of Riueres, Sir John Wodeuille Knight, Jaquette lady Straunge of Knokyn, Anne first maryed to the Lord Bourchier son and heir to the Erle of Essex, after to the Erle of Kent, Mary wyf to William Erle of Huntingdon, John Woodville, Lyonell Bisshop of Sarum, Margaret Lady Maltravers, Jane Lady Grey of Ruthin, Sir Edward Woodville, Katherine Duchesse of Buckingham.[10]

This note is in a chronicle dated *circa* 1480–1500 and has been suggested by Susan Higginbotham as a better source for the birth order of the children.[11] While it is more contemporary than the portrait of Elizabeth, it still makes no mention of dates. It may only mention Anthony as the first sibling as he was his father's heir. There are certainly four confirmed sons alive in a grant from June 1446 – Anthony, Richard and two Johns – but this does not tell us whether it was Anthony or Elizabeth who was the eldest.[12] If the clerk did not make a mistake in naming these sons, then it can also be assumed one of them died young, as only one John is documented later. It is also possible that Lewis, the son who definitely did not survive, may have been the eldest child. Whatever the true birth order, Anthony was the eldest surviving son.

Prior to Jacquetta's marriage to Richard Woodville, she had been married to John, Duke of Bedford, brother to Henry V and Regent of France under Henry VI, when she was about seventeen. This placed her firmly on the Lancastrian side. Bedford and Jacquetta were married on 20 April 1433 in Therouanne, just a year after the death of Bedford's first wife, Anne of Burgundy, who had died during an epidemic in Paris. Following Anne's death, a new marriage was sought for the childless duke. Jacquetta was seen as a suitable match due to her lineage. Her father was Peter of Luxembourg, Count of Saint-Pol. While Saint-Pol was only a small county, sandwiched between Picardy and Boulogne in northern France, its location was strategically important, which made it a useful ally. The pedigree of the House of Luxembourg was also good. It had given kings and queens to various European countries. Most notably, Marie of Luxembourg married Francis of Bourbon, Count of Vendome. They were the great-grandparents of Henry IV, the first Bourbon King of France.[13] As well as these more recent links, Jacquetta's family could also claim descent from Charlemagne.[14] With these important connections, as well as Jacquetta's family lands being so close to France, it is clear what motivated Bedford to marry the young Jacquetta.

Upon their marriage, Jacquetta would have had to learn about the formalities and court rituals of England. It would have naturally taken her some time to adjust to her new surroundings. By June, they were on their way to England. However, the country was in a period of unrest due to the minority of the young Henry VI, and Bedford and the Duke of Gloucester, who were uncles to the young king, struggled to unite in their roles as regents. On 8 July 1433, Jacquetta applied to Parliament for English citizenship, which was granted.[15]

By marrying the Duke of Bedford, Jacquetta was marrying into money and status. John's English income amounted to over £4,000 a year, without taking into account his income from lands in France.[16] This was an enormous sum.[17] As his wife, Jacquetta would have lived a life that reflected her husband's wealth and status. This was not to last, though, as Bedford died in France in 1435. He and Jacquetta had been married for less than two years and had had no children. However short the marriage was, Jacquetta continued to be known as Duchess of Bedford long after John's death.[18]

In his will, Bedford had made Jacquetta his sole heir, giving her all his lands, incomes and lordships in both England and France, apart from one castle and its land in Normandy, which went to Bedford's illegitimate son.[19] This arrangement was not accepted by English law, nor liked by Bedford's family, and so was never enacted. Instead, Jacquetta was awarded the customary widow's third, known as a dower. Considering Bedford's wealth, even a third was still a huge amount, making Jacquetta probably the richest woman in England. In total, the amount she owned was worth 'twice the qualifying level for an earldom'.[20] However, this dower was soon under threat.

Richard Woodville was a lowly squire in Bedford's household and was far below Jacquetta in status. Still, the pair went on to have a long and happy marriage until Woodville's death in 1460. The match could only have been one of love, or lust perhaps, because for Jacquetta, there could have been no financial or societal gain from such a union. Richard was her own choice, not one made for her. It is not clear whether the relationship between Richard and Jacquetta started before or after the death of Bedford. However, it is possible that Woodville was among the retinue that brought Jacquetta back to England following her husband's death in France.[21] Whatever the circumstances, the pair were obviously willing to risk their reputations over such a match as the marriage was conducted without royal assent, causing issues for the newlywed couple. Jacquetta's dower was taken away from her as punishment, which meant that the the couple were soon almost destitute save for the income that Richard was already able to bring in. Henry VI eventually forgave them after a fine of £1,000 was imposed on 23 March 1437, but most of Jacquetta's lands had to be sold in order to pay it.[22]

Despite the issue of marrying without royal assent, it is interesting to note that the marriage was not mentioned in English chronicles until after the marriage of their daughter, Elizabeth, to Edward IV in 1464. It was mentioned before this time by European chroniclers, such as Enguerrand de Monstrelet. Writing during the period from 1444 to 1447, Monstrelet started his account of events from 1400, but he refers to the circumstances of Richard and Jacquetta's marriage:

> In this year [1436], the duchess of Bedford, sister to the count de St. Pol, married, from inclination, an English knight called sir Richard Woodville, a young man, very handsome and well made, but, in regard to birth inferior to her first husband, the regent, and to herself. Louis de Luxembourg, archbishop of Rouen, and her other relations, were very angry at this match but they could not prevent it.[23]

So from Monstrelet's description, not only did the couple not have royal assent from Henry VI, resulting in Jacquetta's dower being taken away as well as the later fine, but Jacquetta's family had also expressed their disapproval of the match. When both of these aspects are taken into account, it is implied that they married in secret, especially as Jacquetta's family were unable to prevent the union. Due to its secret nature, it is impossible to place an exact date on the wedding, but it would have occurred sometime between Bedford's death in September 1435 and March 1437, when Henry VI issued a fine for the match. From this, it is understandable why Monstrelet places it in 1436.

As there is no mention of the marriage in English chronicles, it suggests that there was not widespread concern about or interest in the match until their eldest daughter Elizabeth's marriage to Edward IV in 1461.[24] Then it would raise questions as to the status of Elizabeth and whether she deserved to be a queen. The fact that this royal marriage had also been conducted in secret, just like that of Elizabeth's parents, meant that the marriage between Richard and Jacquetta had inadvertently set a precedent for their daughter. While Elizabeth's marriages do seem to have some similarities to those of her mother, Elizabeth managed to elevate herself to the role of queen upon her second marriage to Edward IV. She married up, her mother married down.

Despite the unequal status of the newlyweds, Richard was raised to the title of Baron Rivers. Before their daughter married Edward IV, the Woodvilles' position was seen as a lowly one and a title appeared to have been invented to counteract the wide social gap between the pair. This left the children they had in a sort of no man's land in terms of social status. However, J. R. Lander argues that the Woodvilles' low social status before Elizabeth's marriage to Edward IV has been somewhat exaggerated, suggesting that their status was 'not as lowly as many historians have assumed'.[25] Before this marriage, Richard owned eight manors, only four of which he had inherited from his father, which would not have generated enough income to reflect his status as a baron (which he achieved in 1447).[26] While of course they were not the most wealthy family, their low-born reputation prior to the royal marriage was the result of the Woodvilles' position alone, without any allowance for the pedigree of Jacquetta. This reflected contemporary views on women taking their husband's status, whether for better or for worse.

With family connections to Bedford and the royal circle surrounding Henry VI, it was no surprise that when the tribulations that would later lead to the armed conflict known as the Wars of the Roses began, the Woodvilles were on the side of the Lancastrians. Alongside Thomas, Lord Scales, Anthony's future father-in-law, Richard Woodville, who held the title of Lord Rivers at this point, gave military support to the Lancastrian King Henry VI. This support stemmed from the connections to the Duke of Bedford, but also Jacquetta's acquaintance with Margaret of Anjou when she first became Queen of England. It would have also been cemented by friendly relations with Lord Scales, who had served in the Hundred Years War under Bedford. Scales is especially known for his participation in the famous Siege of Orleans in 1428–29. In a letter dictated by Joan of Arc to a scribe before her coming to relieve the siege, she named Lord Scales, alongside the better-known William de la Pole, then Earl of Suffolk, and John Talbot, Earl of Shrewsbury, as 'lieutenants of the said Duke of Bedford' and asked them to surrender and return to their own country in peace, as she was 'sent hither by God the King of Heaven'.[27] This direct mention of Lord Scales showed that he had been promoted to a similar rank on the battlefield as men above his social status, indicating how adept he was in a war setting. Scales was also a captain of many of the English possessions in France during this time, so it is thought he did not return to England until these were all lost, with the exception of Calais.[28]

The friendship between both families possibly began after Scales' creation as a Knight of the Garter in 1425, for he subsequently nominated Richard Woodville to join him as a fellow Garter knight in 1450.[29] Later in that same year, both lords participated in the fight against Jack Cade's Rebellion, turning them into brothers-in-arms as well as friends. Cade's revolt was started in Kent by a group of small landowners who felt wronged by high taxes and prices. This, alongside concerns about corruption following the beheading of the Duke of Suffolk while out at sea and travelling into exile, and recent losses in France, caused alarm in Kent.[30] Jack Cade sympathised with Richard Duke of York, rather than Henry VI's regime. A manifesto was produced by the rebels that suggested that the king replace his current council with that of 'the hyghe and myghty prince the Duke of Yorke', as well as 'the myghte prynce, the Duke of Exceter, the Duke of Bokyngham, the Duke of Noffolke'. While the dukes of Buckingham and Norfolk were not described as 'mighty', they were, just as York was, cousins to the king. Like Henry VI, they were related to Edward III.[31] The manifesto suggested that these men were better company and counsellors for the king and that the Duke of York in particular should be recalled to the king's side from his virtual exile.[32] The demands given in the rebels' manifesto followed parliament's attempts earlier in the year to impeach the king's chief minister, the Duke of Suffolk, who was rumoured to have been plotting the downfall and eventual death of the Duke of Gloucester.[33]

There was also a more complex connection between the Scales and Woodville families. Elizabeth Woodville had first married Sir John Grey of Groby, a Lancastrian and the heir to the barony of Ferrers Groby. Sir John's mother eventually married Sir John Bourchier, the first Earl of Essex.[34] Elizabeth Scales, who went on to marry Anthony Woodville, had first been married to John Bourchier's younger brother, Henry, until his death in around 1458. Both of these alliances show a strong affiliation between the families that coincided with their Lancastrian connections.

The exact date of the marriage between Anthony Woodville and Elizabeth Scales is unknown; it would probably have been prior to the Battle of Towton.[35] (This will be discussed further in chapter 4.) If this is the case, then the couple did not have an easy time during their early years of marriage, not least because of the death of Thomas, Elizabeth's father. His death was only one of many in the years that were to come as the conflict, now known as the Wars of the Roses, escalated following the First Battle of St Albans in May 1455.

Scales was part of a Lancastrian force stationed in London when the earls of March, Warwick and Salisbury returned from exile in 1460. The Lancastrians were not popular with the people of London, and Yorkist forces penetrated the city.[36] On 2 July, Scales and his comrades were pushed back and retreated to the Tower of London. The Yorkists began to besiege the fortress. The siege was brutal on both sides. The *English Chronicle* records that after some of the besieging Yorkist forces went to fight at the Battle of Northampton, the Lancastrians inside the Tower 'caste whyld fire in to the cyte', which injured men, women and children.[37] In retaliation, those surrounding the fortress increased their bombardment. With the Yorkist victory at the Battle of Northampton, the Lancastrians surrendered.[38] Scales and three other men decided to make an escape by boat on the Thames.

The group's escape attempt was discovered by an unknown woman, and Scales' naked body was found by Edward, Earl of March, at St Mary Overy in Southwark, now Southwark Cathedral.[39]

Scales had been godfather to Edward, so it is understandable why he, as well as the Earl of Warwick, respected Scales as a soldier and saw his death as regrettable, and they made sure he was buried with honour.[40] They both attended his funeral to show their respect. The *English Chronicle* mourned his passing, considering it a 'grete pyte' that a man 'so welle approued in the warrys of Normandy and Fraunce, shuld dy so myscheuously'.[41] Richard Woodville and the rest of the Woodville family undoubtedly mourned the loss of their great friend and ally. What the family did not know at the time was that Lord Rivers would meet a similar fate himself before too long.

In 1460, following the seizure of ships in Kent in the possession of the Earl of Warwick by Richard Woodville, then known as Lord Rivers, he, his wife Jacquetta, and his son Anthony were captured at Sandwich in retaliation and taken to Calais.[42] In her description of the event, Scofield suggests that the following inquisition did not indicate an exact date for this or name those who captured the Woodville family, but it did imply the capture was probably conducted on Warwick's orders, as the inquisition was held before him.[43] However, the contemporary *New Chronicles of England and France* suggests that the person behind the capture was John Dynham, who led a surprise attack and then sent them to Calais to be paraded before the exiled earls of Salisbury, Warwick and March (later Edward IV).[44]

The *Paston Letters*, which are the most detailed contemporary account of the events at Sandwich and Calais, do not report that Jacquetta was taken alongside her husband and son at Sandwich, so this may have been misreported by other sources such as the *New Chronicles*.[45] In the account given by the *Paston Letters*, when they reached Calais, Rivers and Anthony were escorted by men carrying torches and they taunted Rivers as a 'knave's son', who was 'hymself made by maryage', with similar insults being thrown at Anthony.[46] Their appearance at Calais was a piece of public theatre and is also the first recorded public insult about the status of the Woodvilles; it would not be the last. Whichever account is more accurate, there is no indication of how long either Richard or Anthony were incarcerated. As they were held without much reason other than for Warwick's propaganda, it is possible that they were not detained long. In any case, both Richard and Anthony were fighting for the Lancastrians during the Battle of Towton in March 1461. If Anthony and Elizabeth were married by the time of their capture, it is unclear why she was not with them, so maybe the pair were married between then and Towton. On the other hand, perhaps the couple simply weren't married at that time.

At the Battle of Towton, the Woodvilles, having been imprisoned in Calais by the exiled Yorkists, naturally continued to fight for the Lancastrian cause. And with so personal an attack on their background, despite Jacquetta's links to European royalty, honour was at stake. The idea of a code of honour and its effect on social standing was a common thread during the fifteenth century. Moralistic texts considered this, and codes of chivalry were further elaborated.[47] Having suffered such a personal affront at a time when honour was essential to a person's reputation, it is clear why the Woodvilles remained true to the Lancastrian cause. For the women left behind, most notably the probably newly married Elizabeth Scales, this must have been an extremely worrying time. With the outcome of battle uncertain, fear for the future and for her husband's life would always have been a heavy burden to carry, let alone at a time when she was adjusting to a new married life.

The Battle of Towton was fought near Tadcaster in Yorkshire on Palm Sunday, 29 March 1461. It has since gone down in history as the bloodiest battle to be fought on English soil. Arguments for not fighting on a holy day came to nought, as did any consideration of weather conditions. On the morning of the battle, the wind was behind the Yorkist army, offering their archers the advantage as the Lancastrians were struggling to loose their arrows into the headwind and snow. The battle that ensued turned into chaos and many of the combatants became unable to cope with the wintry conditions. Trevor Royle describes the scene as a 'grim slugging match in which quarter was neither given nor expected'.[48] The chaos meant that neither side could seize an advantage. Only after sunset were the Lancastrians forced to withdraw to the River Cock, a small but surprisingly deep river. Men trying to save their lives by escaping across it were either dragged down by their armour and drowned or cut down in the process. As more and more men were being hacked to death, the Lancastrian ranks broke entirely. In the ensuing rout, Yorkist cavalry slaughtered any remaining Lancastrians they found in their path, earning the site the nickname of the 'Bloody Meadow'.[49] It is believed that between 20,000 and 30,000 men were killed at Towton.[50] In this deadly maelstrom, it is no wonder that Anthony's death was misreported, by William Paston among others.[51] He was not the only man to have his death mistakenly announced following the battle. George Neville, the Bishop of Exeter and brother to the Earl of Warwick, reported the death of the Earl of Devon upon the battlefield; Devon was in fact wounded and discovered on his way to York, where he was later beheaded.[52]

The Yorkist victory at Towton paved the way for Edward, Earl of March to become Edward IV. He was crowned on 28 June, nearly two months to the day after the battle. The Woodville family sought the forgiveness of this new Yorkist king. The reason for their change of heart is not documented, but they were not the only family to switch allegiance during the Wars of the Roses. Many others did, but what was more unusual was that they stuck with their new choice – although following the marriage of Elizabeth Woodville to Edward IV, any other decision would have been political suicide. Perhaps they viewed Edward's victory as a potentially positive development, given that Henry VI was known to have long periods of incapacity, leaving him unable to rule. The sight of such slaughter must also have weighed heavily, knowing that both Richard Woodville and his son Anthony could have easily been casualties, taken prisoner, or executed. George Neville ended his description of the battle in a rather prophetic manner. He contrasted the killing of fellow Englishmen with the crusades against the Turks in the Holy Land, opining that such killing in the latter circumstances was acceptable whereas the 'civil discords' in England at that time were ensuring that 'our riches are beginning to give out, and we are shedding our own blood copiously among ourselves'.[53] Perhaps the Woodvilles saw Edward as a strong figure who would help end the fighting and suffering that Towton exemplified.

Some insight into the Woodvilles' thinking at this time can be gleaned from the State Papers of Venice. The papers record a letter from Count Ludovico Dallugo sent to the Duke of Milan during a visit to England in late August 1461, where he reports on English affairs during his stay. Dallugo mentions those defecting from the Lancastrian cause to join Edward IV, among 'the chief of them' being Richard Woodville and his son, Anthony, who make it clear they changed sides because Henry VI's cause 'was lost irremediably'.[54] Despite voicing regrets about their Lancastrian loyalty as demonstrated at Towton, the pair were briefly imprisoned in the Tower of London. Giovanni Pietro Cagnola wrote to the Duke of Milan, 'The Earl of Warwick has taken Monsig. de Ruvera and his son and sent them to the king who had them imprisoned in the Tower.'[55] The incarceration was not for long, as pardons soon followed for Richard and Anthony. Richard's came on 12 July 1461, while Anthony's arrived eleven days later on 23 July.[56]

The new monarch was showing his trust in those he had once fought against, and the Woodvilles were also proving their new loyalty. They certainly did not appear to be a threat to the Yorkist regime, as Edward granted both Richard and Anthony Woodville various oyer and terminer commissions to enforce law and order in 1463 and 1464.[57] There were other examples prior to this that showed Edward had begun to trust the Woodvilles. In May 1462, Anthony and his wife, Elizabeth, were granted the manor of 'Le Syche' in South Lynn, Norfolk, worth £20 a year, from the forfeited estates of Thomas Tuddenham.[58] This new allegiance seemed secure by the time Anthony became part of a Yorkist force attempting to besiege Alnwick Castle in December 1462.[59] To be given this type of responsibility just over a year after receiving a pardon for fighting on the Lancastrian side showed that Anthony had already earned the trust of members of the Yorkist elite – or, at the very least, he was trying to earn it.

2

AFTER THE ROYAL WEDDING

With Elizabeth Woodville's marriage to Edward IV in May 1464, the Woodvilles' Lancastrian allegiances seemed long forgotten. Indeed, the loyalty shown by the Woodvilles to the House of York would turn out to be long-lasting. Intriguingly, both Lord Rivers and Lord Scales had been part of the band of men who accompanied Richard, Duke of York, when he voiced his grievances before Henry VI in the autumn of 1450.[1] Scales stayed true to the Lancastrian cause until his murder in 1460. Despite the obvious rift that led to the Wars of the Roses, in the days before 1450, there was no definite indication that arguments between York and the Beauforts would lead to violence. The Beauforts, just like York, were cousins to Henry VI, but the family were close advisors to the king. Many, including York, thought they abused this position during Henry's long periods of illness, which made him unable to rule. Initially, certain individuals on either side of the argument tried to maintain common courtesy with the other. This is evident from the fact that Thomas, Lord Scales, despite his known loyalty to Henry VI and the Lancastrians, was also godfather to Edward, Earl of March, who later became Edward IV.[2]

There was widespread opposition to Edward's marriage to Elizabeth because of the lowly social status of the Woodvilles, which was openly commented on with horror by Edward's brother George, Duke of Clarence and his cousin Richard Neville, Earl of Warwick. The main objections focussed on the lack of adherence to traditional matches for Edward, as Elizabeth was not even the daughter of a nobleman, but also the fact that the wedding invalidated Warwick's previous negotiations for a French marriage.[3] However, the *Crowland Chronicle* suggested that while it had previously been thought that the marriage between Elizabeth and Edward was the source of contention between Edward and Warwick, it was in fact the later marriage of Edward's youngest sister, Margaret, to Charles, the future Duke of Burgundy, that 'was the real cause for dissension' for Warwick.[4] Warwick was 'deeply offended' by Margaret's match as Warwick hated Charles, a situation which was only made worse by the Woodvilles' involvement in organising the match in the first place.[5] What made this particular marriage so offensive was the favour already shown towards Elizabeth's large number of siblings, who were elevated by marriages and given positions that would usually have been reserved for the smaller pool of higher-status nobles such as Warwick himself.[6] It would seem that Warwick was being squeezed out, and he was not going to relinquish his influence quietly.

The reality is that things were not quite so black and white as the objections listed above would suggest. First of all, when compared to the Continent, as explained by Alan MacFarlane, there was no 'true hereditary nobility based on a special legal status', meaning that nobility was based on a mixture of bestowed titles as well as land owned, rather than on a legal definition as seen elsewhere in Europe.[7] Nobility was established by the king.[8] In other words, Edward himself could improve a person's rank, so why would the same not apply to his own wife? The problem was that there had not been a previous example of this type of royal marriage, so Elizabeth's status was completely new territory.

In the words of Joanna Laynesmith, it was made even more complicated because Elizabeth's status was already so debateable because of 'the unusual disparity in her parent's lineage'.[9] If a father was noble, then any children would automatically be noble too, but the children's status was not as readily defined if it was the mother, rather than the father, that was noble.

There was no law against inter-class marriages, although, as we have seen, it was frowned upon in certain circumstances, and did cause complications, which was certainly the case for Edward and Elizabeth. Despite the opposition the couple may have faced to their match, there is no denying that there were other cases of inter-class marriages occurring at this time, not least that of Elizabeth's own parents, Richard and Jacquetta. In that case, Jacquetta, as the noble at the time of marriage, was allowed to keep her status. In examples where the woman was not noble at the time of marriage, she would take her husband's rank. Ironically, an example of this type of marriage can be seen in the Earl of Warwick's own great-grandmother, who was the daughter of a merchant.

There is also something else at play in the opposition to the match. Edward's regime had already been hard won through conquest and the deposition of Henry VI.[10] At a time when the divine right of kings played a large part in the idea of kingship, some, particularly those of a Lancastrian leaning, would have seen Edward's accession to the throne as controversial. Edward had much to prove to those of this disposition, having to work harder than other kings to convince his subjects that he was the rightful monarch. The timing of the announcement of his marriage to Elizabeth Woodville, a woman so far beneath him, did little to help his cause so early on in his reign.

Since Elizabeth's marriage, the accusation that marriages were used as a tool by the Woodvilles for their own advancement has often been levelled as an example of Woodville behaviour in general. However, there were many Woodville marriages made prior to Edward and Elizabeth's that do not follow the pattern.

Anthony's own marriage to Elizabeth Scales was one of these, as he most likely married prior to the royal match. If we take this into account, we can see that at least some of the accusations were deliberately circulated to create an overall despicable image of the Woodvilles, although the situation was far from straightforward.

However, not all contemporaries were as unanimous in their condemnation of the Woodvilles as has been previously thought; they were seen as respectable enough, but not necessarily with the standing expected for the wife of a king.[11] The majority of the matches made for the Woodvilles were reasonable, as they mainly strengthened existing ties with families known already to be loyal to the House of York, such as the Herberts and the Greys, among others. While this was usually the case, there were some that did indeed have complications.

Thomas Grey, Marquess of Dorset, the eldest son of Elizabeth Woodville from her previous marriage, was married to Anne Holland, a niece of Edward IV's and heiress to the duchy of Essex. The Earl of Warwick had a personal reason for disliking this particular match as his nephew, George Neville, the heir to Warwick's brother the Marquess of Montague, had previously been betrothed to Anne.[12] After Anne's death, Dorset went on to marry Cecily Bonville, stepdaughter of Lord Hastings, Lord Chamberlain and favourite of Edward IV. Another such problematic marriage was the marriage of the young Duke of Buckingham to Catherine Woodville, sister of the queen, which the duke was later said to have considered as beneath him. The duke's comments had probably been fuelled by his anger at being overlooked by Edward at court, for it was only during the reign of Richard III that he came to prominence.[13] Perhaps the most unusual marriage was between the nineteen-year-old John Woodville to the sixty-eight-year-old Catherine, aunt to Edward IV and the elder of the two dowager duchesses of Norfolk. John was her fourth husband. She was a large landowner thanks to a jointure on her husband's estates, meaning that though her grandson was the Duke of Norfolk, she held more of the ducal lands than he did.[14]

It would appear that the Woodvilles were not as well rewarded following Edward IV's marriage to Elizabeth as has been previously stated. This applied to Elizabeth's father, Richard Woodville, who was promoted from baron to Earl Rivers in 1466 and was also made treasurer. In June 1465, Richard and his heirs, which would have included Anthony, were granted a weekly market and two annual fairs at Grafton.[15] Rivers also received £250, plus income and profits from his role as treasurer, as well as existing income from his own lands. It has been estimated that the minimum income required for a lesser peer was £250 annually, but this would have been much more if they were required to attend court regularly. As father to the queen, Rivers would have been one of those required at court. Despite being given more roles and a better title, Rivers would still have still been heavily reliant on Jacquetta's dowry for his income, just as he had been prior to their daughter's royal marriage. When this is taken into account, the awards granted to the Woodvilles do not seem excessive when compared with those given to the Nevilles, including the Earl of Warwick, since Edward IV's coronation.

The only member of the Woodville family who could be rightly adjudged to have been over-promoted following Edward IV's accession was Thomas Grey, Marquess of Dorset. Dorset benefitted from two advantageous marriages largely engineered by his mother, and he spent nearly all of his time at court. His behaviour was seen as avaricious and grasping, meaning he was often cited as one of the bad advisors surrounding Edward IV.[16] He also had a reputation for womanising, similar to his stepfather and Lord Hastings. Dorset believed that he had risen above others and was happy to make that clear. He was almost entirely reliant on Edward IV for his position, even if he would not have liked to have admitted it. His position became even more elevated following the execution of the Duke of Clarence, brother of Edward IV. Dorset was granted some of the forfeited estates that had belonged to Clarence, as well as the wardship of his son, Edward. Not only were these awards substantial, to Dorset they must have appeared to signify even further aggrandizement.

It is obvious that ancestry and family ties mattered greatly to late fifteenth-century nobility. So it should come as no surprise that Anthony Woodville was no different. During his time as champion of tournaments, he would rely on this ancestry, particularly through Jacquetta's royal continental ties, as a key component of his display and spectacle.[17] These familial ties would help him attain his role as part of the delegation to secure a Burgundian alliance, most notably concerning a match between Margaret of York and Charles, the future Duke of Burgundy, to help consolidate and strengthen the Yorkist throne.[18] Both of these aspects of Anthony's life will be explored in more detail in later chapters.

Anthony is best remembered as being Elizabeth Woodville's favourite sibling. While there is no surviving evidence as to the exact nature of feelings Edward IV had towards any of her family, there are some glimmers of what the relationship was like between her and Anthony. One example is when Anthony was asked in 1465 to participate in a tournament at Smithfield against the Bastard of Burgundy, the illegitimate son of the Duke of Burgundy, who was confusingly also called Anthony, or Antoine in French. The tournament did not take place until 1467, as Antoine had a busy military schedule. In the true spirit of chivalry, Anthony was asked to take up the challenge by Elizabeth and her ladies-in-waiting, while on his knees before them, with his cap doffed. This may not sound much of a spectacle initially, but a collar of gold and jewels was placed around his thigh, featuring the symbol of a flower of souvenance, and a letter outlining the challenge to the tournament was placed in his cap.[19] Both the giving of a flower of souvenance and a letter inviting a participant to a tournament were steeped in chivalric tradition. A flower of souvenance was given as a reminder or keepsake, particularly as a badge for a knightly act.[20] The giving of a lady's colours, or some other keepsake, to her chosen champion is a gesture often portrayed in medieval books, as it is in films in the modern day. This was Elizabeth and Anthony's contribution to the tradition. Still, there is more complexity to these rituals than first meets the eye.

According to A. J. Pollard, Edward IV wished to create his own version of a 'new' Camelot with an emphasis on chivalric ideals.[21] Inspiration came from the literary background of ancient heroic tales, the stories of King Arthur being the most obvious choice as an example to follow. In his description of the much later Georgian and Victorian revival of interest in medieval culture, Michael Alexander discusses the different forms these tales took. Such epics and romances 'celebrated martial action, others celebrated love as well as war'.[22] The giving of Elizabeth's colours to Anthony is not a sign of romantic love, it is a celebration of familial love instead. Between them, the pair were able to recreate tropes of the old tales in the rituals of the court. In the years to come, Anthony himself would be more involved in the creation of this chivalric culture through the translation and printing of chivalry-themed texts, which focused on the need to 'glorify a popular hero', just as the 'new' Camelot required.[23] That Anthony was on good terms with Edward's family at this time allowed him to help create and participate in Edward's version of Camelot.

The letter given as an invitation to participate in the challenge had a similar function. It was more a command from his queen, even if she was his sister, ordering that Anthony fight for the honour of his lady at a tournament in London.[24] A similar challenge, along with the same flower, was sent to the Bastard of Burgundy and upon the acceptance of it, the flower was sent back to be placed onto Anthony's thigh once more.[25] What this ritual shows about the relationship between the siblings is that Elizabeth trusted in the skills and character of her brother enough to indirectly put the Burgundian alliance in his hands. The absolute trust she had in Anthony was also later shown in the decision to appoint him as the head of her son Prince Edward's household in Ludlow while he was the Prince of Wales. This decision would not have been taken by Elizabeth alone, but she would have had some say. It would have largely been Edward IV's decision about how his son, a future king, would be educated.

While there wasn't unanimous condemnation of the Woodvilles over the royal union, it certainly did create tension.[26] This was not the end of troubles for the Woodville family. Warwick was becoming increasingly driven to warn Edward of these new and dangerous advisors that he had allowed into his inner circle. Following a summons to court in January 1468, Warwick specifically refused the order, stating that he would not attend if either Richard or Anthony Woodville was present at court.[27] Warwick was becoming more vocal with his feelings about the Woodville family, but worse was to come.

In April 1469, a rebellion in the north was led by a mysterious figure known as Robin of Redesdale. This 'Robin' appears to have been Sir William Conyers of Marske in Swaledale, who was from a family closely connected with the Earl of Warwick.[28] There was no reason specified for this particular rebellion. John Neville, Earl of Northumberland, quashed it sometime after 26 April. It was not necessarily taken seriously by Edward at first. It was only after more rebellions in the name of Robin began to emerge that he began to take action, albeit slowly. A second rebellion, under the leadership of Robin of Holderness, started not long after. These rebels demanded the restoration of Henry Percy to his family title of Earl of Northumberland to replace John Neville, who had suppressed the previous rebellion. Just as before, John Neville won against the rebels, this time capturing and beheading the leader.[29]

Without a driving force, the rebels could have easily given up, but by June they had returned and regrouped in Lancashire, ready to march southwards. The *Crowland Chronicle* suggests the rebels now claimed to be rising because they were 'grievously oppressed with taxes and annual tributes by the … favourites of the king'.[30] This echoes the objections of the Earl of Warwick about the influence of the Woodvilles and other royal advisors. As Hammond states, if this series of uprisings was 'not instigated by Warwick, it was certainly led by men who sympathised with his aims' – to force the king's hand.[31] What makes the connections to Warwick seem all the more genuine is the men of note who were involved. These included Sir William Conyers, Sir Henry FitzHugh, a nephew of Warwick, Sir Henry Neville, a cousin of Warwick, and Sir John Sutton, a brother-in-law to both Henry Neville and Warwick. There was no denying that there was some connection to Warwick, although he himself could deny this as he was not directly involved.

The rebel forces began to march south as early as the beginning of May and Edward marched north to supress them, although at this point he was not convinced that they were a serious threat. His journey was slow, a great deal of time being spent in East Anglia first. Edward's misreading of the situation can also be seen when he put the Duke of Clarence, Earl of Warwick, Sir Henry FitzHugh and Sir John Sutton, names both directly and indirectly linked with the insurrection, on the oyer and terminer issued for the counties of York, Cumberland and Westmorland, dated 22 May.

Edward's intention was to visit the shrine and Augustinian Priory at Walsingham, a popular pilgrimage site dedicated to the Virgin Mary, despite the unrest that had erupted. The party included Richard, Duke of Gloucester, Richard Woodville, Earl Rivers and his sons, Anthony and John, as well as others.[32] Prior to the group reaching Walsingham, they stopped at Norwich, which during medieval times was the wealthiest and largest provincial city, second only to London. Here Edward ordered Yorkist banners and standards, as well as 1,000 jackets made from the Yorkist colours of murrey and blue with white roses.[33] Norwich was convenient for the group's journey to Walsingham, and news of this Yorkist show of strength would quickly spread from the city. While there, Anthony and John took the opportunity to dine with the Paston family at their Norwich home, where discussion centred around a land dispute the Pastons had with the dukes of Norfolk and Suffolk.[34] At the time, John Paston was betrothed to Anne Haute, a cousin of the Woodvilles.

It was only after this journey around Norfolk, when he had passed the Yorkist stronghold of Fotheringhay Castle in Northamptonshire and then Nottingham Castle in early July, that Edward began to realise the seriousness of the Robin rebels. By now he had possibly been given a copy of the manifesto written by the rebels which was being distributed.[35] This document accused Edward of isolating lords of his blood from his councils, replacing them with those seeking to advance themselves at the expense of others, especially the Woodvilles, including Anthony, and Lord Hastings, among others.[36] The parallels with grievances against Edward II, Richard II and more recently Henry VI would have been impossible to ignore.[37] As if things were not bad enough, on 12 July 1469, the Duke of Clarence, the Earl of Warwick and Warwick's brother, Archbishop George Neville, all put their signets to a letter declaring the veracity of these claims about those surrounding Edward IV. The letter declared that they had heard complaints voiced to them about the 'deceivable rule and guiding of certain seditious persons'.[38]

While at Nottingham, Edward awaited reinforcements from William Herbert, Earl of Pembroke, who brought around 2,000 Welshmen, and William Stafford, Earl of Devon, who brought mainly archers from the West Country. Richard, John and Anthony Woodville had also been at Nottingham but left to raise men for the king. Richard and John went to Chepstow, with Anthony riding to Norfolk. It was this decision that would have tragic consequences for Richard and John Woodville. The rebels managed to come between the king and his reinforcements raised by Pembroke and Devon, who had joined forces near Northampton. The rebels succeeded in pushing these forces back towards Banbury.[39] Both sides met again three miles outside of Banbury, in what has since become known as the Battle of Edgecote though it was really a series of skirmishes. On 25 July, the rebels fought the Welshmen under Pembroke, with the rest fighting the next day. This attack on the first day caused confusion among the Welshmen. Fearing attack by all of Warwick's army, they fled, unaware that they were only facing a small contingent. In the confusion, Pembroke and his brother were captured and taken to Northampton, where they were executed without trial on Warwick's orders, who had just arrived.[40] Richard and John Woodville had also been captured in or around Chepstow and were executed at Gosford Green just outside Coventry without a trial. These executions were clearly an attempt by Warwick to rid himself of as many of his enemies as he could.[41]

As the recent rebellions made clear, Warwick's opposition had become increasingly militant, although initially in the form of uprisings with which he could not be proved to be directly involved. The deaths of Richard and John would of course have been a blow to the family; two members killed at the same time. These losses surely fuelled the animosity between the Woodvilles and Warwick. The earl had sullied the Woodville name in the past, but now he was responsible for the deaths of two of their men. As Anthony had gone to his lands in Norfolk at this time, he was not one of those caught by the rebels. An attempt to find him was made, but he was only tracked as far as Crowland and was able to escape.[42] There is some conjecture as to whether he was actually caught and then released for some reason.[43] Considering his father and brother had been executed, this does not sound very likely, especially as Anthony had already been listed as one of the bad influences on King Edward, just as his father and brother had been.

The execution of his father was probably not the way Anthony would have wanted to inherit the title of Earl Rivers. Still, he had little else to inherit as most of his father's wealth had come from titles, rather than actual land he owned.[44] However, once Anthony had managed to build up his estates, he would go on to give land in 1475 to Eton in memory of John, who had a special affinity with the college there.[45]

With the Yorkist forces either defeated or driven off, Warwick's men took the opportunity to march towards Edward, who was still in Nottingham, and capture him. The king was placed under an armed guard and sent to Coventry and kept there under house arrest. With his capture, the remaining Woodvilles were vulnerable to their enemies, none more so than the now widowed Jacquetta. It was because of this weakness that she was accused by Warwick of witchcraft, which was also known by the blanket term of sorcery.

A squire by the name of Thomas Wake, a follower of Warwick's, made an accusation against Jacquetta. He came into the presence of the king and various lords at Warwick Castle, bringing a piece of lead moulded to look like a man and said that it belonged to Jacquetta, who had used it for 'wichecraft and sorcerie'.[46] This figure was broken in the middle and tied with wire, and it was suggested that this meant Jacquetta intended to harm either Warwick or Edward IV. Wake also claimed that a parish clerk in Northamptonshire called John Daunger had found two similar figures made by Jacquetta bearing a resemblance to Edward IV and Queen Elizabeth, suggesting that these were used 'to perform love magic' and that this was how the pair became married.[47]

The accusations against Jacquetta were serious enough for her to be arrested. While under arrest, she wrote to the mayor and aldermen of London to appeal for help and support. She hoped that as she had appealed to the Lancastrians not to march on London following the Second Battle of St Albans in 1461, they would be willing to help her.[48] They sent a letter of support for Jacquetta to both Warwick and Clarence. An inquiry was held into the charges, with the Bishop of Carlisle, the Earl of Northumberland, the Lords Hastings and Mountjoy and Roger Radcliff in charge of examining the case.[49] It was at this point that the case crumbled and it became obvious that the charges had been a set-up by the Earl of Warwick to try to demonstrate that 'the Woodvilles were enemies of Crown and Country'.[50]

John Daunger's story was very different to that given by Wake. Daunger admitted that he received the figure after it had already been found by another person and passed around multiple towns and even a nunnery. The figure had actually been left in a house where soldiers had recently been billeted. It was only after this that he was asked by Thomas Wake to send the figure to him, thus Jacquetta's name had not been mentioned prior to this. Daunger went on to incriminate Wake by admitting that Wake had told him to say that there were two other figures meant to represent the king and queen and that these images had never existed.[51]

It is no wonder that Jacquetta was officially cleared of any charges of witchcraft in front of the king and his council on 20 January 1470, with the verdict being officially recorded a month later.[52] Such public acceptance of the innocence of Jacquetta was also an acknowledgement that this had been an attempt by Warwick and other opponents of the Woodvilles to get rid of the family and their influence on Edward IV. This had severely backfired. Instead, the attempt revealed more about these enemies and the lengths to which they were willing to go to discredit the Woodvilles, especially at a time when they felt vulnerable following the extrajudicial executions of Richard and John after the Battle of Edgecote. We do not know what punishment Thomas Wake was given following the proceedings. Considering how clear-cut his deception had been when his accusations were placed under scrutiny, he probably would have suffered in some way. At the very least, his reputation has been ruined by the verdict being recorded for posterity.

Accusation of witchcraft was just one of the many ways opponents of the queen's family sought to discredit them. They invariably targeted the behaviour of the Woodvilles in some way or another. Certain accusations were possibly true while others, such as the accusations of witchcraft, were simply lies.

The complaints against the Woodvilles were either generalised, aimed at the whole family, or were aimed at particular members, such as Richard and Jacquetta. While it has been thought that Elizabeth was also one of those named, once she became queen this would not have been possible. Any word spoken against the queen would have been classed as a criticism of King Edward himself. Anthony was included in some of the condemnations, especially those suggesting the brood were evil advisors to the king.[53] These types of accusations reveal more about those who instigated them than they do about the Woodvilles themselves. The Earl of Warwick in particular, as we have seen, was keen to discredit them in the hope of stopping the diminution of his influence over, and favour with, the man he had helped make king.

Despite the many attempts to discredit the Woodville family, Anthony was relatively unscathed. In general, he was not named outright as a troublesome Woodville, although there are some examples where he is. This is because he tended to keep himself to himself. He was still able successfully to carry out his roles and responsibilities with great efficiency. Perhaps this may have been Anthony's way of trying to prove that any of the accusations against his entire family did not apply to him.

While this may be the case, there is one confessed act that was used to attack his character later. In 1465, Maud Stanhope, lady Willoughby, was required in an exchange for a pardon for her husband, Gervase Clifton, who was a Lancastrian, to grant Anthony 400 marks a year, which was around 80 per cent of her inheritance. This situation had clearly played on Anthony's conscience as he mentioned it in his will, wishing that she was recompensed for his servants seizing her personal goods, which were not part of the agreement.[54] From the wording in the will, it appears that Anthony felt a pang of conscience because either he did not punish these servants for their theft (perhaps even turned a blind eye to it), or he may have not known of their actions until it was too late to do anything about it. If he did know, it does show that there was a ruthlessness in this action for which Anthony felt he must make amends. While a will does partly play the role of clearing a conscience before death, this should not necessarily be viewed cynically. We cannot know all of Anthony's motives while writing his will, produced in haste knowing full well that he was to be executed, so it is entirely possible that he did feel regret over this episode.

Despite the warnings given to Edward IV about the company he kept, as well as the accusations aimed towards the Woodvilles in particular, Edward continued to trust the Woodvilles as his in-laws. One of the many events that showcased this trust was in the ceremonial reburial of his father, Richard, Duke of York, and younger brother, Edmund, Earl of Rutland. Both had been killed during the Battle of Wakefield in December 1460 and had been buried in the Priory of St John the Evangelist in Pontefract. The plan was to rebury them in July 1476 in the collegiate church at the Yorkist stronghold of Fotheringhay. It is unclear why it took so long between their deaths and their reburials, but it is probable that a mixture of unrest, Edward IV's exile and reglazing at Fotheringhay Church all contributed to the delay.

The reburial of York and Rutland held import for the house of York. It was to be a moment that was to be remembered as 'one of the most lavish of all Yorkist ceremonies and one that touched the very heart of the house's dynastic pretentions'.[55] In other words, it would show that Edward IV was the rightful king, even though by 1476 he had been on the throne since 1461, other than a brief exile between 1470-71. His throne, although technically won by conquest and military prowess, he wished to be seen to be his by right, and the reburial of his father and brother would be a good propaganda tool to this end.

The bodies were exhumed in Pontefract on 21 July and began their journey south from Yorkshire to Northamptonshire.[56] The bodies were placed inside chests or coffins, which were then placed on top of a platform underneath what was known as a hearse. Unlike the modern meaning of hearse, a vehicle used to transport a body, this was an immoveable structure built to fit the dimensions of a specific church, used to display a body. Hearses were house-like structures with an ornamental wooden roof, underneath which cloth would hang down to provide a canopy for the coffin. The structure would have had barriers around the sides to provide a more private grieving experience for important mourners, and it was surrounded by a multitude of candles.[57] The hearse was richly decorated and covered with various heraldic and religious symbols. These symbols were also repeated on banners carried by those in the procession. Religious symbols representing the Trinity and Virgin Mary were used, alongside Yorkist heraldic symbols like the Falcon in Fetterlock and the White Rose, both badges of the house of York.

A new hearse would have been provided at each church the procession visited on their journey to Fotheringhay. For this reason, each one would have been donated to the church as an alms offering. A separate one is not mentioned for Rutland until the arrival at Fotheringhay, suggesting that the bodies probably shared the same hearse prior to this. While on the road, the bodies were placed inside large four-wheeled carriages that looked like cages, draped with black velvet pulled back enough for onlookers to see the effigies. These effigies would have been the focal point; just as those that still exist in churches today, they were meant to be a lifelike representation of the deceased. York's effigy was life-size and had his hands folded in prayer. He was purposefully dressed in a gown of dark blue, the colour of mourning for kings, which was trimmed with ermine, as well as a purple cap of maintenance, also trimmed with ermine. An angel held out a crown behind the effigy's head, suggesting that York had been king in all but name.

The journey would have taken eight days in total, including stops at Doncaster, Blyth, Tuxford, Newark on Trent, Grantham and finally Stamford, before reaching Fotheringhay on 29 July. The large procession had Richard, Duke of Gloucester as chief mourner, with clergy, noblemen, officers of arms and a large number of poor men, a 'distinguished and wondrous' sight to behold.[58] They would have formed a pretty large group who walked beside the funeral carriage. There were twelve officers of arms alone, made up of a mixture of kings of arms, heralds and pursuivants, including one in Anthony Woodville's employ.[59] While all the mourners in the procession dressed in black hooded robes, the officers at arms were allowed to wear their brightly coloured surcoats on top. All the mourners would have had to attend the masses and services held along the route. The noblemen within the party would have been the ones allowed to kneel or stand within the barriers of the hearse, whereas the offices of arms and the poor stood beyond the barriers. This would have been done at every stop until the group finally reached their destination at Fotheringhay.

Upon reaching Fotheringhay on 29 July, the cortege at Fotheringhay was met by another large party, including King Edward and his queen, along with his brothers George, Duke of Clarence and Richard, Duke of Gloucester, as well as Anthony Woodville and his nephew, Thomas Grey, Marquess of Dorset, and the two eldest York princesses.[60] There was also a multitude of other nobles, including dukes, earls and barons.

Once inside the church, Edward would have privately retreated to his closet (a private pew partitioned off by a curtain). The nobles that were there, including Anthony, were then allowed inside the barriers of the hearse after the coffin and effigy had been placed correctly, having been borne by twelve former servants of the late duke. Towards the end of the service, offerings of cloth of gold were placed across the body. First, Lord Hastings gave his offering on behalf of Edward IV, then Lord Dacre, the queen's chamberlain, who gave on behalf of Queen Elizabeth.[61] All noble mourners were also expected to provide an offering of a quantity of cloth, according to their status. Three pieces five yards long were given by earls, with Anthony being the first, with five pieces given by the dukes. All the cloths were placed in a cross shape.

There is no doubt that Edward had spent a great deal of money in organising not only the reburials, which would have required complex logistics in organising a route, contacting mourners and organising the churches involved, but also the wonderful ceremony and display that went with it. There was a lavish feast held after the official funeral service on 30 July. For this, many canvas pavilions were provided to accommodate the number of mourners in attendance, as well as probably an outdoor kitchen.[62]

The Woodvilles themselves played their part in the ceremony – Anthony, his sister, the queen, and her eldest son from her first marriage, Thomas Grey. It is easy to forget that the Woodvilles were Lancastrians at the time of the Battle of Wakefield. The event was meant to symbolise the continuity, unity and loyalty both to and within the house of York, as well as projecting its future, which was so intertwined with that of the Woodvilles through Queen Elizabeth herself as the mother of the Yorkist heirs, but also through Anthony, Earl Rivers, who had proved himself a capable and loyal devotee of Edward IV's regime, and the man in charge of the Prince of Wales, the future of the dynasty.

The Woodville family, especially Elizabeth Woodville and her son, Thomas Grey, who became Marquess of Dorset, of course benefitted from the royal marriage. It is certainly true that Dorset spent much of his time at Edward's court, and this allowed him to partake in similar boisterous activities as his stepfather. Dorset appears to have entered the fold. For this reason, he has been viewed as one of the bad advisors often cited as being around the king.[63] However, that is not all there is to consider. It risks sounding as though they were the only family to have made such an advantageous marriage. The Nevilles' rise was based on such marriages. In fact, the Earl of Warwick's own great grandmother was the daughter of a merchant, but she enjoyed a similarly propitious marriage. This theme continued with subsequent generations until by the time of the Wars of the Roses, they were cousins to kings. While naturally there are similarities in the rise of both the Nevilles and the Woodvilles, the main difference is that the Woodvilles achieved their status within a shorter timeframe, which is why more attention was drawn to it. The fact that Elizabeth Woodville's parents, Richard and Jacquetta, had married despite their wide disparity in social status, with Richard being a lowly knight and Jacquetta a duchess, made things much more complicated for their children when Elizabeth made a similar match. As there had not been a previous example of this type of royal marriage, many nobles were unsure how to react to it.

Edward did not give everything to the one family alone. He was willing to spread his generosity to all the 'new' families who had supported him in his rise, including those of Lord Hastings, whom he made Lord Chancellor, as well as the Herberts. In fact, William Herbert, son and heir of Lord Herbert, Earl of Pembroke, was married to Mary Woodville, one of the many daughters of Richard and Jacquetta, in September 1466. An indenture of the marriage had been drawn up for the marriage earlier that year and had been between Richard, Earl Rivers, Anthony, lord Scales, and Sir John Woodville of one party, and William, Lord Herbert, Walter Devereux, Lord Ferrers, Sir Richard Herbert, and Thomas Herbert esquire of the other.[64]

As has already been discussed, better marriage prospects for her relations was one of the benefits of Elizabeth's marriage to Edward, but they were not the only family to have thus gained from marriages outside their social class. It was titles and governmental or military roles that concerned nobles, especially the Earl of Warwick, the most. *The Chronicles of the White Rose of York* bluntly proclaims that it was the 'almost unlimited power' of the Woodvilles that caused the destruction of the house of Neville.[65]

If this is really the reason behind Warwick's dislike of the Woodvilles, then it does not apply in the case of Anthony Woodville, as he did not benefit from titles and roles until after 1473. Some of these benefits included being granted lands in Norfolk, Suffolk and Nottinghamshire and elsewhere, through deaths and confiscations.[66] In May 1473, Anthony was also made

Chief Butler of England after the death of John, Earl of Wiltshire, a role closely associated with the manor of Kenninghall in Norfolk.[67] These roles and grants given to Anthony were largely focused on his East Anglia heartland, close to his existing estates, so these new land grants could be easily managed. The rewards he was given were also given in acknowledgement of the time that Anthony had spent in exile with Edward IV and others in Burgundy, as well as his time as governor to the Prince of Wales. So Anthony Woodville was not necessarily rewarded by Edward IV instantly after his marriage to Elizabeth. Very few nobles supported the Earl of Warwick's attempts at rebellion, which were deeply rooted in his dislike of the Woodvilles, although masked as a means of 'defending' England. As Gemma Hollman suggests, this shows that 'the Woodvilles cannot have been as unpopular as has been claimed'.[68]

In general, rewards appear to have been given to Anthony on merit. With this in mind, it is clear others of the Woodville family, most notably Thomas Grey, Marquess of Dorset, and men such as William Herbert or Lord Hastings, hugely benefitted in marriages, titles and roles during Edward IV's reign without such justification. Their social standing was immensely enhanced, and this would have caused antagonism among some of the aristocratic families who had enjoyed their high social standing for much longer than these so called upstarts. This cannot be said of Anthony Woodville, who despite eventually benefitting in titles and roles, appeared to keep himself in the political background and did not necessarily provoke the anger and disdain of others.

3

MARRIAGES AND AN ILLEGITIMATE CHILD

There has been some debate about the exact date of Anthony's first marriage to Elizabeth Scales, the most probable being around the time of the Battle of Towton in spring 1461. If we take this to be true, that would mean that the marriage took place just prior to Elizabeth Woodville's secret marriage to Edward IV in May 1461.[1] With this in mind, it is necessary to try and piece together other possible motives for the match than accumulating wealth and status. Love and affection, as well as improving familial connections, could have been motives.

Elizabeth Scales was daughter and heiress to Thomas, Lord Scales. In Lord Scales' post-mortem inquisition in July 1460, Elizabeth is mentioned as being 'aged 24 and more', placing her birth date around 1436.[2] This would mean she was anywhere between six and eight years older, possibly more, than Anthony. The proposed date of 1461 for the nuptials is based on Anthony's summons to Parliament on 22 December 1462, when he was known to have already been using the title of Lord Scales, a title which would only have come to him following his marriage to Elizabeth.[3] As this gives only a vague estimate of marriage dates, there has been some speculation as to whether the marriage took place before or after the Battle of Towton in March 1461.

While we cannot say when the marriage took place with any certainty, it is possible that it could have followed the Lancastrian victory at the second Battle of St Albans on 17 February 1461. The worried citizens of London had barred their gates following this battle. They sent 'the duches of Bedford and lady Scalys' and others to St Albans to plead with Queen Margaret of Anjou to 'entreate ffor grace ffor the cyte', with the hope that they could spare London from any fighting.[4] An agreement was reached that London would be safe, so long as it provided money to pay soldiers, which was much needed. When a small contingent arrived at the capital to collect the promised money, they were refused entry.[5] The women and others who had been sent to broker an agreement had showed bravery, even if the citizens of London did not go through with it.

Could this 'lady Scalys' sent on this mission be Elizabeth accompanying her new mother-in-law? Cora Scofield disagrees and instead suggests that the 'lady Scalys' mentioned in *The Great Chronicle* was more likely to have been Elizabeth's mother, Esmania.[6] However, no reference is made to her in the post-mortem inquisition of Thomas Scales following his death in 1460, perhaps suggesting that he had outlived his wife. This makes it more likely to have been Elizabeth, even more so when she appears to have accompanied Jacquetta Woodville. Thus, Anthony and Elizabeth would have been married before the Battle of Towton, as has been suggested by Susan Higginbotham, which occurred around a month after this entreaty.

What were the true motivations for the match? Anthony could have married Elizabeth for the money and status she brought as the heir to the Scales fortune, or perhaps it may have been to connect the two families through blood ties, rather than just allegiances.[7] Elizabeth was certainly left a large amount of land in Norfolk, Cambridgeshire, Hertfordshire, Essex and Suffolk.[8] By owning these lands, Anthony would certainly have had more land to support his status than his father could offer him in terms of an inheritance. While gaining these lands and the connections they came with gave Anthony more than any family inheritance, they did little to improve his own influence as they were scattered across the country, rather than being concentrated in a particular county or area. Nevertheless, the lands around the manor of Middleton in Norfolk offered the most potential, as they made up a third of the total.[9]

The Norfolk town now known as King's Lynn lay just five or so miles away from Middleton, the centre of Anthony's Norfolk estates inherited from the Scales fortune. During the medieval period, the town was known as Bishop's Lynn or just Lynn. Its name changed to King's Lynn following the dissolution of the monasteries. In May 1462, Anthony and his wife were jointly granted the manor of 'Le Syche' in South Lynn, worth £20 a year, which had been forfeited by Thomas Tudenham.[10] As their existing lands were in the area, this grant makes logistical sense. It also shows that the Woodvilles were now becoming part of the Yorkist regime.

Lynn's origins date back to around 1100 and it was established on the banks of the River Ouse, which gave it access to inland counties and the North Sea, and so Europe. Bishop's Lynn was largely owned by the Bishop of Norwich, hence its name. It is thought that the word 'lynn' describes the salting pools surrounding the town, which were the first thing that visitors were able to smell upon their arrival. From the thirteenth century, Lynn prospered by exporting wool to Flanders under the jurisdiction of the Hanseatic League, a powerful European trading association.[11] The wealth and trade networks established in Lynn attracted traders from all over the country and continent. Building upon this reputation, the town was granted a fee farm in 1449 by Henry VI, which granted it civic autonomy in exchange for an annual fee to the king. This was a prestigious grant as it was usually awarded to places such as York, Chester and Norwich, which were deemed to have sufficient royal importance.[12] The people, around 6,000 residents and the many visitors, who came from all social backgrounds, mingled together at the market, purchasing and selling a wide variety of goods.

The civic buildings built in Bishop's Lynn were the physical embodiment of the town's wealth and status during the fifteenth century. Some still exist today, such as the Trinity Guildhall and the South Gate. Both of these buildings would have been an impressive sight to visitors. The Trinity Guildhall, the home of the Guild of the Holy Trinity, a merchant group, was located on the marketplace. It was rebuilt following a fire in the previous building in 1421. The new building took sixteen years to build at a cost of £220.[13] The design features a chequerboard-style façade made from flint and chalk, which once would have been adorned with statues, although these no longer exist.[14] The Guildhall was a multipurpose space. It was an imposing building not only designed to show the power and status of the Guild, but also to be a public space for those invited inside. The stone undercroft was used to store items such as wine and millstones.[15] It was the symbolic heart of the mercantile community that the town's wealth was built on.

The South Gate was similarly built to impress visitors. The current South Gate is very different from the one that was intended by the town authorities, after the original gate needed repairs in 1437. There was an invitation to design its replacement and the man chosen to complete it was Robert Hertanger of London. His design was made up of brick and stone and was to include a twenty-foot-high arch with a fan vaulted ceiling, as well as a grand room above, in which important guests could be entertained.[16] Sadly, Hertanger was not the right man for the job as he was a drunk, meaning that when the money ran out, the authorities terminated his contract, citing that it was ended by 'reason of his own poverty'.[17] To make do with what had been built already, a temporary roof was put on top instead, which remained in place until 1520, when Cardinal Wolsey ordered the building completed.

With such close proximity to the town, there was a chance for Anthony and his wife not only to build connections but to also make money. The town often sent the couple flagons of wine and fish.[18] In April 1470 Anthony was given the lifelong grant of the annual rights to the customs and subsidies from the ports at both Bishop's Lynn and Yarmouth, now known as Great Yarmouth.[19] These customs rights for both ports were later exchanged in favour of a grant for the port of London.[20] While these Norfolk customs rights were in place, it was important to bolster his relationship with the townspeople of both of these towns, who were instrumental in his assumption of authority in Norfolk. Lynn was more important and nearer to his lands than Yarmouth, so it would have been a necessity for Anthony to maintain good relations with the residents there. These links that Anthony built with Lynn as a nearby landowner definitely contributed to the use of the port as a gateway to Europe when Edward IV and his followers needed to escape into exile following the brief restoration of Henry VI in 1470.

The main issue Anthony faced in terms of owning land in Norfolk wasn't necessarily to do with how profitable his lands were, but that the earls of Oxford and Norfolk owned more in comparison and were more permanently based there. As his responsibilities took him elsewhere, he had little opportunity develop a deeper relationship with those who lived and worked on his land. The elite were expected to display paternal generosity to the wider community beyond the manor house, just as a noble would to guests or members of his household.[21] It was necessary to create loyalty bonds between tenants and their liege lord. Anthony's roles calling him to court, as well as to different parts of the country and often abroad, would have made it difficult to maintain those bonds. In the words of Anne Crawford, this would have meant he was 'unlikely to command local loyalties' from those in Norfolk.[22] This is difficult to confirm, as loyalties cannot be measured as such. However, he must have been able to command at least some loyalty among those who lived and worked on the land he had inherited, simply because there is no evidence of dissent.

There is one example which suggests that there were some who thought that Anthony Woodville was a person of standing within the county. In 1482, a dispute arose between the City of Norwich and the Abbot of St Benets about water mills on the River Wensom.[23] A petition had been submitted to Edward IV by the Mayor and Aldermen of Norwich about mills that provided corn for the city. Four mills owned by the city had been damaged by a flood, but others owned by St Benets had not. The monks of St Benets argued that the damaged mills should not be replaced. Despite Edward IV taking the side of the monks, the city built four new mills to replace the lost ones. The disagreement did not subside and the Mayor wrote to Anthony Woodville to explain the citizens' position and to ask for assistance in the matter. Anthony wrote back to the Mayor, saying he would help 'to my otmost power and I trost it shall do weel'. Indeed it did, as Edward IV eventually changed his opinion on the matter and took the side of the city dwellers. Anthony had shown he was a capable landlord who was able to intercede in local issues. It is interesting to note that the Duke of Norfolk and the Earl of Oxford, who both owned more land in the county than Anthony, were not mentioned in the case.

Despite Woodville being brother-in-law to the king, he owned less land than you would expect. This meant he had to rely heavily on kinship ties for his reputation and status. This was probably a strong motive for his marriage to Elizabeth Scales. Anthony's father, Richard, had had a friendship and brother-in-arms style relationship with Thomas, Lord Scales, Elizabeth's father. When Richard Woodville was nominated to become a Knight of the Garter, Scales was one of the nominees. The Order was created by Edward III in 1348 and only allowed twenty-six members at a time. The members consisted of soldiers and peers, along with the monarch and Prince of Wales. To become a member, a person had to demonstrate knightly endeavour and gentility of birth.[24] For much of the fifteenth century, members were elected for these reasons, alongside familial ties, and sometimes for reconciliatory purposes.[25] Scales probably nominated Richard for a mixture of these reasons. Scales wanted to prove his trust in Richard. This was something that their children, Anthony and Elizabeth, would have been aware of and took into consideration prior to their marriage.

Whatever the reasons for their marriage, the pair seemed to get on well and to have been comfortable in each other's company. While the court was in Reading in November 1464, John Howard gave Elizabeth 8s 4d so she could gamble in a game of cards.[26] The next month they were at Eltham Palace, said to be one of Edward IV's favourite palaces, for Christmas. Howard gave 12d to 'my lord Scales child'.[27] As Anthony had no legitimate children, this is presumably his illegitimate daughter, Margaret, born prior to his marriage to Elizabeth Scales. This shows Elizabeth's generous or at least considerate nature, as it suggests that Margaret was allowed to be in her household. Howard was certainly in regular contact with, and a good friend to, Anthony and Elizabeth, for he also gave 8d to a servant of Anthony's on the same visit to Eltham, while in September 1464 he gave 6s 8d to a servant of Elizabeth's who had 'browt a lettre' from her.[28]

There are some glimpses of what their marriage was like in some of the very few records that mention both Anthony and Elizabeth. While not much survives, a common outcome from this period, Anthony must have thought well of Elizabeth. In a private agreement between Rivers and the town of Newport on the Isle of Wight, which details that Anthony wishes to pay taxes on behalf of the town, it is agreed that in exchange, the townsfolk would not only 'pay and distribute to the indigent poor 4 pence in sterling', but were also 'to pray for the good and noble standing of the said lord and his consort Elizabeth while they both live and for their souls when they have migrated from this light and also for the souls of their ancestors and heirs'.[29] The use of the word 'consort' is intriguing as it signifies Elizabeth Scales was seen as an important person in her own right, not only in terms of the usual preparation for the afterlife, as is common throughout this period, but also in her role as Anthony's helpmate. It is probable that Anthony himself referred to his wife as such. If this was the case, it would suggest that he viewed Elizabeth as a huge support to him, just as a queen consort would be to her king.

There was a Chancery Court case between Anthony, as Lord Scales, and John Towneshend, a yeoman of Raynham in Norfolk who worked on some land originally owned by Anthony's father-in-law, Thomas, Lord Scales, but which had been conveyed to Towneshend and others to be held in trust.[30] Following Thomas Scales' death, it would appear that his daughter and heir, Elizabeth, as well as Anthony as her husband, attempted to revert the land into Elizabeth's ownership as the Scales heir, and thus under Anthony's name as her husband. The case was to be overseen by the Chancery Court as Towneshend, the only surviving trustee, would not cooperate with this and held on to the land.[31] The dispute followed an unusual legal manoeuvre that ensured that if Elizabeth died before Anthony, the Scales' estate would stay with Anthony, rather than pass to her distant relatives. Despite this being an unusual arrangement, there is no reason to assume that it was one that Elizabeth disagreed with.[32] The distant relatives may have been people she had either never, or hardly ever, met, and so she may have preferred the estates to go to her husband.

This Chancery Court case implies that Anthony and Elizabeth were able to work as a team to try and recover land that they deemed was rightfully theirs, despite the complications of a possible trust. As a female heir, anything left to Elizabeth by her father meant that it would automatically belong to Anthony as her husband. If they worked together on this, it could also mean that Elizabeth trusted Anthony enough to look after her inheritance and rights on her behalf, despite the fact that as a woman she would be written out by the law in this instance.

Elizabeth Scales spent time in the company of her sister-in-law, Queen Elizabeth Woodville. In the queen's only surviving household account book of 1466-67, Scales and the queen's sister,

Anne, were paid £40 each for services as senior ladies-in-waiting.[33] This was quite a considerable sum. The queen's chamberlain, John Bourchier, Lord Bernes, a younger brother of the Earl of Essex and brother-in-law to Anne, was paid the same amount for his services. To have been granted a role in the household of the queen, even if it was a relation by marriage, would have been an honour for Elizabeth Scales. This meant that she was trusted and responsible enough to be able to take on the role. A role within Queen Elizabeth's household was even more of an honour as the number of incumbents was purposefully smaller than under her predecessor, Margaret of Anjou. There were seven ladies in waiting, rather than the ten under Margaret.[34] The other junior ladies were paid £20, half the amount of Anne and Elizabeth, again showing the favoured position that Lady Scales enjoyed.[35]

An account of Queen Elizabeth's churching ceremony following the birth of Princess Elizabeth in 1466, her first child with Edward IV, was given by Gabriel Tezel of Nuremburg. He was part of a retinue of Bohemians following the nobleman Leo of Rozmital, who was travelling around Europe.[36] As Elizabeth Scales was one of the queen's ladies-in-waiting, it is probable that she was one of the 'great company of ladies and maidens' that Tezel mentions in attendance that day.[37] It is also probable that Anthony was there, as Tezel says that his retinue banqueted in the hall alongside 'the noblest lords'.[38] As the ceremony involved Anthony's sister and new niece, as well as his wife being one of the party, it is logical that he would have been one of these lords, although Tezel does not mention names.

Elizabeth Scales played a similar role in October 1472, when Lord Gruuthuse, a Burgundian nobleman who had welcomed Edward IV during his exile, visited England and was presented with an English title in thanks for his hospitality. At a banquet held by the queen at Windsor during this visit, Elizabeth Scales was in attendance, mentioned as 'Lady Rivers'.[39]

Elizabeth Scales had quite clearly become a trusted attendant to the queen and would be much needed at such important events.

She would have had a vital part in portraying the sumptuousness of the Yorkist court, to both domestic and foreign audiences. The trust that the royal circle had in Elizabeth Scales would be further shown when she was chosen, alongside her husband, to be a member of the party of Margaret of York, youngest sister of Edward IV, to escort her upon her marriage to Charles the Bold, Duke of Burgundy.

Elizabeth died on 1 September 1473, while Anthony was away on pilgrimage to Santiago de Compostela in Spain. There is no document to suggest how he felt on the death of his wife, let alone whether he was informed of her death while out in Spain. No matter what the circumstances, Elizabeth's loss would have been a blow to him. They had been married for around twelve years at the time of her death and they had often been seen at court together and had even gone to Burgundy with Margaret of York. She was not forgotten by Anthony; his will suggested that some of the land inherited by his father be used to pay for prayers for her and her family.[40]

Anthony had no legitimate heir. For this reason, it was customary to marry again, usually after the socially acceptable year's mourning period was over. Unusually, Anthony's second marriage was to Mary FitzLewis in 1480, seven years after the loss of his first wife. Perhaps this does show that there was some love between Anthony and Elizabeth Scales, but in between there were also failed marriage proposals, both to foreign women. However, they were more to do with Edward IV's policy of using Anthony as an alternative to his younger brother, George, Duke of Clarence, who was proving troublesome and traitorous.[41] It is unknown what Anthony's own personal feelings were on either of these proposals.

Just as with Anthony's first wife, there were some old familial ties to the FitzLewis family. Mary's grandfather was John Lewis, also known as Lewis John, who was accused alongside Anthony's grandfather, Richard Woodville, of depriving the Earl of Warwick of his captaincy of Calais. For the sake of ease, we shall call him

John FitzLewis, even though the surname FitzLewis was only adopted by the family following John's death in around 1442.[42] The family's wealth had originated from his business as a wine merchant in London. In 1402, he was appointed deputy to the king's chief butler, Thomas Chaucer, son of the famous poet, Geoffrey Chaucer, in the port of London. With this appointment, he received patronage from Thomas that would last throughout most of John's career. This initial patronage seems to have stemmed from Thomas buying wine for the royal household from John, introducing him to those within the royal circle. In his *Survey of London*, Stow suggests that FitzLewis built some form of friendship with the future Henry V and his brothers through this connection, as they were known to feast in his house in the Vintry Ward of London, an area named after the wine merchants there.[43] In 1412, the Close Rolls described him as a goldsmith, but there is no mention of his wine business.[44] It appears this may have been a side venture, although it is unknown how long he kept this up. In February 1413, John was again organising wine to be collected for the royal household. The customs collectors at the port of London were ordered to pay John and Thomas Chaucer £795 10s out of the first money to be collected, for wine bought for the royal household.[45] FitzLewis' reputation grew with the help of Thomas Chaucer. He was elected as burgess of Taunton and Wallingford in 1413 and in 1419, and he became Member of Parliament for Essex in 1420.

Chaucer was a good choice of patron to help kickstart John's political and public service career. First of all, his personality was persuasive thanks to his charisma and shrewdness, meaning he was able to maintain personal and political relationships in a way that benefitted himself and his associates.[46] Thomas Chaucer was well respected by others and had connections spanning across the court and gentry, which no doubt helped develop networks for FitzLewis to climb not only the social ladder, but the political ladder, too. Thomas's cousin, Henry Beaufort, the Bishop of Winchester, helped to build these connections. This association placed Chaucer in the camp of supporters of Henry, Prince of Wales, the future Henry V, but he did manage to maintain his status under the aging Henry IV in retaining his role of chief butler, which had not been a given. While he had originally been granted this position for life, Henry IV briefly removed him in 1407 when he was replaced by Sir John Tiptoft, only to be reinstated a few months later under the condition that he should hold the title at the king's pleasure, not for life.[47] Chaucer also served for five parliaments, an achievement not equalled until the eighteenth century.[48]

Chaucer had the chance to prove himself further when tensions between Henry V and Bishop Beaufort began to rise following a disagreement over unpaid loans Beaufort had given the king, especially after one loan he made of £17,666 13s 4d, despite £8,300 still being unpaid from previous ones.[49] Beaufort angered Henry more when in December 1417 he became a cardinal and papal legate without having the king's leave to do so.[50] While it is thought Henry was willing to let things go until then, this appeared to be the final straw and hostilities continued to grow. Thomas Chaucer was hired to spy on Beaufort and report back using secret correspondence, as well as in a face-to-face meeting in the spring of 1420. Chaucer is to be admired in his dealing with this tricky bind, as at the risk of alienating his cousin, Beaufort, he managed to bring about some form of reconciliation. It was 'a tribute to Chaucer's intelligence that he had been able to discharge so successfully this task of acting as royal watchdog without losing Beaufort's confidence'.[51] It is clear that Chaucer was a man of many talents and someone that FitzLewis would have been glad to have on side.

For John FitzLewis, the networking behind the scenes had begun to pay off by 1413. He was appointed Keeper of the Change and Master of the Mint in both London and Calais. These roles meant that he would have been in 'complete control of the system of foreign exchange' and the production of money, a huge responsibility.[52] As mentioned earlier, it did come with some issues, not only because people accused him of being a social climber but because the Earl of Warwick named him as one of the people, alongside Richard Woodville and Richard Bokeland, who deprived him of the captaincy of Calais. Despite Warwick's complaints, the careers of the three men were unharmed. FitzLewis continued to be the Keeper of Change and Master of the Mint for nine years until 1422. In 1434, he was given a role on the King's Council, indicating the king's trust in him. This would be further indicated when he was sent as part of a diplomatic party to discuss breaches of an Anglo-Scots treaty with James I of Scotland.[53] This was by far the most important task John had been given to date. His time as a diplomat was short-lived, for the diplomatic protection he was offered was quickly revoked when he returned to England to conduct personal business in Middlesex.[54] No matter how long his role lasted, John must have been held in high esteem to have been chosen for this diplomatic mission.

John's career was an interesting example of Welsh and English relations at a time of great tension between the two. John claimed that both his parents were Welsh. Penal law at the time stipulated that a Welshman, unless classed as free, could not hold land. Rumours were spread by those jealous of his status that he was not free. To counteract this, John petitioned for his rights and won.[55] He went on to own land in Essex, Middlesex, Hertfordshire and Kent, mostly in Essex.[56] The amount of wealth and land he accrued is evident in his tax assessment of 1436 of £350, making him the third wealthiest man in the county of Essex.[57] This was a lot of money to be paying in taxation, especially considering he was still yet to be knighted at this point. With the wealth and standing that his career brought, he was able to make advantageous marriages, first to Alice de Vere, daughter of the Earl of Oxford, secondly to Anne Montague, daughter of the Earl of Salisbury. It is no wonder that others may have viewed his wealth and ability to mix with royalty and nobility with envy.

The pedigree that John had established for subsequent generations of the FitzLewis family would not have been lost on Anthony when he chose John's granddaughter, Mary, as his second wife. Both the Woodville and the FitzLewis family's pedigree was only a couple of generations old, although the circumstances were different. The Woodvilles' pedigree came from advantageous marriages and family ties rather than money, like the FitzLewis family. Still, both had grown in standing compared with previous generations; the FitzLewis family had been rising for a few generations now, whereas the Woodville family's high standing was still relatively new by comparison.

According to a calendar in a book owned by Jacquetta Woodville and inherited by Anthony, the birth date of Mary FitzLewis was 30 May 1467, meaning that she was thirteen at the time she married Anthony and just over twenty years younger than him.[58] Mary had many notable connections through various family members, but most prominent were the Beauforts. There were connections through her grandfather, John, who had become associated with Cardinal Beaufort, a cousin of Thomas Chaucer, after being indentured to fight in France during the Agincourt campaign as part of the Cardinal's retinue.[59] The Beauforts were also related to Mary by marriage. With these various links to the great families of the day, whether they were Yorkist or Lancastrian, Mary would have been seen as a good match for creating ties of kinship. This is perhaps a more likely motivation for their marriage rather than land, as the FitzLewis family was male dominant, meaning it was unlikely that any significant inheritance would pass to Mary. According to Lynda Pidgeon, these connections were 'the only value' this marriage could have had.[60]

Even less is known about Anthony's marriage to Mary FitzLewis than his previous marriage. Anthony and Mary married in 1480, about seven years after the death of Anthony's first wife. It was unusual to leave so long between marriages. Perhaps this meant that there was genuine affection between

Anthony and his first wife. Mary and Anthony may not have had much chance to spend time in each other's company because of Anthony's duties as governor in the household of the Prince of Wales in Ludlow, but also because in 1482 he accompanied the Duke of Gloucester's Scotland campaign. Mary was still young to consummate a marriage. Generally, this happened when the female was around fifteen years old.[61]

Due to Mary's age at the time of her marriage, Lynda Pidgeon has suggested that this means Anthony was 'not really interested in having a wife and providing an heir'.[62] But within a few years of their marriage, Anthony would be executed. Anthony of course could not have known this as Mary approached childbearing age. Mary would go onto have children after Anthony's death. She married George Neville, an illegitimate great nephew of Cecily Neville, Duchess of York. Neville was a Yorkist and went on to be an Esquire of the Body during the reign of Richard III.[63] He was living in exile on the continent during the reign of Henry VII and in 1492, Neville lent his support to the pretender, Perkin Warbeck.[64] The couple also had a daughter called Anne. It is possible that Mary and Anthony had not consummated their marriage in the few years they were married.

Mary is mentioned in Anthony's will, in which he bequeathed 'all such plate' – probably items such as cups, bowls and salt cellars – that she had brought into their household and had once been originally owned by her family, as well as any plate given to her upon and during their marriage.[65] He asks for prayers to be said for Sir Henry Lewis, Mary's father.[66] This was little to leave his wife, but as the will was written after Anthony knew he was to be executed, it was uncertain as to how many of his instructions would have been acted upon. This might explain why little else is mentioned.

In between his marriages, Anthony Woodville was considered one of the most eligible bachelors and Edward IV attempted to use him as a means to secure much needed alliances. Edward IV was obliged to offer Anthony as an acceptable alternative to his own brother, George, Duke of Clarence, to high-status noblewomen across Europe. The two women he offered Anthony's hand to were Princess Margaret, sister of James III of Scotland and Mary of Burgundy, the only child of Charles, Duke of Burgundy, and thus a stepdaughter to Edward's youngest sister, Margaret.

Following treaties with Scotland in the 1470s, a marriage between Anthony and Margaret of Scotland was proposed in the hope of stopping conflicts across the border. At the same time, Cecily, third daughter of Edward IV, was betrothed to James III's heir. In December 1478, Edward Woodville, Anthony's younger brother, and John Alcock, the Bishop of Rochester, were sent to Scotland to discuss terms for Anthony and Margaret's match. The identities of these two representatives indicate the negotiations were serious. Arrangements were made for Margaret to arrive in England on 16 May 1479 with an escort of 300 men, Nottingham being chosen as the location for the wedding.[67] Despite these thorough preparations, Margaret's journey to England was delayed because James III's brother, the Duke of Albany, vied for the throne. By 1480, relations with Scotland had deteriorated, making the match unviable, and that same year Anthony married the heiress Mary FitzLewis. Even if Anthony had remained unmarried and stuck to the plan for the Scottish marriage, following the invasion of Scotland in 1482 the match would have been impossible to complete anyway. After peace was concluded, the marriage between Cecily and James III's heir was still meant to go ahead. However, in December 1482, James III changed his mind, possibly because he found it difficult to accept the English control of Berwick, and he was still facing a threat to his rule – albeit diminished – from his brother, the Duke of Albany.[68]

In 1477, the year of the death of Charles, Duke of Burgundy, his only daughter Mary was unmarried. Edward IV sent John Coke and Louis de Bretaylle, a friend of Rivers, to put Anthony forward as a possible husband for the new Duchess of Burgundy. To sweeten the deal, England offered military support if Anthony's proposal was accepted. It was unlikely that this offer would have been accepted though, as Mary was the greatest heiress on the continent. She married Maximilian, son of the Holy Roman Emperor, in August 1477.[69]

Just as with the wives of Anthony Woodville, little is known about Anthony's illegitimate daughter, Margaret. Her mother has been identified by H. T. Evans as Gwenllian, daughter of William Stradling of Glamorgan and his wife Isobel.[70] Edward Lowry Barnwell, who wrote notes during the Victorian era on the various branches of the Perrot family, which included Margaret, wrongly identified Gwenllian as Anthony's second wife.[71] This cannot be the case as despite the fact there is no known birth date for Margaret, it is presumed that she was born prior to his first marriage to Elizabeth Scales around 1461, and a long time before his second marriage to Mary FitzLewis in 1480. It is possible that this may have been a deliberate mistake to gloss over an illegitimate ancestor, a Victorian attempt to mitigate what they saw as a social impropriety.

If Gwenllian was the birth mother of Margaret, Anthony could have met her through a mutual connection to the Herbert family. Gwenllian's nephew had married Elizabeth Herbert, sister of William, Earl of Pembroke.[72] This theory makes sense considering that Margaret's future husband, Robert Poyntz of Iron Acton, had been made a ward of Thomas Herbert in 1467.[73] It suggests that there was some connection to the Herberts, which is entirely possible considering the patronage Edward IV had given the family when he made William Herbert Earl of Pembroke.

As previously noted, Lynda Pidgeon in her assessment of Anthony's will suggests that he did not care for Margaret as his daughter. Her reasoning for this is that he does not appear to leave her anything in his will, so he 'seems to have had little feeling' for her.[74] As a will is a legal document, it is not a necessarily a good source to use as an indication of a person's private feelings. Anthony's will was written in haste, as time was of the essence. It is also possible that, as Margaret had married well, Anthony felt she was already well cared for. In addition, upon Margaret's marriage to Robert Poyntz, Anthony settled eight hundred marks, two hundred of which was to be paid on the sealing of the deed, with the rest to be paid on certain days.[75] Anthony also provided for Margaret by granting her lands that had the yearly value of one hundred marks.[76] From this, it is certain that Margaret did have some financial protection. Anthony also mentioned Robert Poyntz as an executor of his will, suggesting that there was some form of close relationship, so Margaret was not entirely forgotten as death approached.[77]

Margaret's firstborn son was named Anthony after her father, again suggesting there was some affection between father and daughter. The couple also had four daughters.[78] The Poyntz Chapel at St Mark's Church in Bristol, built by Robert, contains his arms quartered with Woodville arms. It appears Robert was not embarrassed to showcase his Woodville connections.

While little is known about the relationships that Anthony had with either of his wives and illegitimate daughter, it is clear that in the case of Elizabeth Scales, Anthony had found someone he was willing to share time at court with. Her role as lady-in-waiting to his sister, and as part of the wedding party of Margaret of York, meant that Elizabeth was clearly welcomed into the family and was entrusted with roles which entailed great responsibility. More is known about Elizabeth thanks to these roles, as well as the fact she was an heiress to the Scales estate.

We cannot be sure of the personal feelings that went with these relationships. Anthony's will did not request burial beside Elizabeth, his first wife, and he only requested the bare minimum be done in the provision for her soul and that of others, suggesting that Anthony 'did not have feelings for anyone else'.[79] But it is worth stressing that Anthony wrote the will just prior to his execution at Pontefract, a situation we might describe as high pressured. As we lack more complete records relating to Anthony, it is very difficult to make a confident negative assessment.

From what we can piece together about Elizabeth Scales and Anthony's relationship, they appear to have enjoyed each other's company, as seen during the time they spent together with the court at Reading in November 1464.[80] They also spent much time together at their estates in Norfolk. Anthony could have equally enjoyed spending time with his second wife, Mary FitzLewis, as well as his illegitimate daughter, Margaret. The problem is that we do not have any surviving sources that may give a definitive answer.

4

MILITARY CAREER

After the marriage of Elizabeth Woodville to Edward IV, Anthony and the other Woodvilles were given more opportunities to express their newfound loyalty to the Yorkist king. According to the Venetian papers, Lord Rivers, Anthony's father, was reported as saying that Henry VI's cause was 'lost irremediably', and this could have been the same opinion held by Anthony himself.[1] If this were true, it would explain the continued loyalty of the Woodvilles. There would be no better way of displaying this new Yorkist allegiance than to fight against the Lancastrian threat following an invasion of Northumberland by forces who had made the journey from their continental exile to seek favour and military assistance from Scotland.

In the autumn of 1462, Lancastrian forces headed for castles in Northumberland such as Bamburgh, Dunstanburgh, Warkworth and Alnwick. Once they had taken control, it would not be easy for the Yorkists to besiege them. *Warkworth's Chronicle* considers the initial French force that the Lancastrians had landed with was around 2,000 strong, before other Englishmen and Scotsmen joined their number after the castles had been taken.[2] As there was no mentioned Yorkist siege at Warkworth, it is possible that their numbers became concentrated at Alnwick. The Lancastrians had received subsidies from Louis XI and were allowed to recruit men from France, alongside the renewed help from the Scots. With these factors in mind, Northumberland would be the best place to start their invasion, even though Scottish support was wavering.

In early November, Edward left London for Northumberland. He had a large force with him. Anthony Goodwood has claimed that it was the one of the largest groups of peers in the later medieval period, with a total of thirty-nine adult nobles among Edward's men.[3] Among them were a number of former Lancastrians, or so called 'neutrals', hoping to gain favour with the new king. Anthony Woodville was one of these men. After pledging his allegiance to Edward following his victory at the Battle of Towton, the Northumberland expedition was a chance for Anthony to prove both his newfound loyalty and his military skill.

Despite this positive start, Edward contracted measles and had to stay in Durham, leaving the Earl of Warwick in charge of organising the upcoming sieges. At Alnwick and Bamburgh there were an estimated 300 men, with Alnwick mainly containing French forces brought over by Margaret of Anjou, and around 120 men at Dunstanburgh. Dunstanburgh and Bamburgh fell quickly, on 26 and 27 December respectively. The siege at Alnwick proved more troublesome.

It was during the siege at Alnwick that Anthony would become involved, alongside William Neville, Earl of Kent.[4] To be given this type of responsibility just over a year after receiving a pardon for being allied with the Lancastrians showed that either Anthony had already earned the trust of members of the Yorkist elite, or this was a test of his loyalty. It was not an easy siege to have been a part of, if you can say that about any siege. The Yorkists at Alnwick had to contend with the harsh winter conditions which a siege in late December and early January brought. *Warkworth's Chronicle* gives a very bleak insight into the morale among the besiegers as they 'had lie there so long in the field and were grieved with cold and rain, that they had no courage to fight'.[5]

As if the conditions were not demoralising enough, there were rumours of a Scottish force being sent to rescue the Lancastrian men holed up at Alnwick.[6] The reports reaching the Yorkists indicated that George Douglas, Earl of Angus, had been amassing his troops along the English border, ready to make his move into Northumberland. According to the Scottish chronicler John Major, Angus had gathered around 13,000 men and chose the very best of them to go to Northumberland.[7] This Scottish force arrived at Alnwick on 6 January 1463. Their arrival caused the Yorkists to withdraw from their besieging positions, allowing part of the garrison inside Alnwick Castle to disappear with the Scots. With part of the garrison rescued, the remaining Lancastrians were able to surrender on good terms. Following this surrender, the campaign in Northumberland came to an abrupt end and the Yorkist forces were moved southwards, other than those who directly served under the Earl of Warwick, who were ordered to stay behind to patrol the border.

This was a disappointment for the Yorkists. Anthony would certainly have felt this. The Northumberland campaign had not fulfilled his ambition to prove himself. To make things worse, the chronicles were critical of the Yorkists' capabilities at Alnwick. *Warkworth's Chronicle* in particular had a lot to say on the matter. The author suggested that the Yorkist performance had been poor, and he found it quite strange that the Scots had not taken advantage of this and defeated the Yorkists while they had the chance.[8] The chronicler was right in his assumptions, but perhaps it was easier for the Scots not to attack as their appearance effectively ended the siege anyway. Major's Scottish chronicle suggests that the English had mixed orders from those in charge about whether to attack the Scots or not, which did not help.[9] Another chronicler was even more critical of the campaign, claiming that it was a failure of 'practically the whole knighthood of England', as it did not achieve much beyond capturing the castles of Dunstanburgh, Bamburgh and Alnwick.[10]

While of course there were failures on the part of the Yorkists, the fact the siege was during a bout of bad winter weather, as well as Edward IV's illness keeping him in Durham, meant that there was a lack of drive and low morale. These things were outside of the Yorkists' control, although if the Scottish chronicle is to be believed, there did appear to be a lack of united leadership, particularly after the arrival of the Scots. Still, the Lancastrians did not manage to keep their hold on Northumberland and the Scots did little to help their cause, other than to help relieve the siege at Alnwick.[11] While the Lancastrians failed to extend their power outside of Northumberland, the threat they posed did continue to drain Edward's resources, meaning he had continually to ask his subjects for financial assistance, as well as rely heavily on the Nevilles in the North.[12] So it was Warwick who was placed in charge of a force to patrol and guard the border.

No matter what failures the Northumberland campaign represented, for Anthony Woodville there was some benefit for having taken part. Not long after the siege at Alnwick, he was made a knight of the garter.[13] By being nominated for this honour, Anthony had proved himself worthy in both military and familial ways. For him, this would only be the first of many chances to prove himself militarily, something which he would do time and time again when the circumstances required it.

In August 1467, just two years before his death at the Battle of Edgecote, Richard Woodville, Earl Rivers, was granted the prestigious post of Constable of England. He took charge of all military affairs alongside the Earl Marshal, the Duke of Norfolk. Upon Richard's appointment, it was agreed that Anthony would replace his father upon his death, under the same conditions.[14] However, following Richard's death in 1469, Anthony instead waived his right to the role in favour of Richard, Duke of Gloucester, Edward IV's youngest brother.[15] Anthony thought that Gloucester was the more capable man for the job, showing that the pair must have known each other well in order for Anthony to have come to this conclusion.

Whatever the reason for Anthony's decision to defer the role of Constable of England to Gloucester, Anthony still continued to offer military assistance when necessary. In 1468, Anthony was given control of 3,000 armed men and 1,100 sailors for raids on the undefended French coast for the term of a quarter of a year.[16] Alongside Lord Howard, it was Anthony's responsibility to supply this royal fleet. Howard had problems sourcing items like barrels and pipes, which had to be sourced from London taverns and loyal friends.[17] Although the expedition did not last as long as the quarter that Anthony and the men under him had been paid for, they were not required to repay anything.[18] These types of expeditions would be something that Anthony conducted many times, including during the Brittany campaign of 1475.

As a direct result of his faithful and successful service, both on land and at sea, Anthony was rewarded with the roles of Lord of the Isle of Wight in 1466 and Constable of Carisbrooke Castle. In January 1474, he was similarly made governor of Porchester Castle, as well as supervising the safety of the town of Portsmouth.[19] With all of these responsibilities, Anthony was in charge of defending most of the Solent between the Isle of Wight and Portsmouth. With his previous experience in organising fleets against Lancastrian rebels, it made sense to place Anthony in charge of the Isle of Wight and Portsmouth, for they could be defended at sea if necessary. He was the right man for the job.[20]

There were rebellions in the North during the Spring of 1470, and England once again was in turmoil. In April, the Earl of Warwick and the Duke of Clarence attempted to flee to France, so they could bide their time and bolster their cause. Their journey took them through Wiltshire. Anthony Woodville had been sent by Edward IV to try and stop them from leaving the country. Anthony was captured and was briefly imprisoned at Wardour Castle, alongside John Lord Audley. Their fate was uncertain, with the rebels gathered in the names of Warwick and Clarence now in disarray. While there was some doubt about what would happen next, Woodville and Audley were 'to be kept out of the way unto a time determinate, that they should have been put to execution'.[21] Upon hearing of this predicament, a gentleman from Dorset named John Thornhill 'came the night following with a good company of hardy fellows and found the means to deliver these two lords from captivity'.[22]

It is curious to note that this incident of Anthony's brief incarceration at Wardour Castle is only to be found in *The Chronicles of the White Rose.* Does this mean that the story is not credible? We do know that Warwick and Clarence did journey through Wiltshire on their way to Southampton to sail away to the continent, and that Woodville had been sent by Edward to stop them. This certainly gives credence to the tale, even more so when it is taken into account that Wardour is around forty miles away from Southampton, a day or a day and a half's ride away. Warwick it should be remembered had imprisoned and executed Anthony's father, Richard, and brother, John, without trial in 1469, following the Battle of Edgecote. If he planned to do the same with Anthony Woodville, that would have ensured Warwick was rid of another member of the family he so hated.

Upon reaching Southampton, Warwick and Clarence were able to put to sea, taking many ships with them, including the *Trinity*, owned by Warwick. However, Anthony was in hot pursuit and determined to fulfil the orders that he had been given by his royal brother-in-law. Anthony managed to cause damage to Warwick's forces and took 'dyverse schyppes of theres and many men therein'.[23] It is probable that he had inside help. The captain of the *Trinity* was later paid an annuity of £20 by Edward IV.[24] Most of those captured were sent to John Tiptoft, Earl of Worcester, for judgement. Twenty were hung, drawn and quartered.[25]

If anyone thought that would be the end of the fight, then they were sorely mistaken. Woodville continued to follow the rebels towards France, which would become their place of exile.

With a combined English and Burgundian fleet, they attempted to block the rebels in the Seine. This sent a clear message to the rebels that not only were England and Burgundy strong allies, but that the treason they had committed would not be tolerated. In total, they seized fourteen of the ships in Warwick's flotilla.[26]

Warwick and Clarence were nevertheless able to reach safe harbour in Honfleur. Louis XI, while not openly welcoming them, decided to cast a blind eye on the English exiles, exasperating the English and Burgundians. While the exiles, including Thomas Neville, the Bastard of Fauconberg, an illegitimate nephew of Warwick, were able to turn pirate and attack Burgundian and Breton ships.[27] In choosing these ships as their victims, it was obvious who they believed their perceived enemies were, those who had followed them to France in the first place.

The piratical behaviour endorsed by Warwick ensured that the Burgundians were being robbed of their 'possessions, merchandise and vessels', guaranteeing that the English exiles were increasing the size of their fleet.[28] The amount of damage they were doing to the Burgundian shipping was not going to go unnoticed. The longer it went on, the more anger it provoked in the Burgundians themselves and their English allies, and it put King Louis in a difficult position. Warwick's arrival, as well as the acts of piracy, infringed on a treaty the French had recently signed with Burgundy. If the French continued to harbour Warwick and his men, then it would have diplomatic repercussions. With tensions growing, it became increasingly unlikely that a safe haven would continue to be offered to these exiles.

As a result of Anthony's successes against Warwick and the rebels who followed him, he was given the role of Lieutenant of Calais in June 1470, which he held until 1474.[29] This was an important role which not only included looking after the crown's interests and the citizens there, but also meant taking responsibility for maintaining control of the English Channel. It made sense to give Anthony this role to ensure continued monitoring of Warwick's exiles and if necessary, he could fight them at sea. Once these pressures had eased, Anthony was replaced in the role by Lord Hastings. This created an enmity between the pair and a war of words ensued that would last for the next decade.

In 1470 Warwick returned for his final act on the political stage. He reinstated Henry VI as a puppet king, ruling through him. Edward IV and his supporters were now the ones in exile, but in Burgundy. With many months spent abroad, eventually the Yorkist exiles received enough military support from Burgundy to return to England. Edward IV's road back from exile in the Low Countries in early 1471 was not an easy one. With Henry VI reinstated to the throne, there were many challenges ahead. The first was to find a safe place to land where the locals would not be hostile to Edward's return. Charles, Duke of Burgundy had subsidised more than 2,000 men for Edward to bring over as part of his forces.[30]

Edward and his party, including Richard, Duke of Gloucester, Anthony Woodville, Lord Hastings and others, initially tried to land at Cromer in Norfolk. With Anthony among their party, this was a logical choice as he was a local landowner, so it was hoped the local community would allow them to move through without hostility. To gauge the feelings of the area, men were sent to investigate, but the locals were found to be anything but welcoming, meaning it was best to move on. After 'great stormes, wynds and tempests', they safely landed on the Holderness coast, albeit in different areas, with around 2,400 men.[31] Edward and Hastings landed together at Ravenspur, with Richard, Duke of Gloucester four miles away and Anthony fifteen miles away. *The Crowland Chronicle* suggests that there is some significance to the group landing along the Holderness coast, as this was the same region where Henry IV, as Henry Bolingbroke, had landed when he returned to England to depose Richard II.[32]

There was less opposition to their landing than was expected, but the people suggested they would only offer Edward support if he wished to claim his right as Duke of York, through the inheritance from his father, rather than as king.[33] Edward agreed to this and he was allowed to continue on his way to York, before journeying south. Edward's forces marched towards Coventry, where the earls of Warwick and Oxford were known to have positioned themselves with a large force. No fighting took place though, as the Lancastrians did not dare to challenge Edward to a pitched battle at this point.[34]

Anthony continued to be one of Edward's group; he was mentioned as a member of the king's party at Banbury when Edward met with his brother, Clarence, for the first time since he had defected with the Earl of Warwick. At this meeting, Richard of Gloucester, Lord Hastings, Anthony and a few select others were taken with Edward to this intimate meeting, with all the other men ordered to stay at a distance. *The Arrivall* indicates that this meeting was thankful and joyous, with an emphasis on unity for 'the Kynge browght his brother Clarence, and suche as were there with hym, to his felowshippe'.[35] To be part of such a personal moment for the York brothers shows the importance that Edward placed upon Anthony's company. Clarence appeared to have settled himself in again as the prodigal son of York. He even tried to convince Warwick to give up his campaign with the Lancastrians against Edward, but this warning was ignored by Warwick.

The route towards the Battle of Barnet was set, and Edward and his men marched south towards London. When the Yorkist forces reached there, they made Henry VI their prisoner once more, showing who was now in control of the country. Once this mission was complete, Edward and his men left London on 13 April 1471 and camped at Barnet, just ten miles outside of the capital, where they would face Warwick's army the following day.

Barnet is remembered in part for the fog that spread across the battlefield. It was this fog that sealed the fate of the Earl of Warwick and the Lancastrian forces. The Lancastrians outnumbered Edward IV's forces and also had the advantage of being on a ridge just outside the town of Barnet. It appeared that the Lancastrians had the upper hand, especially when men led by the Earl of Oxford routed those led by Lord Hastings. With the heavy fog, the Lancastrians mistook the Oxford star badge for the Yorkist sun in splendour, with shouts of treason.[36] This created confusion and with the death of the Marquess of Montague, Warwick's younger brother, the Yorkists began to gain the upper hand. Warwick himself tried to escape but he was killed in the process, as were other nobles. Many others were injured, including Richard, Duke of Gloucester and Anthony Woodville.[37] According to a newsletter written just a few days after the battle by a Hanseatic merchant by the name of Gerhard von Wesel, who was living in London at the time, they were both 'slightly wounded, but thanks be to God, suffered no further harm'.[38] It would appear that Wesel was fond of both noblemen, probably from what he had heard on the streets of London, or had seen of them on the many times they had paraded into the city either on the king's or private business, or on their way to court.

The battle proved to be a turning point in Edward's return to the throne. With Warwick's death, a powerful magnate many had gathered under was gone. As he had been so much a part of the lives of all three York brothers, this must have brought mixed emotions. While his death surely strengthened Edward's hand, Warwick had known Edward and his brothers, George and Richard, since youth, and had been instrumental in supporting Edward's rise to kingship ten years previously. Whatever they may have been feeling, all three brothers triumphantly rode back into London. There were others alongside them, 'large numbers of the magnates and the common folk'.[39] Anthony Woodville, who had taken part and been injured in the battle, would have been one of these many men. It is not certain what injury he sustained during the fighting, but whatever it was, he was clearly recovered by mid-May 1471, as he was defending London against Lancastrian rebels.

The Battle of Barnet would not be the only large-scale battle of 1471. Less than a month later, Lancastrian forces under Margaret of Anjou would meet the Yorkist army at Tewkesbury. Her forces, alongside her son, Prince Edward, had landed on the south coast at Weymouth on the same day as the Battle of Barnet was fought. She made her way to the West Country to meet up with Welshmen led by Jasper Tudor, the loyal Lancastrian and uncle to the future Henry VII. After securing money and weapons from the city of Bristol, the army decided to find a place to cross the River Severn to reach Wales. The most logical place for this was Gloucester. Edward had already sent messengers to the town, convincing the townsfolk to defend themselves against the oncoming Lancastrians.[40] In response, the gates were kept closed, forcing the Lancastrians to head for Tewkesbury.

On 3 May 1471, the Yorkists caught up with the Lancastrians. The next day, battle commenced. All the brothers of York fought, but particular praise was given to the eighteen-year-old, Richard Duke of Gloucester, who commanded the Yorkist vanguard. Tewkesbury was a major blow for the Lancastrian cause as many of the pre-eminent figures of the Lancastrian cause were killed, most notably Edward, Prince of Wales, Henry VI's heir. The executions of many other Lancastrians after the battle were controversial, especially those ordered by Edward after the men had been dragged from their place of sanctuary at the nearby abbey. By breaking church laws, Edward IV showed he thought his word was above the sanctity of the church, even the word of God. Among those executed were the Duke of Somerset and Hugh Courtney, a cousin to the Earl of Devon.

While men under Margaret of Anjou were trying to cross the River Severn, Thomas Neville, the illegitimate son of William Neville, Earl of Kent, known as the Bastard of Fauconberg, was gathering forces in the Kent area in the hope of taking London. According to the *Crowland Chronicle*, a large number of these men were remnants of the Earl of Warwick's followers, now leaderless following his death at Barnet. They were also a mixture of 'Calais regulars, seamen and pirates', as well as ordinary Kent folk.[41]

Fauconberg was unaware of the death of the Earl of Warwick at Barnet, which ultimately meant that Edward IV was once again in control of London. With the threat from Kentish forces, some Yorkists were left to defend the capital if necessary, while the rest went in search of Margaret's troops. At the same time, Queen Elizabeth and her children were staying at the Tower, along with her brother, Anthony. It is often said that whoever controls London controls the rest of England, not only because it is the largest city, but because that is where the central powers of government were and are largely based. And Henry VI was still being held captive in the Tower, so whoever controlled London would also control the fate of the captured king.

The rebels' ships were brought along the Thames ready to transfer any booty they may take during their raid.[42] They would also be handy if a quick getaway was needed. After moving to dry land, the rebels began to congregate on London Bridge and at Bishopsgate. They were intent on causing as much destruction as possible and used both sword and fire to do this. The destruction caused was so much that their 'marks of wickedness are still to be seen' on London Bridge, where many houses had been 'consumed by fire'.[43]

Despite the efforts of Fauconberg, he and his troops faced more opposition than they had expected. Their attempts to enter London were made more difficult as they coincided with the announcement of the Yorkist victory at Tewkesbury. With this news and the expectation that Edward would return to London following his victory, the Lancastrians were refused entry into the city.[44] Instead, they chose to anchor their ships close to the Tower. They once again faced opposition, probably led by Anthony as he was within the Tower, which forced the rebels to anchor elsewhere, with the plan of besieging the city from the other side of the Thames at St George's field. From there they 'assaulted the citie with greate violence' with guns and ships. Still the citizens of

London kept up their opposition, returning fire in such a way that the rebels were pushed back.

With such strong defence facing them, the Lancastrians were forced to turn to more desperate tactics such as burning houses. While this could have easily demoralised the London citizens, the arrival of the Earl of Essex helped to strengthen their morale. Hearing of the news from within the Tower, Anthony 'gathereyd unto him a felashipe' to attack the rebels in Aldergate, joining the mainly ordinary citizens that were defending the gate there. These men, led by Anthony 'mightily laied upon them with arrows, and upon them in hands, and so killed and toke many of them', with the rebels who were left retreating to their boats. The strength of this force led by Anthony was estimated to be somewhere between 400 and 500 men.[45]

The rebels who were caught in the retreat were hanged, but those who managed to reach Blackheath outside the city stayed for three days before dispersing in fear of Edward IV's men, who were close to London. On 11 May, when Edward did ride into London, he knighted the mayor, recorder, alderman, and other London citizens for their efforts in defending the city against the Lancastrian forces. The *Arrivall* notes that these rewards were given 'ryght well and trewly deserved'. Once the celebrations were over, the escaped rebels were tracked down in Kent, where they had come from, most of them being in Sandwich. Edward followed as far as Canterbury but entrusted his brother Richard to deal with them accordingly. Fauconberg was branded a traitor and he had all his goods seized.

The whole of London was said to have 'rejoiced that these lost men had been vanquished and put into flight'.[46] With the amount of destruction caused by the rebels, this is understandable. Anthony was highly praised for his part in defeating the rebels with his 'sudden and unexpected sortie from the Tower'.[47] This praise was recorded for posterity in a poem entitled *On the Recovery of the Throne by Edward IV* (see Appendix 4). The author describes 'The erle Revers, that gentill knyghte', who was able to unite the forces defending London to attack and repel the Lancastrian rebels led by the Bastard of Fauconberg, and thus 'purchesid grett love of the comyns'.[48] Woodville is the Arthurian knight who saved the City of London and its people from destruction and misery. While the poem does acknowledge that he was not alone in fighting the rebels, it suggests that he was the rallying point for the defensive forces. Considering that Anthony did not command huge numbers of men in his own retinue like more powerful magnates, such as the Earl of Warwick or the Duke of Norfolk, this shows Anthony understood the consequences for Edward's return to kingship if the rebels had succeeded in taking London, and that he was able to prove his military skills enough for the fighting men of London to flock to him.

However capable Woodville may have been during the attack on London, there was still a thorn in his side – Lord Hastings, the right-hand man of Edward IV. Years before, the pair had argued over the role of Lieutenant of Calais, a quarrel that was said to have 'lasted not long'.[49] Even if it did not last long, its repercussions were probably felt in the events following the death of Edward IV in 1483. In 1482, things finally came to a head when Anthony and Hastings accused each other, citing informants, that under their tenures they had been plotting to surrender Calais to the French.[50] Something may have happened to make this argument resurface so close Edward IV's death; perhaps Hastings still held a grudge towards Anthony because of the earlier friction, and then saw an opportunity.

In 1472, the Duke of Brittany had asked for English support against the French. Brittany had requested 6,000 archers, but instead, Anthony landed with only a small contingent of thirty archers and a personal entourage. Edward, Anthony's younger brother, was among this number, the first time he was documented as part of Anthony's entourage. By 20 June, Anthony had managed to persuade Edward IV to send more troops, for it was agreed that a further 1,000 men-at-arms should be sent as well as more archers, though all at Anthony's own expense.[51] The extra reinforcements were sent, but by the time of their arrival in August the French had retreated.

On 11 September, the treaty of Châteaugiron was signed between England and Brittany, which was the culmination of negotiations that Anthony himself headed with the Duke of Brittany. The treaty aimed to maintain a joint force against the French. The expedition did not last long, as most of the men that were under Anthony died of illness.[52]

Brittany would continue to be a focal point in English foreign policy, even in 1475. Edward IV promised that he would lead an expedition to France by 1 July that year and would be joined by forces from Brittany and Burgundy. In April, Anthony and Richard Martyn were sent as an embassy to Burgundy to discuss the logistics for such an invasion. At the time of the attack, Anthony Woodville joined a force of 2,000 archers sent to Brittany to fight the French.[53] Anthony himself had managed to raise two knights, forty men at arms and 200 archers, with the other men being raised by the earls of Northumberland and Pembroke, as well as the Dukes of Clarence and Gloucester and the Marquess of Dorset.[54] The planned invasion of France using these forces was to take place from Brittany. On 16 May, a treaty was signed with the Duke of Brittany, promising Edward 8,000 troops as long as Edward could squeeze a substantial subsidy from his people. While Brittany's promise of assistance was substantial, Burgundy's help would also be crucial in any invasion of France, but Duke Charles was cagey about his involvement.

Despite any reservations, Edward IV prepared a will on 20 June, in expectation of fierce fighting ahead. As to be expected, his wife Elizabeth was mentioned throughout, including giving her control of the future marriages of their daughters and their son, Prince Edward, if he had come of age by the time of Edward's death. If his father died during this campaign though, the young prince would be only five years old. It must have been an anxious time, full of uncertainty over how long the campaign would last.

It did not last as long as expected. The help from the Duke of Burgundy was not as forthcoming as expected because the French had already invaded his lands. Despite attempts being made to continue the conflict, including by Anthony and those men he led, peace was quickly an option as Louis XI offered Edward 75,000 crowns, along with an annual French pension of 500,000 crowns, by the treaty of Picquigny signed on 29 August.[55] To seal the peace, plans were also laid to marry the Dauphin to Princess Elizabeth when they were of marriageable age.[56] As soon as Edward had received an upfront payment of 55,000 crowns, he returned to England with his army. While Edward had come out of this fiasco with a lot of money, his army had nothing. It had not been what they had signed up for and there were worries about what would happen upon their return to England.[57]

Even though the campaign in Brittainy was in essence a failure, Rivers still proved to be a rallying point when needed, especially during the invasion of Scotland in 1482. Relations with Scotland had been tense since the 1470s, mainly due to border raids by both the Scots and the English. Despite various treaties in the late 1470s hoping to create peace, and marriage negotiations for Cecily, third daughter of Edward IV, to marry James, the prince of Scotland, as well as for the then widowed Earl Rivers to Margaret, sister of James III, there was no let up. Due to the deteriorating relations, the marriages never happened. Instead, the conflict intensified in 1482. The Duke of Albany, brother of James III, was supported by the English in his claim to the Scottish throne.[58] As Edward IV 'did not take to the field in person', the command was entrusted to his brother, Richard, Duke of Gloucester.[59] A large part of the fighting centred on the border town of Berwick, which at the time was in Scotland.

Earl Rivers played a role in the fighting in Berwick, as he was the one to raise and lead a regional contingent of several thousand men from Ludlow, the home of the Prince of Wales, Anthony's charge at the time.[60] Anthony showed he was still capable of leading a large number of men, whether that be in his own name or that of the Prince of Wales.[61] If his few thousand men were a part of the four thousand besieging the castle at Berwick, then it shows that he was one of the important military leaders of the campaign, something which has been glossed over since. Gloucester continued with the rest of the army towards Edinburgh, which meant that constant communication was needed with those at Berwick. Anthony would have been one of those with whom would have had to be in communication. So there was some form of relationship between the pair prior to Woodville's execution in June 1483.

Berwick Castle finally surrendered on 24 August 1482, at which point the war was supposedly over. Berwick stayed in English hands and has done ever since. The agreement made following the end of the war concluded the marriages between England and Scotland were to go ahead, but by December, James III had changed his mind. It is probable that English control over Berwick was a factor, as well as the Duke of Albany being temporarily brought back into the fold.[62]

As has been shown, Anthony Woodville had many opportunities to prove himself militarily with differing amounts of success. The greatest failure he experienced was during the Brittany campaign of 1475, but circumstances surrounding it were largely out of his control. In general, Woodville showed he was not scared to fight on the frontline wherever he was sent, from 1461 when he fought for the Lancastrians at Towton, then through his continued loyalty to the House of York until the siege of Berwick in 1482, just ten months prior to his death. This gives the lie to the accusation that his brother-in-law hurled at him, suggesting he was a coward in 1471 for wanting to go on crusade with the Spanish against the Moors.[63] The only time that Anthony appeared to vacillate was in June 1476, when he offered his services to Charles the Bold, Duke of Burgundy to fight the Swiss, but in the end did not offer assistance. It is possible that this was retaliation for the embarrassment that Anthony had felt when Charles had done the same thing during the planned invasion of France through Brittany a year earlier.[64]

If we take this to be the case, then it suggests that Edward's attack was probably made in a moment of anger and frustration, especially as the request to go on crusade was made when Edward was under personal stress thanks to the uncertainty following his restoration as king in 1471. In general, when needed, Anthony did not shirk his duty. Edward himself had recognised this just a few months before his description of Anthony as a coward. In a speech he gave before the opening of Parliament, Anthony was especially credited for his 'constant faith'.[65]

No other moment exemplifies this more than his sortie from the Tower of London when the capital was being attacked by Lancastrian rebels in May 1471. The citizens 'rejoiced that these lost men had been vanquished and put into flight'.[66] This victory had largely been down to Anthony, who was able to unite the citizens and others defending London. In rushing from the Tower and entering the thick of the fighting, Anthony proved that he was far from a coward and was loyal not only to the Yorkist cause, but also to the citizens of London.[67] In that moment, Anthony was their saviour and thus was the embodiment of the virtues of chivalry. These virtues were something that on a personal level, Anthony tried his best to abide by, both on the battlefield and in the tournament lists.

5

TOURNAMENT CHAMPION

By the time of the Wars of the Roses, tournaments had come a long way since their almost barbaric inception in the eleventh century. In earlier times, huge groups would compete in tourneys over several days. These tourneys offered many different events, which culminated in the melee. Melees were huge events, sometimes featuring hundreds of men fighting each other in battle-like conditions. The idea of ransoming opponents, just as in real-life battle situations, was replicated. These melees were chaotic and dangerous events that occurred all over Europe, but their popularity eventually dwindled due to the complex logistics, money and space needed to perform them. In fact, they were seen as such a scourge that they were banned under Henry II.[1] Instead, individual activities became more popular, mostly to avoid any further bans, but also to provide some entertainment and practice for knights. Out of this, jousting was seen as the noblest pursuit of them all.

By the fifteenth century, it was widely believed that society had strayed away from chivalric ideals. To rectify this, chivalric language and practices were encouraged.[2] One way to do this was by increasing the number of tournaments held at court. Tournaments were always popular events and were great social occasions, which were well advertised and had the atmosphere of something like a fairground.[3] With such public interest in these events, it is clear to see why they became such an important part of literary representations of chivalry, particularly in the works of William Caxton and Thomas Malory. Both men were keen to encourage and promote admiration for a tournament culture, with a particular focus on legends, especially those of King Arthur. In producing such texts, they created a two-way street, in which literature influenced tournaments and vice versa.

It was hoped that the heady mix of cavalry skills and noble ideals would influence the wider culture at large.[4] Practicality also played a part in the chivalric culture of the day. According to Anthony Goodman, 'The need for cavalry in the Wars of the Roses may have given tournament techniques of controlling a horse in combat renewed relevance.'[5] There is definitely some truth to this, as pitched battles were sporadic throughout the period, and the noble skill of horsemanship in a combat environment did need to be rehearsed. The need to keep up these types of skills, as well as the desire of Edward IV to create a milieu of courtly splendour, contributed towards the increase of tournaments throughout his reign. This included the participation of his in-laws, the Woodvilles.

For the Woodvilles, competing in tournaments was a family affair. Anthony's father Richard competed in many jousts, including one in 1441, where he was challenged by the Spanish knight Sir Peter de Vasques, which took place in Smithfield, the same location as Anthony's most famous individual feat of arms.[6] While Anthony Woodville was the most famous, his brothers, John and Edward, were also noted champions. John became champion during a tournament held in Bruges to celebrate the marriage of Edward IV's youngest sister, Margaret, to Duke Charles of Burgundy. Anthony also took part in this tournament.

Another tournament that the family possibly participated in was held on 27 May 1465 in honour of Elizabeth Woodville's coronation. While it is not entirely certain, as the new queen's relatives it makes sense that some of the Woodvilles would have been among the participants. What better way to showcase the new queen than by displaying her family's skills in the lists? Even if they did, Lord Stanley won and received a ruby ring as a prize.[7] While the tournaments were a family activity, it was Anthony who went further in creating and reinforcing this type of new chivalric order that was being striven for by Edward IV. He more or less personified what jousting was during this period and became one of the most well-known names on the jousting circuit.

The most famous tournament that Anthony Woodville participated in was the Smithfield tournament. It was a two-day event held in June 1467, after meticulous planning and a two-year delay. The tournament was arranged to mark an alliance between England and Burgundy and show that the Yorkists had gained a powerful ally.[8] The tournament was initially arranged by Elizabeth Woodville and her ladies in 1465. As described in Chapter 2, in a scene akin to Arthurian legend, Anthony was given by the ladies in waiting a letter ordering him to honour his queenly sister by partaking in a tournament with Antoine, Bastard of Burgundy, also known as Count de la Roche. When Woodville was given the challenge, a gold collar was placed around his thigh and a letter stating the challenge was placed into his cap.[9] However, at the time the idea for a tournament was conceived, Antoine, an illegitimate son of Philip, Duke of Burgundy, was too busy fighting in the wars against the French. This meant he was unavailable for the next two years.[10] In a letter written by Rivers, he expressed his disappointment at not being able to fight earlier, but that Antoine's actions in the meantime should be commended.[11]

Upon the Bastard of Burgundy's decision to finally take up the challenge in 1467, he arrived in England with a large retinue made up of 400 knights, lords, squires and others.[12] After three days of rest for the Burgundian visitor, he and his large retinue, with much pomp and ceremony, visited Edward IV and accompanied him to the opening of parliament.[13] This pageantry was to set the tone for the whole tournament, and Anthony Woodville, while a devout and pious man, knew how to live it up when it came to tournament spectacle. Even while staying at the Bishop of Ely's palace in Holborn in the lead up to the tournament, Woodville's household was full of prayer and godly worship, but the supplicants were wearing sumptuous silk and cloth of gold outfits.[14] The pageantry didn't stop there. It had been agreed in the rules laid out prior to the start of the tournament that the knights would be allowed to have spare horses. Anthony had nine horses in total. Each horse was extravagantly dressed in various fabrics – cloth of gold, velvets and damasks – all richly decorated with gold or furs.[15] On the first day, both participants showed off all the horses and pieces of armour they had brought with them in a parade of arms. For Anthony, the Dukes of Clarence and Buckingham, earls of Arundel and Kent and Lords Herbert and Stafford carried two helms, two spears and two swords.[16]

The tournament would have been the talk of the town, perhaps the country. Not only would it have been highly anticipated because of the royal connection, but because it involved a Burgundian. At the time, Burgundy was viewed as being a sophisticated culture, one which most of Europe envied and tried to emulate in some way. England was no different. Antoine's entourage of four hundred men included knights, squires and heralds. When his party arrived in Blackwell, they were met by the Lord High Constable with seven barges, before being conveyed to Fleet Street where they were to meet with Anthony Woodville in the presence of Edward IV.[17]

The Smithfield tournament appeared to be something straight out of an Arthurian legend. In fact, it followed an earlier precedent in tournament culture. During the 1240s and 1250s, Ulrich von Liechtenstein travelled around Europe challenging knights to 'Round Tables', which were tournaments based on such legends. In these tournaments, competitors dressed as various Arthurian characters and had to defend a pavilion that had been erected to symbolise the round table.[18] Spectacles like this saw a huge resurgence during the reign of Edward IV. They were considered a good propaganda tool to help improve Edward's popularity and fortify his claim to kingship during a turbulent and uncertain time.[19] The famous William Marshal, dubbed England's greatest knight, who tourneyed on the continent during the reign of Henry II, would have also been an inspiration to the tournaments held during Edward IV's reign.

John, Lord Howard was chosen as a marshal for the tournament at Smithfield. Originally the Duke of Norfolk, a relative of Howard, had been chosen, but he was unable to attend and so chose Howard as his deputy.[20] The tournament cost Howard 300 marks, which was approximately £200, to take this position, worth perhaps £150,000 today. A similar amount was spent just on the construction of the lists.[21]

However glittering the spectacle was, it did not take away from the seriousness of the fight that was to follow. Just as with any modern-day sportsperson, there would have been a lot of training involved in preparing for the big day. Anthony himself practised at Greenwich before moving with his retinue to the Bishop of Ely's palace at Holborn, five miles away. While staying at the palace, the household observed a strict religious timetable and also wore the same fantastical outfits.[22]

On the first try the lances didn't hit so they were replaced with swords.[23] It was at this moment that things seemed to go wrong. The Bastard's horse was spooked for some reason and reared, throwing its rider, pinning him to the ground.[24] He instantly accused Woodville of cheating, but this was probably prompted by the nefarious conduct of a previous opponent, a German squire, who had hidden daggers in his horse armour.[25] To prove he had not cheated Woodville rode over to Edward IV, showing he had no concealed weapons.[26] Edward nevertheless deemed it necessary to dismiss the knights until the following day due to the accusations.[27]

If indeed there was cheating involved, as Susan Higginbotham points out, 'It seems unlikely that the Bastard would have agreed to fight him the next day.'[28] It would not have made sense to continue if there really had been cheating, but the second day of action went ahead as planned. Instead of being mounted, the participants fought on foot with axes. This manner of combat was also a popular choice during tournaments, for hand-to-hand fighting was also a much-needed skill for a knight, just as much as fighting while mounted.[29] Both men fought hard and during the fight Woodville's axe sliced the Bastard of Burgundy's visor.[30] The men still continued to fight and it was only the intervention of King Edward's men that stopped them from seriously hurting each another.

Despite the cheating controversy, the tournament still managed to achieve its overall goal of improving Edward IV's popularity and helping to secure a lasting alliance with Burgundy.[31] This was boosted by Edward IV's youngest sister, Margaret, marrying Charles the Bold, Duke of Burgundy, for which Anthony was vital in an ambassadorial role, helping negotiate the marriage terms.[32] Anthony's involvement in improving relations with Burgundy shows just how vital he was in international as well as domestic matters.

The tournament had to be cut short due to the death of Antoine's father, Philip the Good, Duke of Burgundy, on 15 June 1467. Antoine made a speedy return to Burgundy and Anthony and other nobles escorted him to Dover, from where he set sail from on 25 June. The timing of Philip's death meant that the diplomatic intentions of the Smithfield tournament were now more important than ever. As Philip's legitimate son, Charles, was now the Duke of Burgundy, it would do well to have him on side. John Howard, who had been deputised by the Duke of Norfolk as marshal for the event, conveyed the Burgundian as far as Calais in one of his own ships.[33] He was a good choice as he had many ships to his name, also used later for the marriage of Margaret of York to Antoine's brother, Charles the Bold.

Spectacle was a large part of tournament culture, just as much as military prowess. A participant had to show his worthiness in both skill and chivalry. Personal image was important. During the Smithfield tournament, Anthony's motto of 'nulle la vault' was prominent as part of the regalia.[34] John Ashdown-Hill translated this motto as 'nothing is worth it', with the implicit religious connotation of nothing *earthly* is worth it.[35] Mottos were an important part of late medieval culture. They were used by noblemen to convey 'personal, lineal, societal and political messages'.[36] These mottos were put on public display in various ways, including on personal items of clothing or on the uniform of retainers as identifying markers to show in whose service a person was.[37] In the Smithfield tournament, Anthony's motto was displayed on the blue satin covering of his tent, alongside banners showing his noble lineage. It appears that he may have had more than one motto, for in his thesis, Ralph Moffatt identifies the motto 'La nonchaillance', the nonchalant one.[38]

With the accusation of cheating, the Smithfield tournament was one of the few instances of a slight against Anthony Woodville's honour. For Anthony this slight was taken very personally. For a loyal knight such as Woodville, this would have been a rather devastating and personal insult. However, it did little to ruin the long-term reputation, both on and off the jousting scene, of Earl Rivers. It would mean that both Anthony and Antoine would no longer face each other in tournaments, probably for fear of a reoccurrence of the tense atmosphere that had to be stopped by Edward IV and the marshals.[39]

The Smithfield tournament had been a moment to remember for everyone. A grocer by the name of Thomas Clarell bequeathed a painted cloth depicting the tournament to the parish church in Rotherham, as well as another painted cloth of the Passion of Christ, in exchange for prayers for souls.[40] The donation of the Smithfield cloth at the same time as one of Christ shows how important the tournament had been to Clarell, an event to share with future generations.

Despite the disturbance at Smithfield, caused both by the accusations of cheating and the death of Duke Philip, the new alliance with Burgundy remained unharmed for the time being. As part of the marriage party escorting Margaret of York to her wedding to Charles the Bold in 1468, Anthony took part in a tournament as part of the celebrations. Anthony's younger brother, John, became tournament champion. However, Anthony's performance was still respectable – he managed to break eleven lances during the competition.[41] To ensure that the tournament was as convivial as possible, Anthony and Antoine did not fight each other, for they had 'mad promise at London that non of them both shold never dele with othyr in armys'.[42] It appears that there was no long-lasting animosity between Anthony and Antoine, as the Bastard led Anthony out to the field when he jousted against another Burgundian.[43] This tournament in Bruges would have been another spectacle to behold. According to John Paston, the competitors were wearing 'clothe of gold, and sylk and sylvyr', just like those of the Burgundian court who were in the audience.[44] Paston goes so far as compare the spectacle before him directly to the court of King Arthur.[45]

Tournaments connected with Burgundy were not the only ones that Anthony was known to have taken part in. In April 1467, Sir John Paston noted in a letter to his brother that he was one of the participants in a tournament held at Eltham Palace, where his 'hand was hurte'.[46] Paston said that 'there was upon the one side within, the king, my Lord Scales, myself and Seuenger; and without, my Lord Chamberlain [Lord Hastings], Sir John Woodville, Sir Thomas Montgomery and John Aparre'.[47] The tournament impressed Paston. He suggested that it 'was the goodliest sight that was seen in Ingelande this forty yeares of so fewe men'.[48] As this particular tournament was held a month before the famous Smithfield tournament between Anthony Woodville and the Bastard of Burgundy, it could have been a training exercise for the main event.[49]

Anthony Woodville's final documented foray in the jousting world was at a tournament to celebrate the marriage of the five-year-old Prince Richard, the youngest son of Edward IV, to the five-year-old Anne Mowbray on 15 January 1478. Anne had been escorted to the chapel at Westminster by Anthony and John de la Pole for the ceremony. What followed were lavish festivities worthy of the wedding of a prince, no matter how young the bride and groom. The final part of these festivities concluded with jousts on 22 January. Among the competitors were Anthony, his brother Edward, and his two eldest nephews, Thomas Grey, Marquess of Dorset, and Richard Grey. Anthony fought against Thomas Hansard dressed as a white hermit. His tent looked like a black velvet walled hermitage carried on a cart.[50] This hermit connection would be something that stayed with him for the rest of his life, most notably during his execution. As this was his final foray into tournament combat, was this a sign that the contemplative, religious life was what he had grown to prefer?

When charging down the lists, there was a huge cheer for both Anthony and his opponent, but in the heat of the moment, Hansard managed to 'let fly a spring between the shoulder and helm' of Anthony.[51] Understandably, this pushed Anthony to retaliate and between them the pair accomplished six strokes. Despite their best efforts in the lists, none of the Woodville men won that day. They were unable to collect the prizes of golden letters set with gems given out to the champions by Elizabeth of York. Anthony still rewarded the king's heralds. He gave them twenty marks.[52]

The fact that tournaments had become a huge part of Anthony's life would have meant that his name was well-known by the many people who went to watch these huge events. The participants were almost like the footballers of their day and would have been known by nobility and the commons alike for their sporting prowess. Anthony would have been no different and it was certainly a good way of combining his love of chivalry and pageantry. Anthony played his part in developing something akin to a new Arthurian court based on tournaments and chivalry that Edward IV hoped to recreate.[53]

6

CONNECTIONS WITH BURGUNDY

As we have seen, Edward IV's decision to marry Elizabeth Woodville had undone a possible treaty with France, and so he needed new allies to consolidate his claim to the English throne he had taken from Henry VI in 1461. Who better to choose than France's neighbour, Burgundy, a separate dukedom which covered parts of what is now modern-day Northern France and Belgium? Edward chose his father-in-law Richard and brother-in-law Anthony to be heads of a negotiating party sent to Burgundy in 1466 to negotiate a marriage between Charles the Bold, the heir of Burgundy, and Edward's youngest sister, Margaret of York.[1] Anthony and his father were chosen not just because of new familial ties to Edward, but also because of continental connections to Burgundy through his mother, Jacquetta, and their previous status as ambassadors. Anthony's ability to speak different languages would also have helped negotiations for the match, as he could speak French, the language spoken at the Burgundian court.

The work that Anthony and his father did during their diplomatic mission to Burgundy succeeded, as the marriage between Charles and Margaret went ahead in 1468. Anthony was chosen to head Margaret's wedding party, with his wife, Elizabeth Scales, as one of Margaret's ladies during the wedding celebrations.[2] On her journey to Burgundy, Margaret rode through London 'behind the Earl of Warwick', towards Stratford Abbey, where the party stayed the night before heading to the coast.[3] Warwick was strongly opposed to a match with Burgundy as he favoured France, so this must have been a galling procession for him to participate in. Even more so when the Woodvilles, including Anthony, had played a large role in the negotiations for Margaret's marriage.

A similar procession of a large number of lords and ladies marched to Bruges following the wedding ceremony, which was held in the early hours of 3 July in Damme, three miles outside Bruges.[4] The people of Bruges appeared to love their new duchess as she was received 'worchepfully'.[5] This is understandable as there was a large English merchant community in Bruges, as well as in other places across Burgundy. William Caxton, as a leading English merchant, probably participated in this procession, or at the very least would have been among the crowds cheering Margaret on her journey into Bruges. If so, it is possible that this was the first time that Caxton and Anthony met, a meeting that would produce a long-lasting working relationship. A tournament was also held as part of the celebrations, headed by Antoine.[6]

Not only had Anthony Woodville been around the negotiating table with Burgundy, he also took part in tournaments held in both England and Burgundy to celebrate the new relationship between the two countries. Edward believed Anthony was entirely capable of dealing with important diplomatic missions, especially as he was later sent as a representative of the English court to both Burgundy and France in military, political and diplomatic capacities.[7] Jousting, tournaments and feasting were a huge part of Burgundian culture and this would be something replicated in England during Edward IV's reign, which Anthony was heavily involved with, the connection strengthened by the marriage of Charles and Margaret.[8] It had taken England five months to gather the amount needed for Margaret's dowry; perhaps Anthony had been a placatory voice when the Burgundians inevitably complained about the delay.[9]

The ties created by the marriage of Charles and Margaret ensured a safe haven for Edward IV and his inner circle when they were forced into exile following the readeption of Henry VI in 1471. In Bruges during this time, Anthony stayed with Louis, Lord of Gruuthuse, who had the largest library in all of Burgundy, possibly Europe.[10] As a known lover of books, Anthony must have perused this library and shared ideas with Louis about his collection. A copy of collected works by the French poet Christine de Pizan, passed onto Anthony from his mother, shows that Louis and Anthony must have had some sort of friendship, as it has both of their signatures inside the front cover.[11]

The library of the Lord of Gruuthuse was not the only bookish connection Anthony made in Burgundy. It is uncertain how Anthony and William Caxton, the printer, met, but the most likely explanation is either during the marriage celebrations of Margaret of Burgundy or during the English exile in Bruges. Caxton had moved his printing press to Bruges from Cologne, as Margaret of Burgundy had become his patroness.[12] Before moving into the printing business, Caxton had been an English merchant in Bruges, and was head of the community at the time of Margaret's marriage to Charles.[13] Whatever the circumstances of their meeting, Caxton would become connected with the English nobility and decided to set up a printing shop in Westminster, so perhaps it is possible that Anthony, the known bibliophile, and Edward IV, who was interested in increasing his library after exile, were behind Caxton's decision to move to England.

The library belonging to Gruuthuse has been cited as the inspiration for Edward IV to start his own library at Eltham Palace in 1480. Monarchs before Edward IV did have their own book collections, but it was customary to give many of them away as gifts to courtiers, visiting dignitaries or religious institutions.[14] This meant that little has survived within the royal collection and that more examples of Edward's manuscripts have survived than those of previous monarchs.[15] Many examples in Edward's collection contain heraldry relating to Louis, Lord of Gruuthuse, suggesting he helped Edward to start, or at least add to, his collection.[16]

Anthony's patronage of Caxton's work and role as a translator for him helped chivalric genres to thrive in England. These books were meant to appeal to nobles in a world where a nobleman's education required both military and cultural input to create a well-rounded person.[17] Anthony oversaw the education of Edward, Prince of Wales, so he knew how best to educate young nobles to the required standards. Books would be printed and dedicated to the cause of teaching the young prince.[18] This reciprocation is evident in William Caxton's prologue to *L'Historie de Jason* (1477), dedicated to the young prince, so that 'he may begyne to lerne to rede'.[19] This reflects Caxton's general view on historical texts, as he saw them as 'an essential means of teaching people the best way to live a profitable life, to counsel rulers, and to check tyrannical government'.[20]

Through Anthony's diplomatic connections with Burgundy, a fruitful relationship between the two states was established. While this had its ups and downs, military and cultural connections lasted throughout Edward IV's reign and continued well beyond, especially with Margaret of Burgundy's pledge to help Yorkist pretenders against Henry VII in the 1480s and 1490s.

Anthony's connections with Burgundy stem from that early diplomatic mission he was chosen to head alongside his father Richard in 1466, to negotiate a marriage between Charles the Bold, the heir to the dukedom of Burgundy, and Edward IV's sister, Margaret of York.[21] Any alliance at this point in Edward IV's reign would have helped consolidate his right to the throne, at a time when his suitability for kingship was uncertain, as he had won it through conquest.[22] Anthony was chosen not just for his family connections to the king, but also because of connections to Burgundy through his mother's continental family and their previous roles as ambassadors.[23] Norbert Ohler identifies authority to negotiate on behalf of a patron, the ability to speak different languages and being trustworthy in dealing with sensitive information as the prerequisites of a diplomat.[24] Anthony possessed such traits, explaining why Edward IV often sent him as a representative of the English court to both Burgundy and France.[25]

The ties Anthony Woodville had been a part of creating between England and Burgundy would become essential at the start of the next decade. Following the brief restoration of Henry VI in 1470, Edward IV and his followers needed to escape to relative safety on the continent. The best place for them to go was to their allies in Burgundy. The group of around 2,000 men, including those like Lord Hastings, Richard, Duke of Gloucester and Anthony, who were part of Edward's royal circle, escaped from Bishop's Lynn in Norfolk, a place that Anthony had close ties with. Their route to Burgundy was one fraught with danger. Some of the men travelling with them drowned even before arriving at Lynn.[26]

The group of Yorkist exiles stayed at Lynn for two days, hoping that there would be some good news, but not enough troops could be raised to counteract Warwick and his new Lancastrian friends. Their only option was to leave England, which they did on 2 October 1470, after they had requisitioned enough ships to take them across the Channel to the Hague. With his prior experience in organising fleets, it was probably Anthony who helped the most in acquiring these vessels. However, the men had little money to pay the sailors, forcing Edward to give his furred gown to the master of the ships in lieu of payment, so they could gain passage.[27]

The journey was not a straightforward one, with the wind scattering the ships and Hanse ships pursuing them. Some of the ships, including Edward's, were grounded at low tide at Marsdiep, a channel near to the island of Texel off the coast of Holland, on 3 October. They had been followed by hostile Hanse ships, who hoped to board the English ships at high tide, but with locals helping them to shore this situation was avoided. The ship that had been carrying Richard, Duke of Gloucester and Anthony Woodville had landed many miles farther down the coast at Wilingen in Zeeland. Richard had had to borrow money from local bailiffs at Veere, and both he and Anthony were reliant on the hospitality of officials at nearby Middelburg, where they were served with wine.[28]

The English exiles were not as openly welcomed as they had hoped as Duke Charles was worried about what would happen with France if he openly recognised the exiles. Instead, their main ally was Louis, lord of Gruuthuse, who was the first Burgundian of substance to offer his support once word had reached him of their arrival. It was necessary to have someone of Louis' standing on their side, for he was close to Charles the Bold and could help negotiate for their interests during their stay.[29]

At the time of the arrival of Edward's party, Louis was governor in Holland, but he had first met with Edward IV in October 1466, when he was sent to England as an envoy. Upon the news of their arrival, Louis sent his treasurer for North Holland to meet Edward and the men who had landed with him, with orders to bring them to him. Upon their meeting with Gruuthuse on 8 October, they were given a warm welcome and provided with new clothes.[30] The plan was then to move to the Hague, with hopes of meeting up with Anthony and Gloucester. The group all arrived within days of each other.

Anthony and Gloucester were certainly at the Hague by 13 October, for a messenger had reached Charles the Bold confirming that they had now joined up with Edward.[31] The exiles stayed at the Hague until just before Christmas as guests of Gruuthuse, prior to moving to Gruuthuse's Bruges home on 13 January 1471. It is here that they would stay for many months enjoying his hospitality. The Duke of Burgundy did pay for the expenses needed for Edward and his party, but he did not openly acknowledge them as he was worried about the repercussions.[32] It was the end of December 1470 before they began to be openly recognised. Initially, this acknowledgement came in the form of granting money in preparation for Edward's return to England and a meeting with Isabella of Portugal, Charles the Bold's mother-in-law from his first marriage. Charles himself finally met with them personally at the beginning of January 1471, where talks were held between Charles and the Count of St Pol, Anthony's maternal uncle, to decide the best cause of action for Edward's return to England. By 19 January, Anthony was bargaining for ships in Bruges to ferry them and the 1,200 men they were to leave Flushings with on 2 March.[33]

The favour shown by Louis, lord of Gruuthuse towards Edward IV and his exiled circle, of which Anthony was a part, ultimately saved their lives and paved the way for their return to England in 1471. Their time spent with Gruuthuse at his home with its extensive library certainly influenced the exiles. Twenty-five volumes from Edward IV's personal library are known to have originated from Bruges and Ghent, with half of these being manuscripts reproduced from examples found in Gruuthuse's collection, with some being given by Gruuthuse personally.[34] The English exiles were avid consumers of the library's volumes. Anthony must have done the same, and had a continued interest in Louis' library, for as we have noted, Christine de Pizan's *The Book of the Queen* he had inherited from his mother was given to Louis. His signature appears alongside that of Jacquetta and Anthony.[35] It is uncertain when this book passed on to Louis, but it was probably given as a thank you for his hospitality during Anthony's exile in Burgundy.

The exiled group would have welcomed any news from England, hoping that their families were safe and that there may be a chance in the future to return home. Eventually, in January 1471, Charles, Duke of Burgundy began secret negotiations with Edward as tensions once again began to rise with France and it seemed logical for him to rebuild his relationship with England. To back Edward once more at this point was a strategic move as the restored Henry VI had regained the throne with assistance from the French. During these clandestine negotiations, Burgundy agreed to provide funding and three ships to support Edward's return to England, all while publicly still claiming to support Henry VI.[36] Thanks to this agreed support, the exiles were able to return to England by March 1471, the eventual result being the restoration of Edward as king.

Following the restoration, the Yorkist regime had to be consolidated once more. This had already been helped by the birth of Edward's son in November 1470, also called Edward, born in sanctuary at Westminster during his father's exile. By 1472, it was also necessary to thank and reward those who had showed continued support during the troubled times of the last year. Anthony Woodville was one of these people, for he was particularly elevated by being given the care of the infant prince, once he was made Prince of Wales.

Another person rewarded was Louis, Lord of Gruuthuse. He had been vital for the group's survival in Burgundy during their exile and Edward sought to ensure this was known throughout England. It was Gruuthuse who offered them safety. Not only did he provide for them in their hour of need, he opened their eyes to all that the famous and often envied Burgundian culture and society had to offer.

During a brief three-day visit in October 1472 after he had already visited Calais in September for diplomatic reasons, the Burgundian was to become an honorary member of the English court, with an English title. The visit was to be a magnificent display of friendship between Edward IV and the Burgundian to whom he owed his life, as well as those who had been in exile, such as Anthony Woodville. The introduction of the infant Prince Edward was a symbolic gesture. The young prince 'borne by his chamberlain, called Master Vaughan ... bade the Lord Grauthuse welcome'.[37] In presenting his young son, Edward hoped to show that this special relationship between England and Burgundy would continue for the next generation, and also that through the help offered by Gruuthuse, the Yorkist dynasty was saved.

Just as with any other state visit, Gruuthuse was spoiled with grand hospitality. The party, including Edward IV and Lord Gruuthuse, first moved to Windsor, where they made use of the hunting grounds in Windsor Park, followed by a dinner in the hunting lodge there. Queen Elizabeth then extended her own thanks for the sanctuary that had been offered to her husband by hosting a grand banquet in her chambers. Among her ladies mentioned as being in attendance at this banquet was 'Lady Rivers', Anthony Woodville's wife, Elizabeth Scales, lady-in-waiting to the queen.[38] Curiously, there is no specific mention of Anthony being in attendance during this visit of Gruuthuse. During this banquet held by his sister, there is only a quick mention of 'certain nobles of the king's own court' who were present.[39] Considering who this banquet was held by and that Anthony had been one of the people who had been exiled to Burgundy, it would make sense that he would have been in attendance during these celebrations.

The party then moved back to Westminster to prepare for the opening of Parliament on 13 October. It was this very public display of affection for Gruuthuse that would have the most significance. All of the 'lords spiritual and temporal' were to be in attendance. The Speaker of the Commons, William Allington, thanked Gruuthuse for his 'great humanity and kindness ... shown to the king when in Holland and Flanders'.[40] The king's brothers Clarence and Gloucester were especially praised for their 'knightly demeaning', with Anthony and Hastings also being commended 'for their constant faith'.[41] Following the welcoming speech in Parliament, the group made their way into Westminster Abbey and the tomb of Edward the Confessor, where, once again, the infant prince Edward was conveyed in the arms of his chamberlain, Thomas Vaughan, although the *Chronicles of the White Rose of York* mistakenly names him as Richard Vaughan.[42] There was immense symbolism in showing the soon-to-be honorary Englishman the tomb of Edward the Confessor. The tomb had witnessed many miracles after the Confessor's death in 1066; he was known as 'anglorum decus', or the glory of the English.[43] Edward the Confessor had great importance not only because of his saintly status, but because he was classed as one of the greatest of English kings.

Some think the connections that England made with Burgundy during the latter part of the fifteenth century have been exaggerated. If you were to have asked Edward IV, or those in his royal circle – including Anthony Woodville – what importance they placed on the alliance, they would not have agreed. The connections during the reign of Edward IV successfully 'ensured a continuous traffic between England and Burgundy and facilitated cultural exchange at all levels'.[44] The perceived superiority of Burgundian culture at the time was something England hoped to emulate. It was influenced by Edward IV and his circle's exile of 1470-71. A large part of this was book culture. While books that survive do not paint a whole picture of what was available to consumers during this period, what has survived can at least give some idea. Some two hundred Book of Hours produced by the Low Countries for English and Scottish markets survive.[45]

Certainly, the relationship between England and Burgundy was volatile due to political upheavals and the threat posed by France's attempts at dominance during the late fifteenth century. Despite the marriage between Margaret of York and Duke Charles, the relationship was not as plain sailing as hoped. Charles was often fickle and swung between open friendship with England to being disinterested or at least silent, depending on what was happening with France at the time. However, Louis, Lord of Grutthuse was constant in his friendship with England, especially with Edward IV himself. In 1470-71, he showed them open hospitality, even when Duke Charles did not. For this, Gruuthuse was praised for his 'great humanity and kindness', as well as rewarded with the title of Earl of Winchester.

This relationship, despite lacking consistency, was important to counteract France's threat to both England and Burgundy. For this reason alone, both countries were in need of allies, particularly if France were to invade. The alliance was also important for reasons other than military: trade with the Low Countries was important and generated a large amount of money. Burgundy was a significant importer of English wool and cloth.[46] With the accession of Charles the Bold as Duke of Burgundy, a more open trading partnership was established. In exchange for the wool and cloth and many other items shipped from England to the Low Countries, many high culture items such as illuminated manuscripts, were brought back to England. In the year 1480-81, as many as 900 books were imported into London by foreign merchants, the majority of whom were from the Low Countries.[47] Such items were seen as proof that Burgundy was culturally superior, but with such cultural connections, it was hoped that England could begin to emulate such sophistication and create its own style.

For Anthony Woodville in particular, England's relationship with Burgundy not only meant he was offered a safe haven during his exile with Edward IV, but that he was sent on many diplomatic missions, none more important than those to negotiate Margaret's marriage. During these missions, it is possible that he met William Caxton, the printer he would go on to be a patron of, and collaborator with, who was governor of the English merchant community in Bruges. Without these meetings, in whatever capacity, the printer would not have had the necessary backing to make his business move to England in 1475 or 1476 viable, nor would he have had such an attentive and hands-on patron to assist him. Anthony's time surrounded by Gruuthuse's library inspired him and showed what was possible.[48] Without all of these experiences spanning England and Burgundy, the printing press would not have reached England as early as it did.

7

MAN OF LETTERS AND PATRON OF WILLIAM CAXTON

Prior to the invention of the printing press by Johannes Guttenburg around 1450, books were for the elite, because they were handcrafted and therefore prohibitively expensive. The printing press created more opportunities for a wider audience to access printed material. The introduction of the press meant cheaper and quicker manufacturing methods. This, as well as the increasing disposable income of the middle classes, created a new market for books.[1] Not only were these new audiences now able to afford more books than before, they were also desirous of using their reading skills, which had previously only been used for business purposes, religious instruction, or for entertainment, to expand their horizons.[2] However, as they had not received the same standard of education as the nobility, they were largely limited to English translations. It was this corner of the market that William Caxton would excel in, although he also needed upper class patronage, most importantly through Anthony Woodville, to establish his printing shop in Westminster.

Edward IV is seen as the first English king to widely partake in this new form of book culture, almost inevitable in that for monarchs prior to Edward IV, little has survived from their original book collections.[3] There are nearly fifty surviving large-scale manuscripts which have survived from Edward IV's collection, the majority originating in Bruges. Some of these manuscripts still contain the heraldry of Louis, lord of Gruuthuse, indicating that he helped Edward to start his collection.[4] As Edward later adopted his own heraldry inside his books, it can be seen that some form of 'lesson in cultural propaganda [was] learnt from Edward's contact with the court of Burgundy'.[5]

Edward also owned books prior to his becoming king, almost all of Flemish origin. The ones that have been attributed to Edward as Earl of March are much more practical, such as medical tracts, and are very well used.[6] The later ones are notably different. Not only are they more literary, but they are also large and weighty and in good condition. This suggests that they were probably for display purposes, as Edward, while commended for his work on establishing a library collection, was not known to be bookish.[7]

The first official reference to a working royal library dates back to between 1401 and 1402, when Henry IV ordered a new study at Eltham Palace, where Edward located his library in 1480. A generation prior to Henry IV, Charles V of France was specific as to his aims when it came to his own library collection, totalling 910 volumes at the time of his death.[8] Charles purposefully built up his collection with the intention of not only bolstering his scholarly reputation, but in the hope it would 'enhance the international prestige of France'.[9] It is possible that Edward IV, while as already mentioned did not necessarily have a learned reputation himself, was keen to grow England's prestige in a similar way. By using emblems of the house of York throughout the collection, Edward intended to record the prestige of his family and his subsequent dynasty. Instead, those emblems became historical relics of the past Yorkist rule once the library was taken over by the first Tudor monarch, Henry VII.[10]

The books from this period that survive are only a part of what was available at the time and so they do not necessarily give an accurate picture of what people owned.[11] While it is possible to understand the themes that run through the material that has survived overall, we will focus here on William Caxton's printing press and the influence that Burgundy had upon it. Burgundy was well known for its production of illuminated manuscripts and printed books. In 1480-1481, at least nine hundred books were imported, mainly from the Low Countries, into London by foreign merchants.[12] During the early years of the English printed book trade, there was a strong influence from the already established trade in Burgundy. While not all books owned by English citizens were made in the Low Countries, most of the ones in the English language were, which supports the theory that the two cultures had similar tastes in literature.[13] During the Middle Ages, Burgundy was home to some of the most important Western churches and monasteries, including those of Cluny, Cîteaux, and Vézelay. Cluny, founded in 910, exerted a strong influence in Europe for centuries. This in part explains the early dissemination of manuscripts and then the printed word from the region.

William Caxton's workshop produced some of the earliest vernacular examples of printed texts in England. Edward Gordon Duff suggests while there was a book trade in England, that the production and importation of books was small and scanty.[14] While this may be the case, it is hard to say for certain as our view on the book and printing trade during the late fifteenth century is based on what has survived, not on what was there. What is certain is that William Caxton created a winning formula. Rather than making copies of texts produced on the continent by more skilled foreign workmen with greater capacity, he created English translations of popular literature.[15] Anthony Woodville helped with this business model by translating some of Caxton's early texts. To understand the working relationship between the pair, it is important to follow the links that Anthony established with the printer prior to his workshop being set up in Westminster. At the time Anthony Woodville was travelling around different parts of Europe, ideas from the continent were transmitted to England either via foreigners who visited England, or Englishmen travelling abroad.[16] Anthony played a large role in this process, bringing back unknown texts from Burgundy.[17] Some of these books would be disseminated to people outside of his close connections through his friendship with William Caxton.

William Caxton was born in Kent to a middle-class family and had been apprenticed to Robert Large, a wealthy London Mercer, which is where he began to gain noble and continental contacts.[18] His merchant trade took him to Burgundy, specifically Bruges, a major centre for trade and home to a large English mercantile community. It is clear that Caxton was held in high regard by this English community as by 1463, he was appointed to the office of Governor of the Company of Merchant Adventurers to the English nation in the Low Countries. This entailed supervising the English trade, which mainly dealt in cloth, and acting as a representative for the whole community. It is in this capacity that Caxton probably first became acquainted with Anthony Woodville, when Woodville accompanied Margaret of York to her wedding to Charles, Duke of Burgundy.

Caxton had already been producing manuscripts prior to his decision to learn how to use the fairly new invention of the printing press. A copy of *The Recuyell of the Historyes of Troye,* or the 'Collection of the Histories of Troy' was produced and translated into English by Caxton and presented to Margaret of Burgundy in 1471. In a surviving copy, an image shows Caxton presenting the book to her. A printed version was produced by Caxton in 1473 in either Bruges or Ghent, the first book printed in English. In this printed copy, Caxton explained in the prologue that following the manuscript version he had presented to Margaret, many other notables in Burgundy also wanted a copy of the text.[19] The text is a *recuyell* (compilation) of stories about the Trojan Wars by Raoul Lefèvre, originally written in French.[20]

Caxton goes on to explain that the number of customers vying for a copy of *The Recuyell of the Histories of Troye* made it too difficult to produce manuscript versions, which was a highly skilled and lengthy process, thus he decided to learn the art of printing. In 1471, he was living in Cologne, which is probably where learned how to use the printing press.[21] Upon learning the craft, Caxton returned to Bruges and went into partnership with Colard Mansion, writer of manuscripts, who would have helped him to establish himself in the print trade, and also possibly in the translation and production of texts.[22] In establishing this partnership, Caxton showed an aptitude for working with the right people, those who would help promote his business. Caxton would later do this with Anthony Woodville, following the opening of his printing shop in Westminster in the mid-1470s.

There is debate as to how far in advance Caxton and Woodville became acquainted before embarking on their joint venture of patron and printer. Whenever they met, it would have been quite easy to establish some form of relationship in Bruges as Anthony visited many times after the 1460s. Anthony first visited Burgundy while Caxton was Governor of the English community in Bruges.[23] Even if their relationship was not formed then, Anthony was part of Edward IV's inner circle that was exiled to Burgundy after the brief reinstatement of Henry VI as king, staying in the home of Louis, Lord of Gruuthuse, the Burgundian who added to, or even started, Edward IV's library.[24]

What made Anthony a suitable patron for Caxton and his printing press? Anthony had an existing interest in books and learning, his main interests a mixture of religious and moralistic themed texts, as well as ones of a chivalric and historical nature. Sadly, only two books known to have been owned by Anthony now survive: *The Book of the Queen* and *Roman d'Alexandre*. *The Book of the Queen* was written by Christine de Pizan who was supported by Isabel of Bravia, queen consort to Charles VI of France, in the early fifteenth century. This copy was passed down to Anthony from his mother, Jacquetta, and is now in the British Library.[25] As Jacquetta died on 30 May 1472, Anthony would have inherited it prior to becoming Caxton's patron in England.

This surviving copy of Christine de Pizan's work is interesting because it is a collection of texts thought to have been produced under the author's own careful supervision.[26]

The Book of the Queen was presented to Queen Isabel around 1414 and was purchased, alongside the entire library of Charles VI, by John, Duke of Bedford, in 1424, which explains how the text came to Anthony's mother, Jacquetta, who was married to Bedford prior to marrying Richard Woodville.[27] This French library added to the collection Bedford had built up before becoming Regent of France. He was known to have had religious texts and thirteen volumes of stories relating to King Arthur.[28] The whole library collection was left to Jacquetta upon Bedford's death in 1435.

What makes this book unusually revealing are the signatures inside it, which has made it easy to trace some of the previous owners. Both Jacquetta and Anthony have signed the pages, along with their personal mottos of 'sur tous autres' and 'nulle la vault' respectively.[29] The next owner's signature is that of Louis, Lord of Gruuthuse, again indicating the close links Anthony had built up with not just Burgundy, but Louis in particular.[30] There must be other unknown owners as the other signature included is that of Henry Cavendish, second Duke of Newcastle, with the inscription, 'his booke 1676', so nearly two hundred years passed between the signatures of Louis and Henry Cavendish.[31]

Christine de Pizan, was an immensely popular author, despite being female. Her patronage by French royalty allowed her to become largely accepted despite the strict gender roles of the time. Edward IV owned *Epistre d'Othea* by Pizan, which was one of five chivalric texts placed in one volume for him produced in Flanders.[32] The fact that the text was produced in Flanders but made for an English king shows that Pizan was widely read throughout Europe, not just in France.

Anthony Woodville's *Roman d'Alexandre* is now held by the Bodleian Library in Oxford.[33] This manuscript details in verse various episodes in the life of Alexander the Great. According to Kate Harris, this text was once in the possession of Thomas of Woodstock, first Duke of Gloucester and son of Edward III, as it was mentioned in an inventory drawn up after his death in 1397.[34] Its fate between then and 1466 is unknown, but its next known owner left his signature. That owner was Richard Woodville, first Earl Rivers, Anthony's father. An inscription towards the back shows Richard bought it in London on New Year's Day of 1466.[35] The text is seemingly untraceable following the death of Richard Woodville until a later signature of a man called Thomas Smythe, dating from the late fifteenth century, appears. However, research conducted by Omar Khalaf has suggested what happened to it between the ownerships of Richard Woodville and the mysterious Thomas Smythe. On the same page as Richard Woodville's inscription, there is a rather illegible piece of writing in the bottom lefthand corner, which Khalaf has identified as a fragment of poetry written by Anthony Woodville.[36]

> ARyverys, sujet to hym that hat no peregal remember the kyngis that [now?] byen al not desprysyng ime ... nor to non lay blamys but say the t...uis the tr...[37]

This appears to be moralistic in its tone, something which Anthony Woodville was noted for, particularly in terms of the texts he translated, such as *The Dictes and Sayings*. From that, and the interpretation of the signature to the poem being 'ARiveris 'it seems this was written by Woodville. But this writing had been previously attributed to Richard Woodville, Anthony's younger brother, who became the third Earl Rivers, following Anthony's death, by E. W. B. Nicholson, a librarian at the Bodleian Library between 1882 and 1912.[38] Little is known about the younger Richard Woodville, besides the few pardons he received during his lifetime. Anthony is the more likely scribe.

According to Khalaf's interpretation, the peerless being that the writer is subject to could be a king.[39] The king in question could be either Edward IV or the uncrowned Edward V, his son, who was under the tutelage of Anthony. Khalaf notes that if the king mentioned in the poem was Edward V, then this would date it to 1483, meaning it could possibly have been written by Anthony following his arrest and imprisonment by the Duke of Gloucester.[40] If indeed this was the date, it may go some way towards explaining why the writing is so illegible. This explanation does seem plausible. Anthony usually had a neat signature, as seen in *The Book of the Queen,* but this example is far from that. The easiest way to corroborate this would be to study an original version of the poem we know he wrote in prison, once he knew of his fate (see Appendix 2), but no known original exists. For the moment, Kalaf suggests, we cannot be sure of the identity of the writer.[41] If it was Anthony Woodville, it sits alongside his final poem and another written on the seven deadly sins, since lost.[42] These surviving books and others such as a French copy of the *Dictes and Sayings of the Philosophers* owned by Anthony Woodville show that he was a reader of varied texts.[43]

Gill judges Anthony's role in early English printing to be significant, as 'an acknowledged patron of letters [who] helped shape the cultural milieu, and in turn, the demands of the market'.[44] While noblemen at this time contributed to the culture and trends within their own circles, Anthony Woodville was unique in doing this as a patron and translator at the very start of the printing process in England. However, the significant role Anthony had in bringing printing to England and increasing the popularity of books has largely been underplayed. This is because Anthony's status as brother-in-law to Edward IV meant that his patronage was considered simply as the result of his links to Edward and his son, the Prince of Wales.[45] Knowledge of Burgundy's book culture would have had an effect upon Anthony's education of the young prince. The Low Countries were skilled at creating illuminated manuscripts and the admiration this brought was something that other countries aspired to achieve for themselves.[46] This, alongside a European-wide desire in the upper classes to acquire books in vernacular languages, either in manuscript form or the new format of print, created the right conditions for Anthony Woodville, alongside William Caxton, to attempt to expand book culture in England.

While printing was still not done on a mass scale, it meant that books were no longer manuscript copies usually made by churches and monasteries for their own use or for royalty and other high-status nobles.[47] Baker points out that it would transform 'the world for centuries to come' and is still contributing to our modern world.[48] In England, this is all down to Anthony assisting Caxton to relocate and marks the beginnings in England of the Renaissance tradition of rediscovering 'lost' knowledge.[49]

Without a previous printing tradition in England to follow, it was vital to put an English spin on the Burgundian model of book culture.[50] The first stage for Caxton was to place his print shop in Westminster, so that he could be near to his intended royal, noble and political audiences that attended the Palace of Westminster and Parliament, usually held either at the Palace or at the Chapter House of Westminster Abbey.[51] Manuscript book craftsmen were often freemen of London. This meant that they were in contact with other members of the mercantile community, as well as political and religious leaders, who could provide them with business.[52] Caxton's own connection with the clergy is confirmed by the fact his print shop was permitted to operate by the abbot of Westminster, John Easteney.[53] Caxton was adapting well-used working practices to suit this new type of book production.

The other option was to create genres that would appeal to nobles in a world where increasingly a nobleman's education was supposed to include both military and cultural pursuits.[54] As both a well-known bibliophile and man of military and tournament success, Anthony Woodville was the perfect patron for Caxton, as he already exemplified, as well as taking a keen interest in, the types of genres that Caxton wished to promote. Anthony's role as tutor to the Prince of Wales made him the best person to advise the new printer in what types of books would be useful for the education of noblemen in this new world. In exchange, books produced by Caxton would be printed and dedicated to the cause of teaching the young prince.[55] This transaction would make their working relationship a mutually beneficial one. Anthony used his status to support the works Caxton printed and Caxton would publish Anthony's translations of French texts.[56] Anthony's patronage of Caxton was important as it would set an example for those in England who would follow.[57]

Caxton's output included themes of chivalry and adventure, echoes of Anthony's personality and experience.[58] Chivalry had a long tradition by the fifteenth century, but this had started to change. As chivalry was so intertwined with definitions of aristocratic masculinity at that time, books focusing on chivalric figures were used to provide subtle advice for knights. This meant that books designed to improve a person's morals subsequently would improve their social and chivalric standing.[59]

The work most associated with Anthony Woodville, his translation of the *Dictes and Sayings of the Philosophers*, printed in 1477, was one such moral text.[60] It was a collection of stories and sayings from Ancient Greek and classical philosophers, especially Socrates. The book was dedicated to Edward IV and would have been used for the education of his son. A manuscript edition was produced alongside three editions in print.[61] One manuscript was presented to the king, a moment which is captured in the illuminated image in a copy now held by Lambeth Palace.[62] The image shows Anthony presenting his translation to the king, who is accompanied by his wife, Elizabeth, and young son. Richard, Duke of Gloucester is also in attendance. This illuminated image is the only contemporary image that we have of Anthony Woodville.

There is also a mysterious person beside Woodville in this image. He wears black robes and has a tonsure. Who is this enigmatic figure? Could this be either William Caxton, or Guilliaume de Tignonville, the author of the French version which Anthony used as a basis for his English translation? Both of these, while they certainly are sensible suggestions, are still doubtful choices as both were laymen and not connected to the Church, as the figure's appearance may suggest. However, N. F. Blake offers another candidate, which makes more sense: Haywarde, the possible scribe of this manuscript version of *The Dictes and Sayings*, as his signature appears in the epilogue. Haywarde's true identity may never be fully revealed, but Blake has suggested he could have been a monk from Westminster Abbey.[63] This is entirely probable as monks were largely responsible for producing manuscripts throughout the Middle Ages, even with the advent of printing. It would also make sense as William Caxton's printing shop was located in Westminster, meaning he would have been well placed to commission the manuscript copy and to keep an eye on its production. The *Dictes and Sayings*, while not religious in its theme, was still a moral tract.

The book is the first printed in England to have the date and place of publication attached to it.[64] However, there is another rather intriguing aspect to it that Caxton introduces in his epilogue to the text: he informs us that Woodville removed misogynistic language – the words of Socrates – because of his respect for women.[65] Caxton disapproves, but says that it was so no woman reading would be offended, the result of Anthony's 'affection, love and good will that he hath unto all ladies'.[66] In later editions an additional chapter was added.

A respect and love for women in general was part of Anthony's version of chivalry, which was not always part of the chivalric code of others, at least not in that form. His religious inclination and desire to improve the morality of others were factors in the translating process for Anthony.[67] While on pilgrimage to Santiago de Compostela in Spain, he was given a copy of the French version of the text by a Frenchman, itself a translation of an 11th-century Arabic work. The decision he took to later translate this text exemplifies the fifteenth-century desire to reclaim knowledge. John Travisa suggests that translations of foreign texts were the most obvious and popular way to do this.[68] In choosing the translations, Caxton and Woodville helped to set a precedent for the types of literature considered worthy of notice.[69] They increased the demand for books printed in English, giving greater opportunities not just for Anthony, but all translators.[70]

Anthony also translated 'the wide and holsom prouerbis of christine of pyse', the moral proverbs of Christine de Pizan, published by Caxton in 1478.[71] This selection of moral observations was translated from the original French.[72] In its content, it was very similar to the *Dictes and Sayings*, although this had more modern content as Christine de Pizan was writing during the late fourteenth and early fifteenth centuries, only eighty or so years prior to Anthony's translation. As well as a poet and biographer, Christine de Pizan was a superb and witty controversialist:

> Men who have slandered the opposite sex have usually known women who were cleverer and more virtuous than they are...
>
> Condemning all women in order to help some misguided men get over their foolish behaviour is tantamount to denouncing fire, which is a vital and beneficial element, just because some people are burnt by it, or to cursing water just because some people are drowned in it...
>
> Do not let the bread of the hungry mildew in your larder! Do not let moths eat the poor man's cloak. Do not store the shoes of the barefoot. Do not hoard the money of the needy. Things you possess in too great abundance belong to the poor and not to you. You are the thief who steals from God if you are able to help your neighbour and refuse to do it.

It is easy to see why Anthony, the man with 'affection, love and good will' for all women, was attracted by Pizan's writings.

Another text attributed to Anthony's Woodville in translation is the *Cordyale,* variously spelt as *Cordiale* or *Cordyal*, known in English as the *Four Last Things*, published in 1479. The text focuses on the need for a strong relationship with God in order to fight the devil. Anthony's English translation was based on a French version produced by Caxton in Bruges in 1476.[73] In general, Anthony stayed faithful to the original, however, there are some examples of paraphrasing or mistakes, which can be expected from translations at this time, or indeed any other. All three of these texts are morally and religiously instructive. This would have appealed to audiences who were concerned with their spiritual welfare, and Anthony himself would have hoped this would fulfil his Christian duty to support the spiritual needs of others.[74]

There are other texts produced by Caxton that have not been directly attributed to Anthony Woodville, but there is a possibility he may have been involved. One such text was *Metamorphoses*, an epic poem by the Roman poet Ovid that influenced the works of Dante, Chaucer and Shakespeare. It is another Classical text that mixes myth with fact, retelling the history of the world from creation to Julius Caesar. There is a copy held at Magdalene Collage in Cambridge that was originally fifteen books, but had been split up after their inception.[75] The last six books were bequeathed by the famous Restoration diarist, Samuel Pepys, the other nine being rediscovered in 1964. The prologue was produced in Bruges in 1484, but unlike other examples of Caxton texts, it provides no information on the original printing, such as date or place of publication, or the translation process. The text is also unfinished as only the first four books had completed illuminations, with the rest having empty spaces where images should have been. This is unusual, suggesting that the production was interrupted for some reason, which perhaps explains why it does not include the usual printing or translating information. N. F. Blake speculates that it could have been Anthony Woodville's execution in June 1483 that stopped the work, although he admits that there is 'no evidence to link him directly' to the *Metamorphoses*.[76]

Even if there is no direct evidence to link Woodville, its classical history theme would be in keeping with the other texts he definitely translated for Caxton. For the *Cordyale*, which Woodville translated, a scribe created some of the copies of the text and omitted any mention of Caxton and Woodville, suggesting that as he had no personal dealing with either of them, he found it irrelevant to mention them.[77] This suggests that even if Woodville was involved with the *Metamorphoses*, it does not automatically mean that he would have garnered a mention. It would appear that scribes creating copies did have some artistic licence, as seen in the *Cordyale*.

One of William Caxton's most famous texts was his edition of Thomas Malory's *Morte D'Arthur* in 1485. The text comprises many different Arthurian tales, detailing Arthur's life from his conception to his death, as well as those of the other knights of the Round Table. Malory is originally thought to have compiled the text in around 1470, but it was first published by Caxton. He described it as full of 'many joyous and playsant hystoryes and noble and renomed actes of humantye, genteelness and chyvalryes'.[78] While this may indicate that the tales show only the ideals of chivalry, they in fact show its positives and negatives. It could be read by noblemen as 'escapist fantasy idealising chivalric values' or as a 'propagandist apology for the failure of their class to live up in reality to their declared ideals'.[79]

As *Morte D'Arthur* was produced two years after Anthony Woodville's death, what does this text have to do with him? There is an intriguing theory that has arisen recently that may connect Woodville to the text, one which deserves further exploration. Caxton references an unnamed knight who had in fact left the text to him so he could print it. It is entirely possible that this knight was Anthony, for it would make sense that Caxton was unwilling to name him in 1485 when Anthony had been executed two years previously. According to Weinburg, it is probable that

Anthony gave Caxton a text that he had used as a reference for his reworking of *Morte D'Arthur*, especially if work on Caxton's version had commenced prior to April 1483, the time that Anthony was arrested.[80] The translating and organisation needed prior to printing a text was a lengthy process, so it is possible. The Malory text could have been at the printing stage towards the end of 1484.[81] It is impossible to confirm that Anthony was involved with M*orte D'Arthur*, but its content would chime with the chivalry and Arthurian legends that personally interested him. It is also interesting to note that Caxton's epilogue laments the decline of chivalry and focuses on the need for an improvement in noble conduct within society.[82] These topics were close to Anthony's heart and were themes reflected in the texts he had already translated for Caxton. Perhaps there was some underlying message that both of these issues had been brought to the fore by Anthony's demise. With his opportunities to visit and understand the culture of other countries, especially Burgundy, he was able alongside Caxton to replicate what he had seen in Burgundy in an English mode.[83] This style would reflect the new Camelot that Edward IV tried to introduce to secure his throne in times of peace, after his military capabilities won him the crown.[84]

It is certainly true that the commercialisation of the printing process helped Edward's regime. It meant that 'official channels' could now be used to encourage loyalty to Edward and the Yorkist regime.[85] Anthony Woodville played a role in this by encouraging certain genres in Caxton's works. The works indirectly suggested that Edward IV's reign was a reflection or recreation of Arthur and his Camelot. [86] Though of course not all of Caxton's output was restricted to such themes.

Without a working relationship and possible friendship between Anthony Woodville and Caxton, the printing press and the printed books it produced would have not reached England as early as they did. Norman Blake's argument that Caxton's relationship with the nobility was 'distant' is not entirely accurate.[87] This is only true after Anthony's execution in June

1483. After Anthony's death, Caxton never found a consistent patron, let alone one who actively contributed towards his printing process as Woodville had done.[88] Caxton's early success was due to his relationship with and promotion through Woodville.[89] Anthony was significant to the story and success of William Caxton's business because it was so entwined with the circles of support around Edward IV and his son, meaning Anthony's part was kept low key or hidden after the death of Edward IV and Anthony's execution in Spring 1483.[90] Such close ties to the Woodvilles and Edward IV's court brought Caxton under suspicion. He had to ask Richard III for a pardon in late 1483, after Anthony was executed in June that year.[91]

Caxton did continue his career following Anthony's death, and it was not all doom and gloom. While of course he did not manage to find a loyal patron like Anthony, his printing business did continue. The rent for Caxton's first printing shop was 10 shillings, indicating that initially it was not a large concern, just enough to build a reputation.[92] In 1483, Caxton's business had clearly expanded as he paid for two houses, and a year later, he paid for an additional room over the gateway to the Almonry.[93] This expansion shows that even if Caxton did not find the noble patronage he had enjoyed under Anthony, the smaller books he produced needed larger premises for either selling or producing.

From what has survived of Caxton's printed materials, we know he produced at least ninety-six books in England, including separate editions, with three printed in Bruges prior to his move to Westminster, and the Sarum Missal he had printed in Paris for him by Guillaume Maynyal, taking the total of known works to a satisfying one hundred.[94] Fragments of other texts that survive suggest that there were more produced by Caxton prior to his death in around 1491. While no print run figures survive, each print run would have produced anywhere between one hundred and three hundred copies, although it was not unheard of for print runs to run to a thousand prior to 1480.[95] If we take these estimates into account, Caxton's print shop must have been a hive of activity. Scholars have interpreted the lack of extant copies as evidence of the popularity of Caxton's works – they may have fallen apart as they were well thumbed.[96]

After Caxton's death, more foreign printers worked in England as there was not enough Englishmen in the trade. Most of them undertaking this work, such as Wynkyn de Worde, the successor to Caxton, had already lived in England for much of their lives and were able to become English citizens in the process.[97] Worde took over Caxton's printing operation following the Englishman's death, but it is uncertain what the exact relationship was between the pair. Some have speculated that Worde had been an apprentice to Caxton.[98]

Caxton's press must have been successful if Worde was willing to take on the business, but what exactly had made it so successful? In Caxton's own words, he hoped to create texts that appealed to a mass audience, alongside the obvious noble circles, not just to be read for pleasure, but also to be morally uplifting. His chivalric themes were important to his success. During the fifteenth century, chivalric texts, by no means a new genre, increased greatly in popularity. In his epilogue to the translation of *The Ordre of Chyalry,* taken from a French text written by Ramon Lull, a worldly knight turned missionary, Caxton complains about the idleness of the upper classes, suggesting that society would be better if gentlemen read romances, cared for their horses and entered tournaments.[99]

After the events of 1482 and the deaths of Edward IV and Anthony Woodville, Caxton was unable to find similar noble support. With these seismic changes at the top and the dwindling of Caxton's business, a process was set in motion that left Woodville a background figure in the history of the Wars of the Roses and of early printing.[100] Alongside the Woodville/Caxton axis, it also helped that Edward IV allowed merchants from all over Europe to reside in England, who 'brought with them a taste for literature and the fine arts, which rapidly spread through all ranks of society', thus creating an international 'wholesale book trade'.[101]

Above: 'Earl Rivers Presenting His Book and Caxton, His Printer, to Edward IV' by Charles Grignion. (Yale Center for British Art, Paul Mellon Collection)

Right: Engraving of Queen Elizabeth Woodville from Charles Knight's *The Popular History of England* (1856). (Courtesy of the British Library under Creative Commons 2.0)

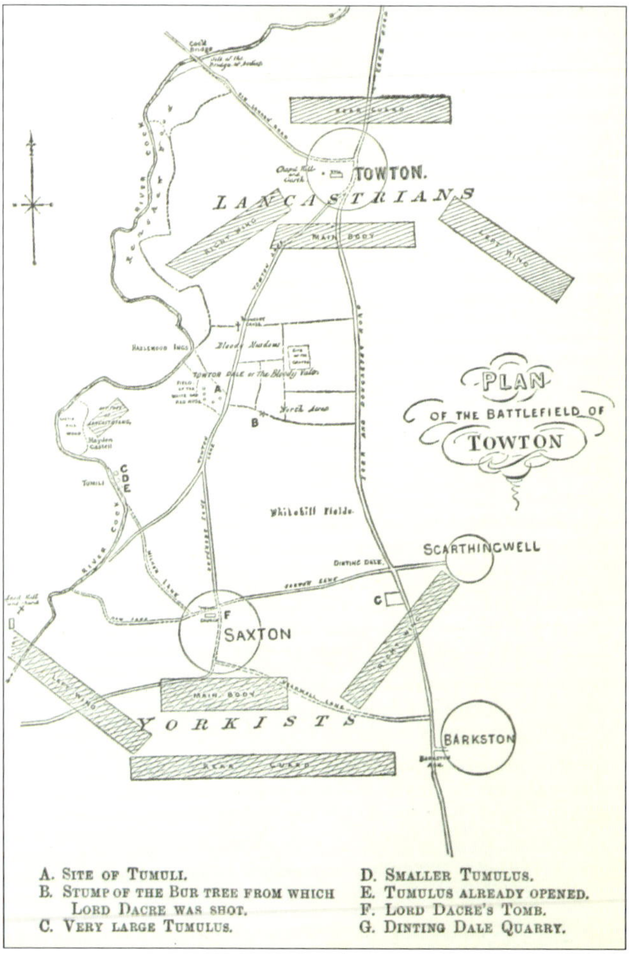

Above: St Mary the Virgin at Grafton Regis, Northamptonshire, courtesy of Amanda Geary

Left: Plan of the Battle of Towton from Alexander D. H. Leadman's *Prœlia Eboracensia, Battles fought in Yorkshire: treated historically and topographically* (1891). (Courtesy of the British Library under Creative Commons 2.0)

Above: Gateway of Carisbrooke Castle, Isle of Wight. (Courtesy of Lara Green)

Below left: Stained-glass window of Edward IV at St Laurence's Church, Ludlow. (Author's collection)

Below right: Richard, Duke of York, depicted in the Talbot Shrewsbury Book. (Courtesy of the British Library under Creative Commons 2.0)

Above: Engraving of St Mary Overy from William Taylor's *Annals of St. Mary Overy* (1833). (Courtesy of the British Library under Creative Commons 2.0)

Left: The manor house at Middleton, once part of the Scales estate in Norfolk. (Author's collection)

Bottom: Later engraving of King's Lynn (Bishop's Lynn) by Henry Ball (*c.* 1690-1711. (Courtesy of the British Library under Creative Commons 2.0)

Above: The White Tower at the Tower of London. Anthony lead a sortie from the Tower against Lancastrian rebels in May 1471. (Author's collection)

Below: William Caxton showing the first page from his printing press to King Edward IV, from Cassell's *Illustrated History of England* (1909). (Courtesy of the British Library under Creative Commons 2.0)

Left: Stained-glass window of Edward V at St Laurence's at Ludlow. (Author's collection)

Below: Ludlow Castle. (Author's collection)

The chapel at Ludlow Castle. (Author's collection)

St Laurence's Church at Ludlow, where members of the Ludlow household may have attended services. (Author's collection)

Above: Denbigh Castle, one of the places other than Ludlow where the council of the Prince of Wales sat. (Author's collection)

Below left: Engraving of Richard III from David Hume's *The History of England to the Revolution in 1688* (1802). (Courtesy of the British Library under Creative Commons 2.0)

Below right: Pontefract Castle. (Courtesy of Laura Adkins)

8

GOVERNOR OF THE HOUSEHOLD OF EDWARD, PRINCE OF WALES

The longed-for Yorkist heir, Prince Edward, was born on 1 November 1470 in the abbot's lodgings at Westminster Abbey, where Queen Elizabeth, along with her three daughters, had taken sanctuary when her husband, Edward, had fled to the continent. With the young Edward's birth, it would seem there was now some ray of light amidst all the uncertainty over the restoration of Henry VI. It was noted that those supporters of Edward IV who remained in England during the Yorkist king's exile were now able to draw 'some consolation and hope' from the birth of his young son.[1]

The young prince was now the ultimate symbol of God's favour upon the House of York. As soon as his father returned from exile, his life would have immediately changed from having to live cooped up in sanctuary for his own safety to living as the heir to the throne. At the age of eight months, he was given his own chamberlain, chancellor and steward. Initially, these roles would have been given to people trusted by the king and queen, most notably Thomas Vaughan as chamberlain, who had been treasurer of the king's council.[2] Not only had he been treasurer, but he had been in royal service since at least 1446, under both Henry VI and Edward IV. He was a substantial landowner within the Home Counties, as well as holding previous offices such as squire of the body to Henry VI and Edward IV, master of the ordinances, keeper of the great wardrobe, ambassador, J.P., M.P. and sheriff.[3] All of these roles show the variety of experience that Vaughan could draw on in matters of the court, law and state. With this in mind, it is clear to see why Vaughan would keep the role of chamberlain to the young prince of Wales until his execution in 1483, not long after the 'accession' of the prince as Edward V.

Prince Edward was officially given the title of Prince of Wales at the Palace of Westminster on 11 June 1471, along with the dukedom of Cornwall and earldom of Chester. (Edward I began the custom of granting the title of prince of Wales to the heir apparent to the English throne in 1301. Today, Prince William is the Prince of Wales and the Earl of Chester.) With these grants, a council and household appropriate for his new status were also established. Those included in the appointments were Anthony Woodville, George, Duke of Clarence and Richard, Duke of Gloucester.[4] Other notables appointed were Thomas Milling as the prince's chancellor, who had given Queen Elizabeth sanctuary, and Lord Dacre of the South as steward, a royal favourite. All appointees were to keep their position until the prince 'be of the age of 14 years, provided that they shall grant no office for life or for a term of years but only during the pleasure of the prince'.[5] As Hicks indicates, these men were already royal councillors, so the prince's council during this early phase was 'little more than a committee of the royal one'.[6] In other words, the council was meant to be temporary until the young prince was deemed to be old enough to appoint his own household. Despite this, his father kept the income granted from the prince's estates and was responsible for delegating the administration of these estates by giving temporary appointments to the council.[7] This set-up would be gradually changed from November 1472, when the prince was granted the issues of his estates in full and was authorised to recruit his own retainers.[8]

The Lords Temporal and Spiritual were obliged to pledge their loyalty to Prince Edward, as a sign of their continuing fealty to the York dynasty. On 3 July 1471, a council met with Edward IV at the Parliament chamber in Westminster to swear an oath of loyalty to the new Prince of Wales. Archbishop Bourchier, the prince's great-uncle, led the oath with a speech, before signing his name. He was followed by forty-two others who were present: Archbishop Neville and eight bishops (including the Chancellor and Bishop of Bath and Wells, Robert Stillington), five English dukes, five earls, including Anthony Woodville, sixteen barons and eleven knights.[9] A similar pledge was given in the presence of the then seven-year-old prince after a dinner on 8 November 1477. The Dukes of Gloucester, Buckingham and Suffolk, Marquess of Dorset and Earl Rivers pledged their honour again to their future king. Gloucester went further than the others by going on his knees and placing his hands around those of the young prince.[10] This went further than was necessary, but the young prince appreciated this gesture. This was during the trial of the Duke of Clarence, brother of Edward IV and Gloucester, meaning the gesture was to show there was still some unity in the House of York.

Prince Edward had been moved to Ludlow in 1473 at the age of two and half. Initially, his mother, Elizabeth, joined him, to help him settle into his new surroundings. As prince of Wales, the young Edward would become a beacon for the future of the Yorkist regime, as well as the focal point for the Welsh marches. Ludlow was a centre of government designed to keep peace in Wales through a mixture of direct and indirect authority, in cooperation with independent lordships throughout Wales and the marches. Chester, Flint and the border shires had direct authority, the lordships of the Duchy of Lancaster and the Earldom of March had indirect authority with the use of chancellors as councillors, and independent lordships were cooperated with.[11] So the power emanating from Ludlow, whether through direct or indirect authority, covered a lot of ground. It replicated the power a king exercised over his kingdom, alongside that of parliament, albeit on a smaller scale. This was why it was important to establish a council that consisted of all three estates, roughly the clergy, the nobility, and what we might call the bourgeoisie, 'ranging from the royal family through select peers (spiritual and temporal) to knights, doctors of law and lawyers'.[12]

These councillors would have moved around the lands owned under the authority of the prince at Ludlow, making decisions on his behalf. Edward IV clearly trusted the prince and these councillors, as in 1476 he arranged for the marcher lords to meet at Ludlow.[13] The councillors would have made decisions in places besides Ludlow. For example, on 10 April 1481, Bishop Alcock, Earl Rivers and other council members were at Shrewsbury town hall, with the assent of the townsfolk, to impose new ordinances that the town had to abide by.[14] Woodville would also have had the responsibility of being a representative of the prince on his own. He was known to have had held sessions in person in South Wales in 1474 and 1478, as well as deputising at Pembroke and Denbigh in 1477. Representatives of the king were often sent to make decisions or hear cases in the king's name, and the prince's council worked in a similar way.

While Ludlow was where the prince would have spent most of his time, it is not the only place he was known to have stayed. His entire itinerary is hard to trace as there is only one surviving household account book. All landowners, and he was one despite his tender age, were expected to travel around their lands. This was even more expected of a prince, who should be known to his subjects. Edward travelled to Haverfordwest in 1473, Warwick and Coventry with his uncle, George, Duke of Clarence in 1474, Chester in 1476, Shrewsbury in 1478-79 and 1480, Worcester and Wigmore Castle in 1479 and Bewdley, Gloucestershire in 1482.

Prince Edward was also with his parents and siblings on visits, particularly at Christmas. As these visits were not consistent, one can imagine a lonely existence for the young boy surrounded by adults, rather than children of his own age. Some of those adults were parental figures to him, certainly in the case of his uncle, Anthony Woodville, and his chamberlain, Thomas Vaughan, with whom he would have probably spent the most time.

While at court in Westminster, Prince Edward stayed in the house of Thomas Vaughan that lay within the precincts of Westminster Abbey. In July 1472, this house was granted to both Vaughan and the prince for their lifetimes.[15] Vaughan spent a great deal of money constructing this dwelling and its connected garden, which neighboured the abbey's infirmary. The house was meant to be a place of rest for the young prince where he could 'quit all entertainment of magnates or of officers and minsters'.[16] So this was a place for both the prince and his trusted chamberlain to enjoy, away from the pressures of their roles.

The prince's household was in charge of every aspect of Edward's life, his clothing, food, health, education, recreation and travel. It was purposefully meant to emulate the king's household, performing much the same function. Life at Ludlow would have been vibrant, even hectic; there would have been a large number of retainers, expensive to keep, and all would have to be utterly trustworthy.[17] All of those employed in the household were expected to live on the premises and whether on or off duty they were meant to be representatives of the young prince, so their behaviour should reflect the royal personage.[18]

As a future king, it was necessary to equip the prince with all the skills essential to this role. In some ways, the education of a prince was similar to most noblemen, certainly in the learning of history, languages and the classics. While nobles were educated to assume the title they would go on to inherit, a prince needed to be educated to take on the political responsibility he was to have as a ruler of a nation. The main difference would have been the speed. Michael Hicks points out that it would have been 'accelerated, enhanced and intensified for a king-to-be', who would have to have finished his education by his mid-teens.[19]

The education that the young Prince of Wales had was quite different from that of his father, Edward IV. As Edward had been born the son of a duke, he would have still had a very good education, but it was not to the same level that a future king required.[20] To ensure that the young prince gained the education needed, instructions were given by the king to ensure a certain standard was maintained at all times:

1. He shall arise every morning at a convenient time, and till he be ready, none but Earl Rivers, his chamberlain, or chaplain, to enter his chamber, and one other chaplain to sing mattins, then to go to his chapel or chamber to hear mass.
2. That he hear, every holiday, divine service.
3. That on principle [sic] feasts, sermons be preached before him.
4. That he breakfast immediately after mass, and be occupied an hour at his school before he go to meat, and to be at his dinner at a convenient hour, and that be reasonably served, and his dishes borne by worshipful folks in our livery.
5. That no man sit at his board, but as Earl Rivers shall allow; and that there be read before him noble stories, as behoveth a Prince to understand; and that the communication, at all times in his presence, be of virtue, honour, cunning [knowledge], wisdom, and deeds of worship, and of nothing that shall move him to vice.
6. After his meat, in eschewing of idleness, that he be occupied two hours at his school; and after, in his presence, to be shewed, all such convenient disports and exercises, as belongs to his estate to have experience in.
7. To go to his even song at a convenient hour; and soon after that to be his supper.
8. After supper, that he have all such honest disports as may be conveniently devised for his recreation.
9. That he be in his chambers, and for all night; and the travers (curtains) to be drawn by nine of the clock, and all persons then from thence to be avoided, except for attendance.

10. That sure and good watch be nightly had and kept about his person for safeguard.
11. That discreet and convenient persons be appointed to give attendance on his person, from his rising to his going to bed.[21]

As seen in rule five, Anthony Woodville's role in the upbringing of the future king was hugely important. It was he who in November 1473 was appointed as 'governor and ruler of the king's first-begotten son'.[22] While it is clear that this was an important role, for he is the only person specifically named in these set of rules, what exactly did his role of governor entail? In short, it meant that he was responsible for the adherence to these rules set out for the young prince, as well as ensuring that all those within the household were also abiding by the roles they had been given. In essence, Anthony was in charge of prince Edward's day-to-day life, education and wellbeing.

It also meant that Anthony was also given permission as a 'right trusty and well-beloved' person by Edward IV to remove the prince at his own discretion if he felt it necessary.[23] This safe environment ensured that education could be given in a way which would have made the young Edward grow into a cultured young man, as per the instructions of his father.[24] The importance placed on education can be seen in the role of John Alcock, Bishop of Rochester, as teacher and president of the council to the young prince, who was to ensure the king-to-be was to 'be brought up in virtue and cunning [knowledge]'.[25]

John Alcock was another good choice to have in the prince's household, not only for religious education. He had a been a diplomat during the negotiation of a possible match between Rivers and Princess Margaret, sister of James III of Scotland. This meant that the two men knew each other, and both had experience of the political aspects of the English court and other kingdoms. Both had been ambassadors, and Alcock had been chancellor. Alcock also clearly took education seriously, for he founded a grammar school in Kingston-Upon-Hull in Yorkshire, as well as the illustrious Jesus College at Cambridge.[26] His own works had been published. He was surely a good choice of teacher who would carry out Edward IV and Anthony Woodville's educative vision for the young heir.

Edward, Prince of Wales would have been taught using that growing genre of texts aimed at advising and educating princes. This genre had until the late fourteenth century been largely created by clerics.[27] By the late fifteenth century, the focus had shifted from solely religious aspects to include personal attributes and public interactions, such as the proper use of councillors.[28] These texts aimed to be 'handbooks for princes who wished to rule successfully'.[29] They indicated that a prince had royal prerogatives and monarchical authority. There were different methods to explain the concept. Historical examples were given, usually either Greek or Roman, or allegories delivered the same message.

A particular favourite philosopher to quote on this matter was Aristotle, as can be seen in the work of John Fortescue. Fortescue was a lawyer closely connected to the court of Henry VI. He became chief justice of the King's Bench in 1442 and later gained a knighthood for his services. He fled with Henry VI to Scotland following the Lancastrian defeat at Towton. It is thought that this is when he received the appointment of Lord Chancellor to the exiled government.[30] Fortesque also lived with the exiled court of Margaret of Anjou in France, meaning he would have known her son, Edward of Westminster, who was part of the exiled party. Fortescue most famously wrote *De Laudibus Legum Anglie*, which devalued Roman law in favour of English law. This text also had some allegorical elements, in which a chancellor advises a prince on how to rule, suggesting that it was written to advise Edward of Lancaster. The chancellor gives specific advice as to how to rule a kingdom which has rejected one's father, which rather ends the debate as to whether it was written for Edward, the son of the deposed Henry VI.[31] In chapter five, Fortescue explores the idea that 'ignorance of the law caused contempt for it', which is an Aristotelian theme.[32] The recommendations made throughout are a reaction to what had happened to Henry VI, so they are perhaps more specific to case than other texts used to educate princes, but they show how the genre could apply the popular classical themes of Greek and Roman law and history to contemporary issues for future monarchs. Such references were not obscure, as people 'produced and consumed an impressive number and variety of historical texts ... biblical, classical, national and personal histories'[33]

While it is unknown which specific texts were used in the education of the Prince of Wales, it is logical to assume that some of the texts were those produced by Caxton, even more probable of course as the printer was a recipient of Anthony Woodville's patronage. The texts produced by Caxton certainly had themes of romance, chivalry, adventure, and moral improvement. All of these themes would be helpful for providing the broad style of education needed for a young prince. Anthony's *Dictes and Sayings of the Philosophers* definitely fits in with idea of moral improvement, seen as an integral part of a prince's education. Aristotle features heavily, and as he was a source keenly used by authors of other texts advising princes, it does not feel like a big step to think that the *Dictes and Sayings* was used.

The young prince's education would not have been solely focused on academic pursuits. Acquiring a specific knowledge, particularly in classics and history, was only part of the education needed for any young noble or future king. As seen in rule no. 8, he would also have participated in 'such honest disports as may be conveniently devised for his recreation'. These may initially appear to be extracurricular activities, but physical education was a necessary part of schooling.[34] This expectation was even higher for princes. The type of physical activities the young Edward would have taken part in were riding, hunting with dogs and 'other youthful exercises to invigorate his body', hawking, hunting, archery – and singing and dancing. [35] As his Woodville uncles were jousting experts, he could have been learning this too.

He would have been taught foreign languages, using a mixture of book learning and conversational practice. While Latin and probably Greek come to mind, there would certainly have been French. Prior to this time, French was viewed as the language of the English court, but less so by the young prince's lifetime. Instead, it would have been the language of diplomacy, which would have been essential for a future king. These were taught not by John Alcock, but by the schoolmaster John Giles, who by 1476 was also teaching Prince Edward's younger brother, Richard.[36]

There would have been no better person to ensure both the academic and physical part of the young prince's education were successfully carried out than Anthony Woodville. As a bibliophile, a tournament champion and a militarily successful combatant, his uncle would have been a good role model for the young prince, particularly as Anthony would have been the only male family role model he would have been around on a regular basis.

Anthony would not have been expected to spend all of his time with the prince at Ludlow. Although he would have spent a large amount of his time there, there were systems in place to ensure the prince's safety and education without the need for his continuous presence. Not only would he have moved around with the prince's council, but just as with any nobleman of the period, he would have also travelled to fulfil the responsibilities he had for his own estates and titles whenever possible. The roles he was given increased after he became the governor of the prince in 1473. It was because of his position in the prince's household that he was able to gain more roles and titles, which he could exploit.[37] He became receiver-general of the duchy of Cornwall in 1473 (later becoming steward of the duchy from 1476), sheriff of Caernarvonshire and master forester of Snowdon, and receiver of Chester in 1482. Some of these positions were given to him to diminish the influence of the Herberts in Wales. Anthony also presented a chantry in the prince's name and used his own signet as sufficient warrant to move the seal of the Carmarthen chancery. It does appear that these were related to his role at Ludlow and may not be as dubious as they first appear. Anthony was also able to reward men who were connected to the prince's office and exploit connections to both princes to return his men to Parliament.

Prince Edward was knighted on 18 April 1475, alongside his younger brother, Richard (who had been named after his grandfather), two older stepbrothers from their mother's first marriage, Thomas and Richard Grey, and twenty others, including their youngest maternal uncle, Edward Woodville, and Thomas Vaughan, Prince Edward's chamberlain. Later that same day, Thomas Grey was also made marquis of Dorset. All of those knighted that day were being rewarded for their Yorkist loyalty or familial relationship with Edward IV. In terms of the two Yorkist princes, considering their young age, the knighting ceremony was more of a symbolic gesture as they were not of fighting age, but it was a means to prepare them for their future responsibilities. For Anthony Woodville, this must have been a proud moment. His young charge, whom he must have viewed very much like his own son, was now growing into his future role, even though he was still only a five-year-old. It must have brought back memories of not just his own knighting ceremony, but those of others he had known, perhaps even of his late brother, John.

The first test that the young prince had was during the short invasion of France in 1475. For many years, Edward IV had been building alliances with Burgundy and Brittany, in the hope of a joint effort to fight France and hopefully regain lost territory there. The king decided it was best to lead his forces in person, leaving the question of who would be in charge of England during his absence. Unlike continental systems, it was rare for a queen to be left in charge as regent. So the then five-year-old Edward, prince of Wales, was to be left in charge as keeper of the realm. This meant that of course others officially governed for him, in the form of a council of twenty people, nine of whom were already on the prince's personal council.[38] To modern eyes, this may seem corrupt or at least corruptible, but this was how the parliamentary system worked. It is entirely possible that Anthony was using his position with the prince to his own advantage, but he would not be the first or the last to do so. It was seen as normal practice in the late fifteenth century.

The prince's responsibilities – which meant the council's responsibilities – included the issue of licences for cathedrals and monasteries to elect superiors, to approve elections, restore temporality, receive fealty of minor prelates, to present to church livings valued between twenty marks and forty marks (the chancellor presented to livings of smaller value, with the king presenting to greater), and to appoint a suitable person to hold the pleas of the Marshalsea.[39] These were only limited and temporary powers.[40] While council members held their positions as the prince so wished once he was deemed to be of an age to make such a decision, it was probably Queen Elizabeth, Earl Rivers and Thomas Vaughan who decided who filled what vacancies within the prince's household at this time.[41]

It was important that these rulings were done in the name of the Prince of Wales. It was vital for the prince to act as the embodiment of the Yorkist dynasty, especially because of the possibility of his father's death while fighting in France. This did not happen, as peace was concluded in fifty-six days, with Edward IV returning home to England within thirteen weeks. The Burgundian promise of support never entirely materialised. Instead, Duke Charles was fighting elsewhere and without this support, Edward knew his army would be outnumbered by the French. He accepted terms of peace, which included the betrothal of one of his daughters to the dauphin, as well as a French pension.

As the council for the Prince of Wales was an offshoot of the king's, with members generally already having proved themselves in the king's council, or in their service to the king in some way, this could cause trouble. Some of the members would not have necessarily only had loyalty to the prince, something desperately needed following the death of Edward IV in April 1483. Michael Hicks argues that because Edward saw everyone as loyal, he turned a blind eye to, or was unaware of, factions and friction among those under him.[42] In many ways this is true, as proved years before with the Earl of Warwick. Edward IV had not entirely understood the friction between Warwick and the Woodvilles and others, such as William, lord Hastings, and the Herberts.

It has long been thought by many that the Woodvilles used Edward, Prince of Wales to their own advantage, seeing him 'as their instrument, their means to domination'.[43] There is no denying that in general, the Woodvilles were, and have subsequently been viewed as, a thoroughly grasping and ambitious lot. However, Edward's uncle Anthony, Earl Rivers, appears to have seen things differently. Unlike the rest of his family, particularly his oldest nephew and half-brother to the prince, Thomas Grey, Marquess of Dorset, Rivers kept himself above the politicking, certainly away from court for most of the time, spending most of it in Ludlow, attending to the education and welfare of his nephew and undertaking duties in the prince's name. With such a position of authority and responsibility, Anthony would have benefitted, but so would anyone else in the same role. By gaining more titles and roles following his appointment to the prince's household in 1473, it is possible that he was being rewarded for a job well done, not just because he held the position. In fact, Anthony's behaviour in general does not indicate a desire to dominate, instead he appears to have been willing to get on with any job he was given, whether it was as the prince's representative, as a pilgrim, or a literary translator. However, without any sources to reveal Rivers' motives, neither judgement can be confirmed.

9

PIETY

The belief that good works could reduce time spent in purgatory was more or less universal in Christian Europe.[1] And paying for masses after a person's death could also speed a soul's journey to heaven. Wills often included instructions to give money to the poor or bequests to religious institutions, as well as to pay for masses for themselves or family members, to this end. In this respect, Anthony Woodville was no different.

The death of his father and brother after the Battle of Edgecote in 1469 must have affected Anthony and his family greatly. Following their execution without trial, Anthony gave land to the provost of Eton in exchange for prayers to be said for his brother John's soul.[2] In life, John had had a special affinity with the college that had been established by Henry VI in 1440, which suggests that if the bodies had been returned to the family following Edgecote, John's body may have been buried there.[3]

Similar prayers were given for Anthony, his wife Elizabeth Scales, and both of their families, living and dead, at the altar of the Virgin Mary at the Chapel of St Thomas the Martyr in Newport on the Isle of Wight, in lieu of the payment of taxes.[4] Anthony was lord of the Isle of Wight. In his will, Anthony also asked for prayers to be said for Elizabeth and her family, paid for with some of the land inherited from his father.[5]

For Anthony, pilgrimage was an integral part of his life. He often journeyed to English sites, such as Canterbury and Walsingham, and visited Rome, as well as places in France on his journey to Compostela in Spain. All of these other pilgrimages are listed in William Caxton's epilogue to one of Anthony's translations, *The Cordyale*. In the prologue to *The Dictes and Sayings of the Philosophers*, Caxton suggests that the motivation for Anthony's pilgrimages was the many adversities and hardships he had faced in his life.[6] Anthony certainly did have troubles, such as the loss of his mother, father, brother, and first wife, exile with Edward IV – and the general chaos of the times he lived in.

Anthony's faith was a huge part of his life and would stay with him until the very end. His piety while facing death was noted in contemporary descriptions. His will, while we are unsure whether it was ever enacted, specified money to be donated to pray for his soul and that of his father, mother and brother.[7] While this was not uncommon, Anthony's mention of the donation of silver basins and the specific wish to be buried near any image of the Virgin Mary, indicate that he was not simply following form.

The motives of pilgrims were not always purely devotional. They could simply wish to travel and experience other cultures, alongside the religious reasons.[8] Anthony's pilgrimage to Santiago de Compostela was undertaken in remembrance of his recently deceased mother, so it was not merely a jaunt.[9] However, as Behrendt suggests in his study of the aristocratic experience of pilgrimage, specifically those of princes, social contacts were important during such journeys.[10] These encounters could also be an informal diplomatic effort to improve understanding between the pilgrim's own country and the country visited.[11]

In June 1469, after the Robin of Redesdale rebellion had broken out, Edward IV undertook a pilgrimage to the famous Shrine of Our Lady at Walsingham. Edward was accompanied by his brother, Richard, Duke of Gloucester, Richard, Earl Rivers as well as Anthony and his brother John.[12] Founded in 1061 after Richeldis de Favarches, the lady of the manor, received a vision from the Virgin Mary, when she was instructed to build a replica of the 'Holy House' of Nazareth, an Augustinian priory was built to look after this holy site.[13] The shrine became a popular pilgrimage destination.

Anthony seems to have felt a particular devotion to the Virgin Mary. The Virgin had obvious connections with birth and the relic held at Walsingham was supposedly some of her breastmilk.[14] Visiting pilgrims prayed to Mary to intercede with God, but they also gave thanks for a child or prayed for future ones. It is entirely possible that during their visit, Edward IV gave thanks for the safe delivery of his third daughter, Cecily, just a few months previously, but prayed – perhaps with greater fervour – for a future son and heir. As Anthony had been married for around eight years at the time of this pilgrimage and his wife, Elizabeth, had yet to bear a child, it is possible that Anthony also gave up his own prayers for a future heir.[15] Anthony may have visited Walsingham more than once, either alone or with others within the royal circle, as the shrine was only about twenty-five miles away from his estates surrounding Middleton in Norfolk. He bequeathed black cloth of gold to the shrine in his will.[16]

Anthony was in a privileged enough position to be able to undertake pilgrimages abroad. He visited the tomb of St James in Santiago de Compostela in North-East Spain in July 1473. In one of the very earliest travel guides, written by a Frenchman, the journey to Compostela and the town itself are described.[17] During Anthony's pilgrimage to Compostela following the death of his mother Jacquetta a year previously in 1472, death would again darken Anthony's door. This time it was his wife, Elizabeth Scales. It was while on this journey that he first read the *Dits Moraulx des Philosophes* by Guillaume de Tignonville, which he would later translate into English as the *Dictes and Sayings of the Philosophers*.

Anthony would again go on a pilgrimage to Rome in the winter of 1475/76. While in Italy, Anthony visited other religious sites, such as shrines in Naples and the shrine of Saint Nicholas in Bari.[18] He would have also visited other holy places in Southern Italy. Before his departure from England, Anthony had been given a letter to guarantee safe passage by Edward IV. This letter became very useful when Anthony was robbed at Torre di Baccano, just north of Rome. The items stolen were 'jowelles and plate', which would have been used as gifts, or as offerings at various shrines along the way.[19] Some of these stolen items were eventually tracked down in Venice, where they had been sold on.

The authorities there, thanks to Anthony's letter from Edward, vowed to undertake a thorough investigation and return as much of the stolen property as could be identified.[20] By the time of the investigation, some of the items had already been sold, but these items were to be returned to their rightful owner, in accordance with civil law as well as out of deference to the King of England, without any cost to Anthony himself.[21] Buhler ponders the motivation of the authorities, suggesting they wanted to advertise safety in Italy to other English pilgrims.[22] It also would not have looked good for the Venetians if an Englishman as important as the king's brother-in-law had not had his case heard and investigated. The goods were promised to be returned within two months. It was also agreed that if any of the purchasers who had brought the stolen goods were found to have purchased them without knowing they were stolen, then they would be compensated via a bill of exchange with three Venetian noblemen via the consul in London.[23] There would be fines to pay if this agreement was not kept. All in all, it seems that Anthony's pilgrimage to Rome had proved to be a costly one for many. Pope Sixtus IV clearly saw something in Anthony that he liked very much. Sixtus bestowed upon him the title of defender and director of papal causes in England.[24]

Anthony had a particular connection to the chapel of Our Lady of Pew in Westminster within the precincts of the Palace of Westminster. It was a small and self-contained chantry chapel that was accessed through the Chapel of St John.[25] As its name suggests, it was dedicated to the Virgin Mary, which would have appealed to Anthony because of his particular devotion to her.[26] He was a patron of the chapel and had helped rebuild it after a fire in 1452.[27] He was singled out as having a special connection to the chapel by the Pope in a fifteen-year indulgence: 'Anthony Wydeville, Earl of Rivieres, brother of Elizabeth Queen of England, and other faithful of those parts have a singular devotion.'[28] This may have been somewhere that Anthony had hoped to have been buried.[29]

Anthony had made plans to go on crusade against the Saracens. During discussions about this journey, John Paston had 'promysed to be ther with hym'.[30] In October 1471, a general request was made for safe conduct for Anthony to go on crusade 'to fight the infidels'.[31] The suggestion of such a venture angered Edward IV greatly. In fact, it enraged him so much that he accused Anthony of cowardice.[32] This was definitely an overreaction on Edward's part, for Anthony had already proved he would not shirk his duty when required. Anthony's timing was appalling. Edward had not long since been restored as king and his situation was still precarious, especially considering the conflict that had ensued following his return from exile in the spring. It is uncertain whether Anthony ever made this journey, for Paston reports that some 'men seye that the Lord Ryverse schypped on Crystmesse evyn' on his way to Portugal, but he was 'not certeyn' as to the validity of these claims.[33] If Anthony did go on crusade, he could not have been there long, as by April 1472 he was in Brittany fighting with the Duke of Brittany against the French.

In Anthony's will, hastily written during his imprisonment at Sheriff Hutton, there are mentions of the institutions connected to the Virgin Mary, such as Our Lady of Pew, but also Saint Mary of York.[34] Anthony requests that a 'hospitall at Rowchestyr' be established to assist fourteen poor folks, and allocates funds to 'to pay prisoners fees' and for the burial of the dead in London.[35]

These bequests could cynically be thought of as attempts to ease a guilty conscience, but as some of them continued the work he had already done in life, such an appraisal does not hold water.

According to William Caxton, Anthony 'desireth with a greet zele and spirituaell love our goostly helpe and perpetual saluacion' and felt it his duty that in translating moral and Christian texts he should guide people in their faith.[36] Religion filtered through to all aspects of his life, even during his tournaments, where he was known to dress as a hermit. It is possible that he preferred the contemplative life. Dominic Mancini commented that Anthony was 'always considered a kind, serious, and just man' who was 'tested by every vicissitude of life'.[37] It is these many trials that focused his mind on the afterlife. Even though he was concerned with his own spiritual wellbeing, as well as that of others, nothing could have prepared him for the way he would enter the afterlife following the events of spring 1483.

10

STONY STRATFORD AND EXECUTION

Edward IV died on 9 April 1483, a few weeks before his forty-second birthday. While Edward was 'not affected by old age nor by any known type of disease which would not have seemed easy to care in a lesser person, took to his bed about Easter time' and did not recover.[1] His death caused huge shock, not just because he died so suddenly, but because his son, also named Edward, was only twelve years old, meaning inevitable political uncertainty. One reason given for Edward's death was reiterated by the Italian visitor to England, Dominic Mancini, in his *Usurpation of Richard the Third*. Mancini says that a fishing trip on the Thames allowed 'the damp cold' to cause an illness in King Edward 'from which he never recovered, though it did not long afflict him'.[2] Mancini wrongly gives Edward's death as 7 April, rather than 9 April, which can be accounted for by the fact that rumours of his demise were in circulation from the 6th.

As centuries before had taught, a young boy king was always a cause for concern. He could be easily manipulated and for this reason it was imperative to ensure a safe transition was made, so that the country was governed as well as could be in the fraught circumstances. The first thing to discuss was what the late king's wishes had been in term of governance. Edward IV's will made around the time of his death no longer survives, making it tricky to follow the discussions about who would govern and how,[3] and what may have been the king's preference.

There were two options that were the most plausible. The first was to allow Richard, Duke of Gloucester, to become the Lord Protector, a type of regent, who would be in control of things in the young king's name until he came of age. The second would have been a type of council, where a certain number of peers would have governed together, with Gloucester being the head of said council. Both of these options made sense and appear to have been discussed, albeit in the absence of the new king or Gloucester, who were both living around two hundred miles away from London at the time.[4] It has been believed that Edward IV openly asked for Gloucester to become Protector, but again, in the absence of a will, this is hard to corroborate.

It was decided that a council, with Richard at the helm, would govern.[5] This followed convention, but there was no written rule as to how to proceed. The pressing lesson from history in everyone's mind would have been that when Henry VI had become king as a baby in 1429, factions had battled over control of him, ultimately resulting in the Wars of the Roses.[6] Nobody wanted a repeat.

With no Lord Protector, then no one person could manipulate the boy, and a ruling council would have council members with a variety of different skills, knowledge and experience to guide the young king in his new role. The makeup of the council and how it would govern was not only of concern to the Woodvilles, who had enjoyed such influence over the young king during his time as Prince of Wales in Ludlow, but to others, such as Gloucester and Hastings, who would also have something to lose if the 'wrong' government was chosen. Everyone had fears for the future for different reasons. It was this fear that explains the mysterious events of the spring of 1483.

The Prince of Wales was officially proclaimed in London as Edward V on 11 April, with plans being set in motion for his coronation to take place on 4 May. The news of Edward IV's death did not reach Ludlow until 14 April, five days after his passing. It is clear that within this timeframe, the Royal party at Ludlow could have easily made it to London in time for Edward IV's funeral, around 18-19 April, but instead they did not even set out from Ludlow until 24 April, leaving a much tighter window to arrive in the capital. Why this happened is still a bit of a mystery, but the usual explanation given is because there were St George's Day celebrations on 23 April.

Hugh Bicheno in *Blood Royal: The Wars of Lancaster and York, 1462-1485* gives an alternative explanation for the delay. In his opinion, it was largely down to the trouble that Lord Hastings had been stirring up in London about a possible Woodville plot.[7] Hastings claimed to the Council that if Anthony was allowed near the capital with some form of army, he would flee to Calais.[8] There is certainly no indication that this was Anthony's intention. Some years previously, there had been bad blood caused between himself and Anthony, after Edward took the role of Lieutenant of Calais away from Anthony and gave it to Hastings.[9] Naturally, this caused some tension between the pair. Was this another attempt by Hastings to lash out at Anthony over an old quarrel? There was a lot of ill will between Hastings and the Woodvilles, particularly Queen Elizabeth and Anthony. Susan Higginbotham goes so far as to claim that this bad blood between Hastings and the Woodvilles made him more of a threat than Richard, Duke of Gloucester, who is often cited as the family's main enemy.[10] Hastings had written to Gloucester (and possibly the Duke of Buckingham as well) about the death of Edward IV, expressing his belief that the Woodvilles may be planning to seize power.[11] Hastings was concerned about Elizabeth Woodville taking revenge on him for his womanising antics with her husband, another reason for Hastings' disquiet about the situation following the death of Edward IV. For this reason, Mancini suggested that

Hastings pushed Gloucester to make haste towards London and not to leave Edward V in the hands of the Woodvilles.[12] Hastings had a particular dislike for Thomas Grey, Marquess of Dorset, the queen's eldest son from her first marriage, whom he thought particularly greedy for power.[13] Following Edward IV's death, Hastings no longer had the protection he had while the king was alive.

The problem is that as with so much of the events of spring and summer of 1483, there is uncertainty. In reality, Hastings did exaggerate his own importance, as he believed he could maintain his high status without Edward IV, but this could also be said for the Woodvilles.[14] All of them had been made who they were by the patronage of Edward IV, and so stood to lose something. Whatever the real reasons behind the delay in setting out to London from Ludlow, it made it look as if the Woodvilles wanted control of the king. Alison Hanham conjectures that this delay ignited the touchpaper that ultimately 'lost Edward his throne'.[15]

As mentioned, the council decided that Edward V be proclaimed king in London on 11 April, with plans being made for the coronation to be held on 4 May, being made in the absence of both the new king and Richard, Duke of Gloucester, his paternal uncle and the possible Protector of the Realm. The news of this and Edward IV's death would have taken a while to travel around the country. Richard, who was residing at Middleham in Yorkshire at the time, heard the news after the burial of his brother at St George's Chapel in Windsor. When the duke heard the news, he wrote to Edward IV's widow, Elizabeth, ensuring her of his loyalty to her son, the new king. He also organised a memorial service in York in honour of the late king, where an oath to Edward V was proclaimed not just by Richard, who was the first to swear his loyalty, but all the men of note in attendance.[16]

The logistics of transporting the new king to London in preparation for his coronation would have needed to be meticulously worked through. It was imperative that Edward V reach the capital safely, and the journey was a long one. How this would happen was the source of some tension. A large force was needed as an escort, but there was an argument about just how large. Lord Hastings raised concerns about this, probably in fear of the Woodvilles. He suggested that the figure was kept at 2,000 men.[17] Although the exact number that did form the escort is unknown, this figure is thought probable. Whatever the eventual number of men in the escort, Anthony's compliance shows that he had no quarrel with or fear of Gloucester.[18]

In an account of what happened at Stony Stratford, *The London Chronicle* initially wrongly says that it was Thomas Grey, marquis of Dorset, who escorted the young King Edward out of Ludlow and towards London. It even wrongly calls him 'uncle by the moders side', which is what Anthony Woodville was, despite Dorset being the king's half-brother and nowhere near the young king at the time.[19] However, within a page, the author does correctly identify the person in charge of Edward V as Anthony Woodville and that he, alongside Richard Grey, Thomas Vaughan and Richard Haute, were all executed at Pontefract.[20] Perhaps the author misunderstood the familial relationships of those involved. Richard Haute is mentioned as being among those executed, but he was not. According to Kingford, it has been estimated that the particular chronicle this information was taken from was written around 1496, some fourteen years after the events at Stony Stratford, which perhaps explains some of the confusion.[21]

In the words of Horace Walpole, in his attempt to undo Tudor propaganda surrounding Richard III, the Duke of Buckingham 'was the devil that tempted Richard', as he was the first to arouse suspicions of the young king's Ludlow party.[22] This is an opinion that has been given elsewhere, including by the late John Ashdown-Hill in his book, *The Mythology of Richard III*. Ashdown-Hill suggests that the arrival of Buckingham changed the atmosphere between Anthony and Richard, which indicates that the Duke had some influence.[23] It is true that Buckingham did not hold the Woodvilles in high regard, mainly due to his being forced to marry into the family at a young age, as well as his dislike for the family's ambition. These may be motives behind the events at Stony Stratford.[24]

What type of relationship did Anthony Woodville and Richard, Duke of Gloucester have prior to the death of Edward IV? This is surely vital to an understanding of the events at Stony Stratford. The pair would have been known to each other as they were both part of Edward IV's inner circle. They had also both been members of the party that had accompanied the king into exile in 1470. There was nothing mentioned in regard to any previous open discord between the pair prior to the meeting at Stony Stratford. In fact, just a month prior to this meeting, Woodville had been willing to 'nominate Gloucester to arbitrate a dispute', showing that they were on good terms and that Woodville 'did not perceive Gloucester to be his enemy'.[25] When Anthony and his nephew Richard Grey arrived for their arranged meeting with Gloucester, 'they were greeted with a particularly cheerful and merry face' and they were able to have a polite dinner together, which was full of 'very pleasant conversation'.[26]

There appears to be some consensus that the meeting with Gloucester was a pleasant one, even if there are slight variations. According to Dominic Mancini, Anthony met with Gloucester alone and had been sent there by the young king himself. The pair spent a 'great part of the night in conviviality' before retiring to bed.[27] This is confirmed by Thomas More in his *History of Richard III*. More again suggests that their meeting was a friendly one and the group retired without a harsh word being said.[28] It is possible, of course, that this friendly meeting was part of a ruse to lull the arriving Woodville party into a false sense of security.

There is certainly a case for some form of friendship between Anthony and Gloucester. They spent a lot of time in each other's company as they were both very close to Edward IV and were given suitable titles and roles by the king, as brother and brother-in-law. They also had spent time in exile in Burgundy together. Not only had they gone through similar situations together, including on the battlefield, particularly when both of them were injured at Barnet, but the pair had other things in common. Both men were known for their piety and scholarly pursuits, and they also had a keen sense of loyalty. With similar personalities and personal circumstances, there were no previous indications that there was any animosity between Gloucester and Rivers prior to 1483.

No matter how friendly the meeting of 29 April was, it would appear that things changed on the morning of 30 April. According to Thomas More's account, the mood had changed significantly when the gates of Northampton were ordered to be closed and guards were placed along the road to Stony Stratford, on the orders of Gloucester and Buckingham. When Anthony Woodville discovered this to be the case, he asked what was happening. The response given to him was that it was because 'hee intended to sette distaunce beetwene the kynge and them, and to brynge them to confusion'.[29] Before Anthony had much of a chance to put his side forward, he was arrested and locked up.

Once Gloucester and Buckingham reached Stony Stratford, they told the servants to keep to their rooms while they met with the king. After greeting their ruler on their knees, they accused Richard Grey, the king's half-brother, of colluding with his brother, Thomas Grey, Marquess of Dorset, and their uncle, Lord Rivers, to 'rule the kinge and the realme', to cause more conflict and to 'destroye the noble blood of the realm'.[30] Dorset was accused of stealing the treasury and putting sailors out to sea. These decisions undermined Gloucester's command.[31]

It is intriguing that despite More's keen dislike of Richard III, his narrative gives a glimpse of the possible friendship he had once enjoyed with Anthony Woodville as Duke of Gloucester. During the evening of 30 April, following the arrests of Rivers, Grey and Vaughan, Gloucester sent a dish from his own table to Anthony, 'praying him to bee of good chere, all should be well inough'.[32] Was this the action of a man who had known Anthony for a long time and had been on friendly terms before and was feeling sorry for the circumstances? Or was it a means of goading a man who was under arrest? If it was the latter, then it is even stranger that Gloucester also did the same for Richard Grey, saying that Grey would find 'such aduersitie' to be 'strange'.[33] More writes critically throughout his work on the scheming motives of Gloucester as both a duke and later king, but this moment does not quite run true with the pantomime-like villain that More wishes to portray.

The fact that Stony Stratford was chosen as the rendezvous point for the meeting of the Ludlow and Gloucester parties is significant. It was a detour from the direct route that would have taken the young king directly to London. As pointed out by Alison Hanham in her analysis of early historians writing on Richard III, she suggests that there are a few consequences to take away from this detour. It could mean that there was some trust between the Ludlow party and Richard at the time of the meeting, and 'there was therefore nothing to gain by discourtesy to Gloucester'.[34]

While it is generally accepted that Stony Stratford was the place of rendezvous between the Woodvilles and Gloucester, Annette Carson has put forward an alternative, Grafton Regis, the Woodvilles' ancestral home.[35] Grafton lies just five miles away from Stony Stratford and would have provided more protection and space to the household of the new king than the small village of Stony Stratford. If we are to accept the reason for Stony Stratford being chosen for lodgings was because there was not enough space in the much larger town of Northampton, it does not make sense to choose the village, when the ancestral home of Grafton was so close by. Perhaps this may have created suspicions for Gloucester, for it was not exactly neutral territory, even if it was a good choice to keep the new king safe. Mancini does acknowledge that Gloucester and Buckingham had arranged to meet the king on the way to London but does not specify where this rendezvous point was.[36] This may have been because his knowledge of places in England outside of London was pretty limited, but it could also mean there was some uncertainty at the time.

Anthony had been in charge of the young prince in Ludlow, as well as all of the household, for nigh on a decade. It was noted by one Italian visitor that the Prince of Wales was 'well versed in most of the standard Latin classics', indicating that his education programme was proceeding well.[37] As young Edward had spent much of his life in Ludlow, Anthony was probably his nephew's most influential father figure. As Anthony never had a son of his own, Edward could have filled a vacuum in his life, too. If we take this to be the case, then surely Anthony had a lot to lose if he became involved in any Woodville plot. If he didn't, he could have easily slotted into any council created to share control during the minority. While some on the already existing council believed Richard should have been made sole protector, the majority view was that there should be a number of people involved, with Richard as chief councillor.[38] Anthony would have been a perfect choice to have sat on this council. Not only had he already had previous experience of the machinery of state at Ludlow, from where the Council of Wales was run, but he already was a trusted figure for Edward V. If a shared council was the way forward for the regency government rather than a protectorate under Richard alone, then Anthony would have been an asset rather than a hindrance.

Hugh Bicheno suggests that Northampton was chosen as the rendezvous point for Richard, Buckingham and Anthony Woodville. The rest of the party accompanying the king carried on to Stony Stratford, but Anthony Woodville, only brought his nephew, Richard Grey, who had made the journey up from London, with him, met with Gloucester and Buckingham there. The fact that the pair visited Gloucester and Buckingham without any of the men-at-arms that had accompanied the king from Ludlow does not seem to support the notion that these were men plotting against Richard. In fact 'men planning to seize power would not have left the security of the 2,000 men who remained with the king'.[39] There was certainly a friendly dinner between the men, so perhaps there is something in the argument that Bicheno puts forward laying suspicion on Buckingham, especially as he suggests the meeting at Northampton had been at Buckingham's behest.[40] This certainly gives some credence to the theory that Buckingham was stirring things between both parties. After the dinner and Buckingham's arrival, all the men retired to their own lodgings for the night.

The following morning, they were to move on to where the young king had stayed, so the whole party could present themselves to him. Instead, the arrests of men of the Ludlow party were made: Anthony Woodville, Richard Grey and Thomas Vaughan.[41] These three men held the highest offices in the household at Ludlow. Vaughan was 'an aged knight' who had been the chamberlain of the Ludlow household. He was known to have been in royal service since at least 1446, some thirty-seven years, under both Henry VI and Edward IV, although he had pledged his allegiance to the house of York from 1460.[42] Richard Grey had been promoted to a position of control within the household earlier in 1483, and so had not been in the role long before the events of that spring. However, he had been the most visible Woodville in Wales during the mid-1470s, probably because Rivers was busy with pilgrimages and personal marriage negotiations after the loss of his first wife, among other things.[43] It was probably for this reason that Grey was promoted. There is some debate as to whether another man, called Haute, was also arrested. There was no mention of his execution, so if he was arrested he may have been released at a later date.

Other attendants within the household were dismissed and told not to come near the king again, which caused the king much weeping.[44] Perhaps Haute may have been one of these men who were dismissed, rather than one who was arrested. There would certainly have been a great many men, both within the household and those who were there to escort the king to London, so it is possible that as he was a named person in this crowd, he was given more significance than those men whose names were not known. It is also possible that the Haute in question was Richard Haute, who was a distant cousin of the Woodvilles. If so, he was not executed at the same time as Anthony, Grey and Vaughan. He was one of the named executors of Anthony's will and had been one of the members of the council of the Prince of Wales. It appears that his name is mentioned in some of the confusion that surrounded the executions.

Thomas More argued that in removing the Woodvilles from the king, Richard allowed 'the lesse noble to be left aboute him'.[45] He adds that the removal of those known to the king had been justified because those around him at the time were not focused upon his safety but instead were seeking to advance themselves, which threatened to break 'the amitie and peace' that Edward IV had fought hard to keep between those who had surrounded him, and who would now surround his young son.[46] There is perhaps some truth in this as there was a lot of fear and uncertainty in the air during this time on all sides. The problem with Thomas More's version of the events of spring 1483, however, is that he relied heavily on the recollection of events by people who may or may not have been eyewitnesses. He was writing at some point between 1510-1518, when undersheriff of London. More had also worked for a few years in the household of John Morton, a Cardinal and previous Bishop of Ely, who had been promoted by Henry VII. This suggests a lot of his source material had come from Morton – who had not witnessed a lot of the events featured in More's work – or those who had a similar viewpoint.[47] The events of 30 April had to be explained to the young king. More suggests there was a quarrel with Richard Grey about a possible Woodville plot, which occurred in the king's presence. In response to these accusations, Edward V supposedly said that he had no knowledge of these plans but believed those accused to be innocent.[48]

It is beyond the scope of this book to consider what the eventual fate of Edward V was, so all that is left to be said is that he was taken to London in preparation for his coronation. What is possible to deduce is that it was certainly a time of huge sadness for Edward, the young boy king. He had lost those who he had been close to and trusted, including his Uncle Anthony.

It is possible that the Woodville family caused their own downfall, if there was a plot as discussed. Upon the arrest of Anthony, when Gloucester and Buckingham had arrived to arrest Richard Grey at Stony Stratford, Walpole suggests there was a quarrel in which Anthony, Grey and Grey's brother, the Marquis of Dorset, were blamed for plotting and Dorset for stealing from the treasury.[49] Mancini also reiterates the rumour that the Woodvilles had got hold of the treasure. He puts the blame on Queen Elizabeth and her son, Dorset, for stealing it, but suggests that they split it with Elizabeth's brother, Edward, who had been out at sea at the time because of threats from France.[50]

Still, there is another explanation that has been put forward that does not necessarily include those from Ludlow. The theory is that it was in fact Elizabeth Woodville and her son, Thomas Grey, Marquess of Dorset, who attempted to arrange resistance against Richard, Duke of Gloucester, following the death of Edward IV.[51] Indeed, there was a cartload of weapons with a Woodville crest on, which was paraded around 'as proof of a Woodville conspiracy', but according to Dominic Mancini, these weapons had been collected for war against the Scots and the people of London knew this.[52] Even if we take these weapons as evidence of a conspiracy however, this would not tell us which of the Woodvilles were involved. The parading of the weapons was done in the hope of persuading people the arrest of those from the Ludlow household had been for legitimate reasons.

Dorset clearly had a motive for such rebellious activity. Michael Hicks correctly identifies that prior to this point, both he and his uncle, Edward Woodville, 'had so far been denied much opportunity', suggesting that they were now seizing their chance while the country was in a state of uncertainty.[53] Dorset had tried to push his opinion about what should happen to the young king and he certainly did not like the idea of waiting for Gloucester to be consulted on related matters.[54] For this reason, Dorset, and to some extent Edward Woodville, appear to be more likely suspects behind a Woodville plot than Anthony Woodville or Richard Grey, who had been arrested under this accusation. Rivers and Grey had been based in Ludlow for around ten years by this point and were largely away from court. As they had become so integrated with the Prince of Wales' household, they both had much more to lose from a plot at this point. Neither had displayed particularly rebellious behaviour before. Dorset, however, had already shown himself to be an abrasive and more ambitious character than either his brother Richard Grey, or his uncle Anthony Woodville.

With so much time passed it is difficult to say with any certainty whether there was any ambush, or Woodville plot. It is entirely possible that Gloucester had acted hastily because of fear of one. This is certainly a view that has been put forward many times, by J. R. Lander among others.[55] Fear does make people do irrational things, so perhaps this is an instance of that. *The Crowland Chronicle* does point the finger at Gloucester as the instigator of the arrests. The chronicler suggests that the reason given for the arrests by the duke to the young king was to 'safeguard his own person' because 'there were men close to the king who had sworn to destroy his honour and his life'.[56] There are, however, conflicting reports about what Gloucester said to the king. It could be that Richard had genuine fears for his safety, perhaps fuelled by those around him at this time. As High Constable of England, Gloucester was entitled to have made the arrests. Part of the role involved protecting England from treason.[57]

Following the arrests, Rivers, Grey and Vaughan were all held in the North for many weeks prior to their executions. If, as Annette Carson has suggested, this was done to exert 'pressure on the remaining Woodvilles' to come to terms,[58] which is a probable explanation for the time lapse between their arrests and executions, it suggests that those arrested were not the main instigators of any plot. Instead, they were being used as leverage with hopes that some agreement or compromise could be made going forward. This never happened, which is why they were executed as scapegoats.

It was a nobleman's prerogative that if charged with treason, he would be tried by his peers. This would have been the expectation of Anthony Woodville and the others arrested. However, if there was no trial for Woodville and his colleagues, it would follow a precedent. Many prominent nobles had been executed without trial throughout the Wars of the Roses.[59] If Anthony, Grey and Vaughan were indeed executed without trial on the orders of Richard, it was more to do with the 'crimes of the age than of the man'.[60]

It is hard to prove whether there was a trial or not as there are no extant documents. We don't even know what the indictments were. Someone, of course, had given the orders for the executions. Dominic Mancini does not give any names for those who may have been behind the orders, though he says that the actual executions were carried out by 'dependable officers'.[61] Mancini makes no other reference to the executions at Pontefract, limited as he was to what information was reaching London. His writings were targeted at his patron, so he may have felt that giving any further details about these executions was superfluous.

While Mancini may not have put forward any possible candidates for who ordered the executions, others have. One such candidate is Richard Ratcliffe. *The Crowland Chronicle* names him directly and says he ordered the executions without a trial, implying that Ratcliffe had innocent blood on his hands.[62] Thomas More also suggests that the executions lay at Ratcliffe's door, the beheadings were all done 'in the presence & by the oder of syr Richard Ratclif'.[63] Once they were led out upon the scaffold, Ratcliffe personally told those assembled that the prisoners were traitors and would be beheaded. More says that the prisoners were not allowed to speak any final words to 'declare their innocence lest their words might haue inclined men to pity them', implying that this also had been done on Ratcliffe's orders.[64]

In the Louvain Latin version of Thomas More's account of the events of 1483, Richard Ratcliffe is noted as being at Stony Stratford at the time of the arrests.[65] Strangely, Ratcliffe is not mentioned at Stony Stratford in the English translation, which suggests that something had been lost in between the two versions, or redacted. Ratcliffe's appearance in the Latin version gives more credence to Ratcliffe's possible presence during the executions. In *Richard III,* William Shakespeare has Ratcliffe appear at Pontefract conducting Rivers, Grey and Vaughan to their executions, so perhaps he had used the Latin version of More as one of his sources.[66]

John Ashdown-Hill instead suggests that there was a trial and that this, along with the executions, were presided over by the Earl of Northumberland.[67] This is also possible as Northumberland was one of the most important landowners in the north, and as Gloucester was a crowned king by the time of the executions rather than a major northern landowner as he had been as Duke of Gloucester, Northumberland could have been filling a power gap. In distributing punishment, he would be seen as demonstrating this.

It is uncertain whether or not the terms specified in Anthony's will written at Sheriff Hutton before he was transferred to Pontefract for his execution were ever followed. However, Richard III did not forget Anthony's widow, Mary FitzLewis. He ordered that her tenants make the payments due to her under her jointure.[68] As this was her legal entitlement, whether or not her husband was executed, Richard was simply helping to enforce the law. It is also similar to Richard's treatment of Hastings' widow following his execution. Mary FitzLewis went on to marry George Neville, an illegitimate great nephew of Cecily Neville,

Duchess of York. Neville was a Yorkist and went on to be an Esquire of the Body during the reign of Richard III.[69] Clearly there was not as much animosity between Mary and Richard following her first husband's execution as you would think. Perhaps there was some regret and Richard was ensuring some security for Anthony's widow, but that is something that can never be proved. As Matt Lewis points out, 'The will reads more like a stream of consciousness rather than a carefully prepared document, which is perhaps not surprising in the claustrophobic circumstances.'

In his description of Anthony's execution, John Rous mentions that he was wearing a hair shirt.[70] Hair shirts symbolised in some small way the pain that Jesus had suffered on the cross. By emphasising the hair shirt Anthony was wearing, John Rous was purposefully contrasting his devotion to the miscarriage of justice he suffered. Rous claims that the execution of Anthony and his fellow Ludlow men was for a thing they had never contemplated, but they had 'innocently, humbly and peaceably submitted' to their fate.[71] However, this simple tale of good and evil begins to lose credibility when we remember that Anthony and Gloucester had known each other and had often spent time in each other's company for many years, meaning there must have been some sort of polite familiarity, if not some form of friendship, prior to the events of 1483.[72]

Anthony's man of letters persona carried on until almost his last breath. After learning that he was to be executed, he wrote one final poem, lamenting how the wheel of fortune can change at any moment and pondering on life and death.[73] This theme of hopelessness in an unjust situation is an age-old one, which can be seen in the work of the fourteenth-century writer, Geoffrey Chaucer.[74] While this may be an old theme made new in Anthony's final poem, Hugh Bicheno says that it reminds us 'what a shining exception Rivers was to the dull aristocratic norm'.[75]

Anthony's hair shirt became consecrated, hung before the image of the Blessed Mary at the Carmelite Friary in Doncaster, also known as Our Lady of Doncaster.[76] It was not out of character for Anthony to wear such an item, as he had dressed as a white hermit during tournaments.[77] The friary was destroyed during the Dissolution of the Monasteries, so it is now impossible to prove that Anthony's shirt was bequeathed to the Carmelites. However, as Anthony had a reputation for wearing such a shirt and in view of his personal affiliation with the Virgin Mary, it would certainly be in keeping.

The Carmelite Friary at Doncaster was established in 1350 and had become a popular place of pilgrimage thanks to its venerated image of the Virgin Mary. In 1486, Henry VII stopped there on his way to York, where he 'harde masse at the freres of Our Lady and evensong in the parishe chirche'.[78] Among those accompanying the new king were relatives of Anthony Woodville, Richard, Earl Rivers, Sir Richard Haute and Sir Robert Poyntz.[79] Could these family members be visiting for reasons other than to see the image of Our Lady? If the hair shirt was left as a relic, perhaps they were there to pay their respects to Anthony, especially as with King Henry VII now enthroned, they may have felt that it was safe to do so.

In Anthony's will, it was specified that he would like to be buried before an image of the Virgin Mary alongside his nephew, Richard Grey.[80] Does this request have any bearing on the shirt given to Doncaster? It does appear to be more than a coincidence that the shirt was given to a shrine dedicated to Mary. However, we do not know specifically what happened to Anthony's body following his execution. We do know that Richard III paid 46s 4d for the burial of Richard Grey, as the expenses appear in the financial accounts prepared by Geoffrey Franke and sent to auditors in Middleham.[81] Unfortunately, the entry does not provide any further information as to the circumstances or place of burial. Perhaps the final resting place of the hair shirt was some sort of compromise, considering the circumstances.

There are even more questions raised about the final resting place of Anthony Woodville. It has largely been thought that Anthony,

Grey and Vaughan were all placed into a mass grave at Pontefract following their executions. As discussed above, there is evidence that Grey was buried with some dignity, albeit from the amount spent it was probably just burial and nothing else. Thomas Vaughan was buried in St John the Baptist chapel in Westminster Abbey. It is thought that the tomb was erected on the orders of Vaughan's daughter, Elizabeth, wife of John Grey of Wilton and later Sir Edward Stanley.[82] The tomb itself is now in a state of disrepair, but a Latin inscription once ran around the rim which translated as 'Thomas Vaughan, treasurer to King Edward the fourth and chamberlain to his first born son. Rest in peace. Amen'.[83]

When both of these burials for Grey and Vaughan are taken into account, it does appear strange that there is no glimmer of what may have happened to Rivers' body. Perhaps he was buried at Doncaster and after the Dissolution, the location has been lost. We may never know, but there are other possibilities at Pontefract: an unconsecrated grave within the boundaries of the castle, All Saint's Church and St John's Priory. If the grave is within the boundaries of the castle, it's well hidden. The ground level has altered much since the fifteenth century, mostly due to Civil War sieges, after which stone was sold to the local community, and later Victorian alterations.[84] There has been no body found yet that would match the description of Woodville, although many bodies have been found during various archaeological excavations.

All Saint's Church was largely destroyed during the many skirmishes and sieges that the town and castle at Pontefract underwent during the English Civil War. The church is most unusual in that a modern church was constructed inside the ruins of the original in the 1960s. With so much destruction and alteration to the original church and its burial ground, there is no evidence of this as a possible burial site for Woodville. However, its proximity to the castle itself is tantalising.

The Priory of St John the Evangelist is also very close to the castle, less than a mile away. This has more chance of being a final resting place for Anthony as it was the place where Thomas of Lancaster (also executed at Pontefract) and Richard of York and Edmund, Earl of Rutland had all been buried. The priory was the most important religious house in Pontefract and had been founded by Robert de Lacy in 1090. Following the Dissolution, the site was turned over to tenant farming.[85] Today, the outline of the remains of the buildings can be seen in a field that now lies in the middle of a housing estate close to Pontefract Monkhill train station. What makes this such a tempting option for Anthony's burial is that not many burials were known to have been recorded here. An assessment given during the 1870s states that 'probably the remains of many political victims during the fourteenth and fifteenth centuries were interred in this ground'.[86]

Following the burial of Thomas of Lancaster, who had been executed for treason in 1322, the priory became a place of pilgrimage after miracles started to be seen at the gravesite. The numbers had become so large that a royal order was passed to bar access to the tomb. It is possible that there were fears that a similar situation could follow Anthony's death. Perhaps this is why Anthony's burial place was not recorded, even if it had been at St John's priory. Or is there a chance that some of Anthony's relatives did ask for his body and he was placed somewhere they wished him to be? Considering that this is what happened to Thomas Vaughan, this possibility cannot be ruled out. We do not have any evidence for a request of this kind for Anthony, which, considering that his family members were numerous, is strange in itself.

The changes made to all of the possible burial sites make it entirely likely that his body, whatever its fate, has been lost. However, if at any point in the future a body that may be that of Woodville is found, then it would be feasible to identify him, as mitochondrial DNA research has been conducted into the Woodville family. Age, sex, location and cause of death would also help to prove identity if this were to ever happen.

The majority of sources imply that Anthony Woodville was innocent; a victim and scapegoat for his own family. His eldest nephew, Thomas Grey, Marquess of Dorset, does appear to be the most avaricious among them and was the most unwilling to compromise following the death of Edward IV.[87] In agreeing to reduce the number of armed men in the escort of Edward V to London from Ludlow, Anthony had shown that he was willing to compromise to ease the already tense situation. His diplomatic skills shown since becoming Edward IV's brother-in-law also indicated that he knew the importance of compromise and negotiation in such political circumstances.

It appears that something or someone had changed the psychological and political landscape by the time the Ludlow party reached Northamptonshire. It is likely that the Duke of Buckingham and Lord Hastings were part of this, for both had reason to dislike the Woodvilles, certainly more than Richard did. Gloucester had little reason to be in conflict with Anthony, for he had been in close contact with him for many years, most notably when the pair were in exile in Burgundy together. Amity was in evidence in the meeting between Woodville and Gloucester at Northampton, where the pair 'were greeted with a particularly cheerful and merry face' and they were able to have a well-mannered dinner together, full of 'very pleasant conversation', before things changed the morning after and the Ludlow party were arrested.[88] As Anthony, and possibly Grey also, had left the rest of the escort party to personally dine with Gloucester, this suggests that Anthony was not privy to any possible Woodville plot as it did not make sense to put himself in the hands of a man he was 'allegedly conspiring against'.[89]

Perhaps after the arrival of Buckingham there were some accusations thrown around and Buckingham added to the words of warning that Hastings had already given about the Woodvilles wanting power after Edward IV's death. And as we know, Hastings also had a longstanding issue with Anthony over the Lieutenancy of Calais.[90] It would appear that now Edward IV was out of the picture, anger and thoughts of revenge that had simmered for many years had bubbled to the surface, with tragic consequences for Rivers, Grey and Vaughan.

To back up these suspicions and rumours spread about the Woodvilles during this fearful time were the weapons with a Woodville crest on, which could have been collected for war against the Scots.[91] These would have increased the tensions and uncertainty the regime of a young king always brought, as had the boy Henry VI in living memory. It would only be natural that fears were in circulation that history would be soon repeating itself. Gloucester would have had some of these fears, and those around him amplified them and encouraged him to act in a certain way: to lash out at Anthony, Grey and Vaughan, which ultimately resulted in their executions.

11

LEGACY

Who was the real Anthony Woodville? He has very often been stigmatised as a man of ruthless ambition, a trait which has often been attributed to the Woodville family as a whole. This has largely been due to his execution for treason at Pontefract Castle on 25 June 1483. This viewpoint has not taken into account the fact that most contemporary sources suggest those executed on that day were innocent.[1]

Anthony was quite different from most of his family. He largely stayed out of political intrigue at court, especially after he was appointed as head of the household of the Prince of Wales in Ludlow. Instead, Anthony was a man who was keen to demonstrate his jousting prowess and literary skills, very much like the ideal medieval knight people can picture today. In the words of Horace Walpole in the eighteenth century, Anthony Woodville was a man who was 'as brave as the heroes of either rose, without their savageness; studious in the intervals of business, and devout'.[2] In this respect, he lived up to the ideals of a well-rounded nobleman, who was expected to be capable in both military and cultural pursuits.[3]

While there is truth in Walpole's description of Woodville, we cannot be too idealistic as we are dealing with a real man, who would have had his own vices and flaws, just like any other man. He would have done wrong things, as was the case in his treatment of Maud Stanhope, when he took a bribe for a pardon for her husband and his servants subsequently stole her personal belongings that were not part of the deal.[4] However, this is perhaps one of only a few instances where he might be adjudged 'meticulous, predatory and ruthless'.[5]

What appears to have been the true personality of Anthony himself is cautiously approached by Susan Higginbotham: 'Anthony may not have been the cold and chilly creature his detractors depicted him as.'[6] It is hoped that this book has at least gone some way towards showing that he had a varied skill set, as diplomat, tournament champion, governor of the Prince of Wales, pilgrim, literary and religious patron, and translator.

Even Thomas More noted that Anthony's written skills were matched by his verbal rhetoric 'as hee was a very well spoken manne',[7] as was demonstrated in his role as arbitrator in the dispute in 1482 between the City of Norwich and the abbot of St Benet's. Thanks to Anthony's involvement, Edward IV did eventually alter his opinion on the matter and took the side of the City of Norwich, as Anthony had advised.[8] The Pastons also trusted Anthony's skills as an intermediary, for he is cited as discussing an ongoing dispute between the Pastons and the Dukes of Norfolk and Suffolk over who owned various parcels of land in the county of Norfolk that once belonged to Sir John Fastolf.[9] These instances show, alongside the many times he was chosen as a negotiator in diplomatic matters with Burgundy, that Anthony was a successful mediator, regardless of whether the matter at hand was on a local or international level.

Perhaps the main reason that the role Anthony Woodville played during the late fifteenth century has been underappreciated is that it was largely intertwined with the young Edward V, while he was Prince of Wales. Anthony had successfully acted on Edward IV's instructions to bring his son up as required. Of huge importance to Edward IV was to choose someone who would fit 'the virtue, honour, cunning [knowledge], wisdom, and deeds of worship' aspects he cherished as part of the the prince's education, which is ironic considering these were not attributes that could describe Edward IV himself.[10] He did not want his son to repeat his own mistakes.

Anthony Woodville was chosen as the man to deliver this ambitious education plan, for he exemplified the qualities that needed to be instilled in the young prince. He had a varied amount of experience in diplomacy, battles and tournaments, the book trade, languages and translating, pilgrimages and patronage of both the religious and literary kind. All of these things would prove vital in being a role model to his young nephew. But as this task was out of the limelight, and despite all of his other lifetime achievements, Anthony has become known for his arrest and execution in 1483.[11] Just a month prior to this meeting, Woodville had been willing to 'nominate Gloucester to arbitrate a dispute', showing that they indeed were on good terms and that Woodville 'did not perceive Gloucester to be his enemy'.[12] It is clear something had changed and perhaps the behaviour of other Woodvilles, especially Thomas Grey, Marquess of Dorset, had made Rivers guilty by association, a target easier to reach than those who had really exacerbated the tense situation following Edward IV's death.

As noted earlier, Hugh Bicheno describes Anthony's last poem as a reminder of what a shining exception Rivers was 'to the dull aristocratic norm'.[13] These words describe who Anthony was in a single sentence. There is no denying that Anthony Woodville lived a life that appears to have come straight from a medieval romance novel. He was the fictional chivalric knight and tournament champion made flesh, who wrote and studied all manner of adventure and romance literature, as well as undertaking deep spiritual reflection both on a personal and public level.

In William Shakespeare's *Richard III*, Anthony, Earl Rivers, is portrayed as someone who is loyal to his family and whoever is the reigning king. Rivers even goes so far as to explain to Gloucester that if he should become king, he would also be loyal to him.[14] The execution scene is one full of emotion, with Rivers proclaiming to the end that he is innocent and that he was about to die 'for truth, for duty, and for loyalty', words that could almost have come from a poem written by the real Anthony Woodville himself.[15] Rivers also comes back as a ghost to haunt Richard III on the eve of the Battle of Bosworth.

In Amy Licence's recent novel, *The York King*, the second book in a trilogy about the life of Edward IV, Anthony features as a background character. In it, Licence portrays him in a sympathetic light; while he is in the background, he appears to have been an important member of Edward's circle, particularly during the Burgundian exile. He is portrayed as competent and level-headed, whereas Edward is not always so. Amy Licence includes a scene on the return boat journey to England from exile. In it, Richard is suffering from a bout of seasickness, with Anthony Woodville by his side. While of course we do know that the pair were part of Edward's party in exile, our understanding of the relationship between Anthony Woodville and Richard has become distorted by our knowledge of the end of Woodville's life and his execution. This scene, and others, try to show this relationship in a different light.

Another author who portrays Anthony in a positive light is Anne Easter Smith in her novel, *Daughter of York*. This book tells the story of Margaret of Burgundy, the wife of Charles, Duke of Burgundy and the youngest sister of Edward IV. Margaret is rightfully portrayed as an intelligent woman who became actively involved in the courtly culture of Burgundy. Anthony Woodville features heavily through his connections with Burgundy (as discussed in chapter seven). He is accurately portrayed as a cultured man with a keen interest in books and jousting, but his gentlemanly and knightly character is also shown. It is this mix that attracts Margaret to Anthony.

A key part to the story is her love affair with Anthony, which resulted in an illegitimate child, who can be recognised as Perkin Warbeck, the pretender to the throne who emerged during the reign of Henry VII. This plotline is in part used by the author to explain both Margaret and Anthony's patronage of William Caxton, the book printer. It's a neat device, but this love affair between them both is completely made up. There is no historical basis for such a relationship between the pair. In fact, Anthony took his role as negotiator and then head of the wedding party for this Burgundian match very seriously. His wife, Elizabeth Scales, also accompanied Margaret to Burgundy.

A very different Anthony is portrayed in Conn Iggulden's Wars of the Roses series. In the final book, *Ravenspur*, which tells the story of Edward IV's return from exile and the rise of the Tudors following Richard III's accession to the throne, Anthony is portrayed as a ruthless and brutish man, who takes part in Edward IV's whoring and drinking sessions, and revels in causing pain and destruction. A particularly gruesome scene is depicted when he leads a group of men to burn a village. Anthony supposedly took great delight in this, particularly when cats and dogs were running away with their fur alight. This is of course a work of fiction, and the author can depict Anthony's personality in any way he likes for his own purpose, here most likely to indicate why the Woodvilles were disliked. This is certainly not the historical Anthony Woodville, far from it.

Perhaps the most famous recent televised version of Anthony Woodville is in the BBC's adaptation of *The White Queen* (2013), where Woodville was played by Ben Lamb. The series was adapted from Phillipa Gregory's Cousins War series of novels, *The White Queen*, *The Red Queen*, *The Lady of the Rivers*, *The Kingmaker's Daughter*, *The White Princess* and *The King's Curse*. In both the book and televised versions, Anthony is portrayed as a charming man, not involved with political intrigue, in comparison with the majority of the other characters. Instead, he is much more interested in the acquisition of knowledge, and in poetry. In the television series this is only vaguely indicated, but he is shown to be quite a serious man. In reality he was, but from his jousting exploits it is clear to see that this was not the whole of his character. Despite this, Anthony's loyal nature is shown extremely well. In the book, Gregory does make Anthony a likeable character, emphasising his thirst for knowledge and books and his innate desire to go on pilgrimages. These portrayals are closer to depicting the real Anthony Woodville, but they are of course still works of fiction. In the television adaptation, Anthony's marriage is never mentioned; instead, he appears to be complicit in Edward IV's womanising, for which there is no evidence.

In a recent documentary on the Princes in the Tower mystery by Lucy Worsley, the historian Michael Hicks commented on the relationship between Anthony Woodville and his nephew Edward, Prince of Wales, during their time in Ludlow. While his work does not go into the details of the fate of the young princes, it is interesting to note Hicks' opinion on this part of the life of Prince Edward. Hicks agreed with Worsley that as the young prince was living away from the rest of the family, his uncle Anthony would have been the closest thing he would have had to a father. Anthony lived up to this role as head of the young prince's household, in charge of his general welfare and exhibiting the kind of authority provided by a father. Surely the young prince would have felt traumatised by the arrests and subsequent executions at Pontefract, even more so considering they came only months after the death of his real father, Edward IV.

Is it likely that Edward's uncle Anthony would have put his own nephew in danger by becoming involved in a plot against the paternal uncle, Richard of Gloucester? If he did, then he not only risked his beloved princely nephew (as well as his other nephew, Richard Grey, who was supposedly implicated and arrested with Anthony), but himself. Anthony had already proved himself highly capable of looking after the welfare of Prince Edward in Ludlow, which would have recommended him as part of the minority government. Woodville would have been a key person for Richard, Duke of Gloucester to have had onside. It would have also helped that the young king would have entrusted matters of state to Woodville as he had already spent a decade with him.

The most difficult part of any study of those who lived during the period known as the Wars of the Roses is that the sources are fragmented and 'observations in characters and motives are few'.[16] As has hopefully been shown here, while it is hard to form a full picture of the real Anthony Woodville, enough can be found to create some kind of true image. He definitely had an important role to play as governor of Edward, Prince of Wales, alongside his responsibilities as a diplomat and his fame as a tournament champion, but perhaps his most important contribution to posterity was as translator and patron of William Caxton, the first book printer in England. The irony is not lost on the author that if Anthony Woodville had not worked with Caxton, the sources on his life would have been even more meagre.

Appendix 1

ANTHONY WOODVILLE'S WILL

Susan Higginbottom comments that

> It has been claimed, falsely, that Anthony named Richard III one of the executors of his will; rather, as the will plainly shows, Anthony named others as his executors and asked that Richard serve as supervisor. [It has been] suggested that this provision showed Anthony's confidence in Richard's integrity. It is more likely, however, that Anthony simply recognised that probate of his will would be impossible without Richard's cooperation and named him supervisor in hopes that Richard would feel morally bound to allow Anthony's last wishes to be carried out by his executors.

In the name of our Lord amen I Antony Widevile etc In hole mynd and Fressh memory in the Castell of Shiryfhoton the xxiij day of Juyn and the vigil of seint John Baptyst the yere of our lord m^{l}cccclxxxiij make my testament and Last will in the fo[ur] me folowyng Furst I bequeith my soule unto the grete m[er]cy of Jhu Crist and to his dere moder our Lady seint Mary and to the glorious company of hevyn And my hert to be had to our Lady of Pewe beside Seint Ste[-]phyns College at Westmynster there to be buried by thadvyse of the Deane and his brethern And If I dy be yend trent than to be buried before our Lady of Pewe aforseid Also I will that all such land as was my Lord my faders Remayne holy to his right heyres w[i]t[h] my cupp of gold of Colombyne which was Lefte me by bequest to that entent it shuld remayne to the right heires of my seid Lord my Faders And such lond[es] as were the Lady Scalis my fyrst wyfe be unto my brother syr Edward and to his heyris male. For faut of such heyres male unto the right heyres of my seid lord my fadre / This is my will and entent therin to take effecte as ferre as consciens and Law will / And that to be sene and determyned by ij doctours of London and ij of Oxford and of Cambrigge / or doctors at the lest w[i]t[h] ij of the chefe Juges and ij of theldest s[er]vaunt[es] of the Lawe And if they fynde that this myn entent may not with conscience and Lawe and any part thereof that it be guydid after their demyng. / And if they think that my seid brother may have it all / or for fawt of hym any of my seid Lord my fadre heires he that shal have the lond to pay or he have possession VC marcas that to be employed for the soules of my last wyfe Lady Scalys and Thom[a]s hyr brother and the soules of all the scales blode in helping and refresshing hospital[es] and other ded[es] charitable / And if all the Land may not be so had than to pay but aft' the Rate of such lond as I may bequeath. Also I will that all my good[es] goo to the paying of my dett[es] And all my fee simpill Lond that is to sey the maner of Tyrington Hall in Middylton with the Hundreth of Frebrigge the man[er] of Wolv[er]ton with thadvow[-]son in the Counte of Norfolke the Maner of Rokey in Barway in the Counte of Hert[-]ford to be sold to the same entent and for to make an hospitall at Rowchestyr for xiij pou[er] folk[es] / and other ded[es] of Charite as to pay prisoners fees and finall dett[es] to visett the prisones of London and help to bury the dede w[i]t[h] other werk[es] of mercy And as for my dett[es] I knowledge I owe to the bisshop of Worcester lx li which I will he be truely paid Also I knowledge that I owe a somme of mony to Loumer mercer of London as it wele apperith both by his billes and by my boke in my closett at London which I wyll be content after consciens Also

I knowlege that I owe abowght xl li to Ocles Mayce goldsmyth as Butsyde of London and Griffith my servaunt can tell which Coles I wllbe truely content Also I knowlege that I owe to the Mayo[ur] of Lynne and to divers creditours in Norfolk And to Abrey drap[er] of Norwich s[er]teyn sommes of money as apperith by waraunt[es] signed by my hand to Fynch[a]m myn receyvo[ur] which shuld pay theym of my lyvelode and fees in Norfolk and Suffolk growing from Mychelmas last passed which warant[es] I wilbe paid in any wyse. Also I remembre there was a preest claymid to be executo[ur] to a boucheer of London callid Lamys As Andrew Dymmok knowith and that I shuld owe the same bocheer money which I will in any wyse be paid And that ther be a preest founde a yere at our Lady of Pewe to pray for the sowle of the seid brocherer and all cristen soules And an other for the sowles of syr Henry Lowes And a preest to be fowde to syng at the Chapell of the Redes in Grenewich to pray for my soule and all [Crist]en sowlys And that my wyfe have all such plate as was the same Henry Lowes / And other of my plate to the valure of asmoche thing as I hadd of his Also that she have all such plate as was geven hyr at our mariage and the sparver of white sylke w[i]t[h] iiij peyre of shet[es] ij payre of fustians a federbed j Chambring of gresylde And except that stuffe all other stuffe of howsehold in the mote and at my place in the Vyntree to be to my seid lord my faders heyres advising theym on godd[es] behalve that thabbot of Seint Jamys beside Northampton And the Nonnes beside Caunturbury be allwey dewley answerd of their Claymes And syr John Gilford to content it as it apperith by the evidence[es] that Richard Haute hath. Also I will seint Mary of York have my grete gilt basons And such a somme of money as myn executours shall think goode to pay for my soule Also I owe to syr Thomas Vaugh[a] n CC marc' wherof I have paid xx[ti] marc' here in the north And he hath to plegge my balys in Colombyne with v perles Also I will that all my household serv[au]nt[es] in the Chekyr Roll have trewly ther wag[es] for Mydsom[er] quarter And every one a blak gowne And as I remembyr I owe Willi[a]m Butler xx s which I will he be paid And as for myn evidenc[es] Andrewe Dymmok knowyth them And canne shewe how all my lond standith And if Willi[a]m Aubrey which was Coferer to the Kyng which now is whan he was Prince Thomas Wytman the seid Andrew Dymmok Butsyde and John Gryffyth know any moo dett[es] that I shuld owe I require for them to shew it And I will myn executours in any wyse to pay to whom it be owyng And I desire on godd[es] behalve that no man int[er]rupt my seid execu[-]tours in fulfilling this my will as they will answere at the dredefull day of Dome geving to my seid executours power by this my seid will to take a Rekenyng and Levy all such sommes of money as is owyng me of my lyvelod fees annuitees or otherwyse And they to employe such good[es] as shall come to their hand[es] after this will and moost consci[-]ent for the wele of my soule And I will that all myn Aray for my body and my horse harnes be sold And with the money thereof be bought shyrt[es] and smokk[es] to pouer folk[es] And my gowne of Tawney cloth of gold I geve to the priour of Royston / my trapper of blakk cloth of gold I geve to our Lady of Walsingham Also I desire and charge on godd[es] behalve and upon payne of damnacion that my feoff[es] make none Astate nor Relese Ne my tenaunt[es] make no reto[ur]ne but acording to theffect of this my Last will. Also I will that all such lond as I purchasid by the meane of syr Jamys Molaynes preest Remayn still w[i]t[h] the Man[er] of Grafton toward the fynding of the preest of thavuntage Also the lond[es] that I purchased beside the mote to Remayne to my lord my faders heyres /

Also I will that my Lady Willoughby late the wyfe of Syr Gerveis Clyfton be co[m]mond w[i]t[h] all by myne executours towching such stuff' as syr Ewan p[ar]son of Wolverton and other my serv[au]nt[es] had awey from hyr place and she to be delt w[i]t[h] therin and answerid acording to goode right and conscience And I will in no wyse that the Nonnes of Blakborough be hurt in such Lond[es] of theires as Lieth w[i]t[h]in the Roche Fenne of Myddylton which I Late closid Also I will that syr Jamys Molaynes and Emson Late Attorney of the Duchie of Lancastre be co[m]mond w[i]t[h] And that it be sene if so be that I have occupied bra[-]don w[i]t[h]out good right that myn executours se the contentacion and Refo[ur]myng therof acording to right and conscience And I will that thadvowson of the parissh church of Bewdeley Remayne the Patronacion therof to the right heires of my lord my fadre Theym to present to the benefice whan it shall fawle voyde an able preest to pray for the sowles of my seid Lord my fadre my Lady my modre my brother S[ir] John me and all Cristen sowles Also I wull that Wyttyngton College of London have a somme of money to pray for my soule and myn executours see that such tythes as I owt to have made be Answerid in the moost behofefull wyse for my sowle Also I will that Tybold my barbo[ur] have v mark And I will my s[er]v[a]nt Jamys [*blank space*] have xl s Also I make myn executours the Bisshop of Lincoln Chaunceler of England the bishop of Worcestyr / Husy the Chefe Juge of the King[es] benche /Bryan the Chefe Juge of the Comyn place Willi[a]m Tunstall Robert Poynz Richard Hawte Willi[a]m Catesby Andrew Dymmok and Thom[a]s Thorysby To which all And at the Lest to thre of them I geve full auctorite and power And prey them at the Reverence of Jhu' to see this my will may be fulfilled Over this I besech humbly my Lord of Gloucestyr in the worshipp of Crist[es] passhion and and for the meryte and wele of his sowle to Comfort help and assist as sup[er]viso[ur] for very trust of this testament that myn executours may w[i]t[h] his pleasur fulfil that my Last will which I have made the day aboveseid In wittenes syr Thomas Gower knyght Willi[a]m Tunstall Docto[ur] Lovell Syr John Esingwold vicar of Shyryfhton syr Willi[a]m Teysedale Thomas Wawer preest[es] and Richard Lepton gentylman. /

My will is now to be buried before An Image of our blissid Lady Mary w[i]t[h] my Lord Richard In Pomfrete And Jhu' have mercy of my soule etc

TNA, PROB 11/8/579,
kindly transcribed by Neil Bettridge

Appendix 2

FINAL POEM

Somewhat musing,
and more mouring,
In remembering
Th'unsteadf'ness
This world being,
of such wheeling,
Me contrarying,
What may I guess?

I fear doubtless,
remediless,
Is now to seize
My woeful chance;
for unkindness,
and no redress.
Me doth advance

with displeasure,
to my grievance,
and no surance

of remedy;
Lo, in this trace,
Now in substance,
such is my dance,
willing to die.

Methinks truly
Bouden am I,
and that greatly.
To be content;
seeing plainly
Fortune doth wry
All contrary
from mine intent

My life was lent
Me to one intent.
It is nigh spent
Welcome, Fortune!
but I ne went
Thus to be shent
but she it meant;
such is her won.

Written by Anthony Woodville while imprisoned at
Pontefract Castle in June 1483

Appendix 3

LIST OF LORDSHIPS AND MANORS

The following is a list of lordships and manors granted to John Howard, 1st Duke of Norfolk, by Richard III, which used to be held by Anthony Woodville, taken from British Library's Add Ch 16559.

Middleton
Item in the account xlv li vi s viii d received from William Gelyn, baliff and farmer [tenant] there, from his farm, according to his recognizance, as shown in his account for this year
Total: xlv li vi s viii d

Scaleshowe
And for xxvii li x s received from Isabell Bastard, farmer there, from her farm, according to her recognizance, as shown in her account for this year
Total: xxvii li x s

Islyngton (baliff)
And for xxiii s v d received this year from Nicholas Bowman, bailiff there, from the issues of his office, according to his recognizance, as shown in his account for this year
Total: xxiii s v d

Islyngton (farmer)
And for xi li xv s iii d received this year from Gilbert Segrave, farmer there, from his farm, according to his recognizance, as shown in his account for this year

Tylney
And for l s v$\frac{1}{5}$ d received this year from Peter Keade, bailiff there, from the issues of his office, according to his recognizance, as shown in his account for this year
Total: l s v$\frac{1}{5}$ d

Clencheverton
And for lxiiii s 0$\frac{1}{5}$ d received this year from Adam Battely, bailiff there, from the issues of his office, according to his recognizance, as shown in his account from this year
Total: lxiiii s 0$\frac{1}{5}$ d

Raynham Scales
And for xiiii li received this year from Robert Wolvey, bailiff and farmer there, according to his recognizance, as shown in his account for this year
Total: xiiii li

Stowebedon
For monies received for the profits of the demesne there he renders no account this year, nor will he henceforth because the aforesaid demesne is granted to Lord Willoughby and his heirs in perpetuity
Total: nil

Hokwold Wilton
And for vii li iiii s vi d received this year from John Bukton, bailiff there, both from his arrears and from the issues of his office, according to his recognizance, as shown in his account for this year
Total: vii li iiii s vi d

Frebrigge Northquarter
And for iiii li iii s xi d received this year from Thomas Hekett, bailiff there, from the issues of his office, according to his recognizance, as shown in his account for this year
Total: iiii li iii s xi d

Febrigge Southquarter
And for lxix s xi d received this year from Richard Proweberd, bailiff there, from the issues of his office, according to his recognizance, as shown in his account for this year
Total: lxix s xi d

Frebrigge Marslonde
And for lix s ii d received this year from Nicholas Thomson, bailiff there, from the issues of his office, according to his recognizance, as shown in his account for this year
Total: lix s ii d

Bailiff of the Hundred of Frebrigge
And for iiii li xii s viii d received this year from Nicholas Dey, bailiff there, from the issues of his office, according to his recognizance, as shown in his account for this year
Total: iiii li xii s viii d

Farm of the fish ponds at Wiggenhall
And for lxx s received this year from John Porter, farmer there, from his farm, according to his recognizance, as shown in his account for this year
Total: lxx s

Scroteby
For monies received for the profits of the demesne there he renders no account for this year, nor will he henceforth because the aforesaid demesne is granted to Lord Lovell and his heirs
Total: nil

Hillyngton
And for liii s iiii d received this year from Robert Thursby, farmer there, from his farm, according to his recognizance, as shown in his account for this year

Hikkelyng
And for vi li received this year from John Hawes, bailiff there, from the issues of his office, according to his recognizance, as shown in his account for this year
Total: vi li

Wydlyngton
And for x li xi s viii d received this year from James Parker, bailiff there, from the issues of his office, according to his recognizance, as shown in his account for this year
Total: x li xi s viii d

Haselyngfeld
And for x li received this year from William Skylman, bailiff there, from the issues of his office, according to his recognizance, as shown in his account for this year
Total: x li

Berkewey
And for xvi li v s i d received this year from John Potter, bailiff, from the issues of his office, according to his recognizance, as shown in his account for this year
Total: xvi li v s i d

Newsell
And for xvi li received this year from John Royston, bailiff there, from the issues of his office, according to his recognizance, as shown in his account for this year
Total xvi li

Rokehay
And for vi li xiii s iiii d received this year from John Newman, farmer, from his farm, according to his recognizance, as shown in his account for this year
Total: vi li xiii s iiii d

Berton Bendich
And for xvii li xiii⅕ d received this year from John Swifte, bailiff there, from the issues of his office, according to his recognizance, as shown in his account for this year
Total: xvii li xiii½ d

Market tolls of Lynn
For monies received from the bailiff there for market tolls, he renders no account this year, because he has received nothing from this source
Total: nil

Woodhamferres
(recently Margnye Dors)
And for xxv li received for this year from John Woderof, bailiff there, from the issues of his office, according to his recognizance, as shown in his account for this year
Total: xxv li

British Library's Add Ch 16559, reproduced in Crawford, Anne (ed), *The Household Books of John Howard, Duke of Norfolk*, pp. xlviii-li.

According to Post Mortem Inquisitions for Anthony's land in Cambridgeshire and Hertfordshire held in June 1486, Howard was only granted these lands temporarily until a close relative of Anthony's father-in-law, Thomas, Lord Scales, was found. After the Battle of Bosworth, Howard was replaced by the Earl of Oxford. TNA, C 142/1/36 and C 142/1/37.

Appendix 4

EXTRACT FROM *ON THE RECOVERY OF THE THRONE BY EDWARD IV*

In Sothwerke, at Bambere heth, and Kyngston eke,
The bastarde and his meane in the contre abowte,
Many grett men in London they made seke,
Man, wyff, ne childe there durst non rowte.
Oxin, shepe, and vetayle, withowtyn any dowte,
They stale away and carrid ever to and froo.
God suffers moche thing, his wille to be doo.

Moche sorrow and shame the wrecchis thay wroughte,
Fayre placis thay brend on the water side.
Thayre myschevus dedis avaylid ham nought,
Schamfully they wroughte, and so thaym betyd.
Thay wolde not leve ther malice, but therin abyde,
Thay cryed kynge Edward and Warwick also.
Thus the wille of God in every thynge is doo.

At London brygge thay made aswate, and sham to see,
The utter gate on the brygee thay sett on fyre;

Extract from On the Recovery of the Throne by Edward IV

Into Londone shott arows withowte pete.
With gunnus thay were bett that sum lay in the myre.
Thay askyd wage of the brygge, thay paid them thayre hire.
Ever amonge they had the worse, then wakyned thaire woo,
False men most be poyneshyd, the will of God is soo.
At Londone brige anodyr sawte thay made agayne,
With gunpowder and wildefire and straw eke;
Fro the gate to the drawbrygge thay brent down playne,
That x. myle men myghte se the smeke.
Thay were not of thayre entent the nere of a leke,
For into the city thay myghte not com for wele ne for woo;
God restid thayre malice, the wille of hym was soo.

At Algate thay sawtid in an ill seasoun;
Thay brente fayre howsis, pete was to se.
Thus these false men did opyne treason,
Supposynge evermore to enture the cite.
God and good seyntes thereof had pite.
Thayre malice was sesid and turned hem to woo.
Thus in every thynge, Lorde, thy wille be doo.

The earl of Esex, and also the aldermen,
At Bysshopsus gate togedder thay mette,
And owte therat sewed like manly men.
Thay bete hem down, no man myghte hem lett;
Freshely on thayre enmyes that day did fyghte.
Thayre false treson broughte theym in woo;
Thus in every thynge, Lorde, thy wille be doo.

The erle Revers, that gentill knyghte,
Blessid be the tym that he borne was!
By the power of God and his grett mygte,
Throw his enmyes that day did he passe.
The maryners were kellid, thay cryed 'Alas!'
Thayre false tresoun brougte hem in woo,

Thus in every thynge, Lorde, thy wille be doo.
There aventurid the erle then into the honde,
Contravelde the welefaire of London that day;
When the comens the skomfertour did understonde,
Thay seuyd owte freshly, thay kepud none araye;
Glad with the Kentyschmen thay were for to fraye.
Thay kyllid down, away thay mygte not goo.
Thus the wille of God is evermore doo.

God wolde the earle Revers there should be;
He purchesid grett love of the comyns that seasoun;
Lovyngly the cetysens and hee
Pursuyd thayre enmyes, it was but reason,
And kyllid the people for thayre false tresoun,
Or the chase were do, CC and moo.
Thus in every thynge, Lorde, thy will be do.

This extract mentions the Bastard of Fauconberg's attack on London in May 1471, including the Yorkist counter-attack from the Tower of London, led by Anthony Woodville. Wright, Thomas (ed), *Political Poems and Songs Relating to English History*, pp. 277-279.

Appendix 5

MEMBERS OF THE COUNCIL OF EDWARD, PRINCE OF WALES

Queen Elizabeth, Prince Edward's mother

Cardinal Thomas Bourchier, archbishop of Canterbury and the Prince's great-uncle

George, Duke of Clarence, the Prince's older paternal uncle

Richard, Duke of Gloucester, the Prince's younger paternal uncle

Robert Stillington, bishop of Bath and Wells, Chancellor of England

Laurence Bothe, bishop of Durham

Anthony, Earl Rivers, the Prince's eldest maternal uncle, also tutor and governor (from 1473)

Thomas Mylling, abbot of Westminster and chancellor of the Prince's household

William, lord Hastings, chamberlain of the king's household

Richard Fiennes, lord of Dacre of the South, steward of the Prince's household

Sir John Fogge, treasurer of the king's household

Sir John Scott, controller of the king's household

John Alcock, dean of Westminster, later bishop of Rochester and Worcester, also the Prince's teacher and president of his council (from 1473)

Richard Fowler, chancellor of the duchy of Lancaster

Edward Storey, bishop of Carlisle, the queen's chancellor

John, Earl of Shrewsbury, distant cousin of the Prince

Walter Devereux, lord Ferrers of Chartley, distant in-law of the Prince

Sir John Needham, justice of the king's bench

Sir Richard Choke, justice of common pleas

Dr Richard Martin, chancellor of the earldom of March

William Allington esquire, royal councillor (later chancellor of the duchy of Cornwall)

Richard Haute esquire, maternal cousin of the Prince

John Sulyard, serjeant-at-law

Geoffrey Cottesmore, lawyer

The list includes the original members from 1471, and the enlargement of 1473. CPR, *1467-1477*, 8 July 1471- Westminster, p. 283; 20 February 1473- Westminster, p. 366

ENDNOTES

Introduction

1. Lander, J. R., *Crown and Nobility 1450-1509*, p. 62
2. Mancini, Dominic, *The Usurpation of Richard the Third*, p. 83
3. Ibid
4. Ibid
5. As one indication of the opinions of London citizens, see Appendix 4 for an extract from a contemporary poem praising Woodville for his skill and ingenuity during the defence of London.
6. Sylvester, Richard S. (ed), *The Complete Works of St. Thomas More*, Volume 2, *Richard III*, p. 14
7. *The Cordyale*, reproduction (Nijmegen: 1914), p. 150
8. Pidgeon, Lynda, 'Antony Wydevile, Lord Scales and Earl Rivers: Family, Friends and Affinity, Part 2.', *The Ricardian*, 16 (2006), p. 15
9. *Ingulph's Chronicle of the Abbey of Croyland, with the Continuations by Peter of Blois and Anonymous Writers*, p. 445
10. Griffiths, Ralph A., 'The Crown and the Royal Family in Later Medieval England', in Griffiths Ralph A. and Sherborne, James (eds), *Kings and Nobles in the Later Middle Ages*, p. 18

11. Walpole, Horace, *A Catalogue of Royal and Noble Authors of England with Lists of Their Works*, p. 68
12. TPL, 778, vol 5, p. 106; Higginbotham, Susan, *The Woodvilles: The Wars of the Roses and England's Most Infamous Family*, p. 76
13. Pidgeon, Lynda, 'Antony Wydevile, Lord Scales and Earl Rivers: Family, Friends and Affinity, Part 2', p. 28
14. Ibid, p. 41
15. Will of Anthony Woodville, TNA, PROB 11/8/579 (see Appendix 1 for will in full)
16. Hicks, Michael, *The Prince in the Tower: The Short Life & Mysterious Disappearance of Edward V*, p. 75
17. Hicks, M. A., 'The Changing Role of the Wydevilles in Yorkist Politics to 1483', in C. Ross (ed), *Patronage, Pedigree and Power in Later Medieval England*, pp. 74-75
18. Higginbotham, Susan, *The Woodvilles*, p. 93

1 The Woodville Family and Their Connections

1. Hicks, M. A., 'The Changing Role of the Wydevilles', p. 60
2. Ibid
3. Pidgeon, Lynda, 'Antony Wydevile, Lord Scales and Earl Rivers: Family, Friends and Affinity, Part 1', *The Ricardian*, 15 (2005), p. 2; Baker, George, *History and Antiquities of the County of Northampton*, Volume 2, pp. 162 and 252-253
4. Hicks, M. A., 'The Changing Role of the Wydevilles', p. 62
5. Pidgeon, Lynda, 'Antony Wydevile, Lord Scales and Earl Rivers', Part 1, pp. 2-3
6. Munro, Cecil (ed), *Letters of Queen Margaret of Anjou and Bishop Beckington and Others* (London: Camden Society, 1863), p. 35
7. Ibid, p. 39
8. Pidgeon, Lynda, 'Antony Wydevile, Lord Scales and Earl Rivers', Part 1, p. 4
9. Higginbotham, Susan, *The Woodvilles*, p. 14

10. Hunter Blair, C. H. (ed), *Visitations to the North, Part III: A Visitation of the North of England Circa 1480-1500*, p. 58,
11. Higginbotham, Susan, *The Woodvilles*, p. 14
12. *CPR 1441-1446*, 8 June 1446- Westminster, p. 453
13. Baring-Gould, Sabine, *The Lives of the Saints*, Second Edition, p. 86
14. C. Weightman, *Margaret of York, 1446-1503*, p. 26, cited in J. L. Laynesmith, *The Last Medieval Queens: English Queenship, 1445-1503*, p. 53
15. *Rotuli Parliamentorum, Volume 4 (1783)*, p. 439; Pascual, Lucia Diaz, 'Jacquetta of Luxembourg, Duchess of Bedford and Lady Rivers (c.1416-1472)', *The Ricardian*, 21 (2011), p. 70; Hollman, Gemma, *Royal Witches: From Joan of Navarre to Elizabeth Woodville*, p. 166
16. Hicks, M. A., 'The Changing Role of the Wydevilles', p. 62
17. According to the National Archives, this is estimated to be worth just under £2.5 million today.
18. Pascual, Lucia Diaz, 'Jacquetta of Luxembourg, Duchess of Bedford', p. 71
19. Nichols, John (ed), *A Collection of All the Wills now Known to be Extant of the Kings and Queens of England*, pp. 270-276
20. Hicks, M. A., 'The Changing Role of the Wydevilles', p. 62
21. Hollman, Gemma, *Royal Witches*, p. 170
22. *CPR 1436-1441*, 23 March 1437- Westminster, p. 53
23. *The Chronicles of Enguerrand de Monstrelet*, Volume 2, p. 46
24. The Paston Letters do make reference to Richard and Jacquetta's marriage as a target of ridicule and insult when Richard and Anthony were captured at Sandwich and taken to Calais before the earls of Warwick and March (later Edward IV), but there is no other mention of the match in English. TPL, 400, vol 3, p. 204
25. Lander, J. R., *Crown and Nobility*, p. 94
26. Hicks, M. A., 'The Changing Role of the Wydevilles', p. 63; Pidgeon, Lynda, 'Antony Wydevile, Lord Scales and Earl Rivers', Part 1, p. 4.

27. Harrison, Kathryn, *Joan of Arc: A Life Transfigured*, p. 123.
28. Luminarium: Encyclopaedia Project, 'Thomas de Scales, 7th Baron Scales'
29. Higginbotham, Susan, *The Woodvilles*, p. 78.
30. Harvey, I. M. W., *Jack Cade's Rebellion of 1450*, pp. 73-74
31. Stowe, John, *Three Fifteenth Century Chronicles with Historical Memoranda*, ed. Gardiner, James, p. 97; Griffiths, Ralph A., 'The Crown and the Royal Family in Later Medieval England', in Griffiths Ralph A. and Sherborne, James (eds), *Kings and Nobles in the Later Middle Ages*, p. 16
32. Britannica, *Jack Cade*
33. Gardiner, James (ed), *The Historical Collections of a Citizen of London in the Fifteenth Century*, p. 189
34. Pidgeon, Lynda, *Brought Up of Nought: A History of the Woodvilles*, p. 149
35. Higginbotham, Susan, *The Woodvilles*, p. 78
36. Luminarium: Encyclopaedia Project, 'Thomas de Scales, 7th Lord Scales'
37. Davies, John Sylvester (ed), *An English Chronicle of the Reigns of Richard II, Henry IV, Henry V and Henry*, p. 96
38. Higginbotham, Susan, *The Woodvilles*, p. 79
39. The name originally meant St Mary's over the river. *An English Chronicle*, p. 98
40. Scofield, Cora L., *Edward IV*, Volume One, reprint 2016, p. 92
41. Ibid p. 98.
42. Scofield, Cora L., 'The Capture of Lord Rivers and Sir Anthony Woodville, 19 January 1460', *The English Historical Review*, 37.146 (1922), p. 254
43. Ibid
44. Fabyan, Robert, *The New Chronicles of England and France*, ed. Ellis, Henry, p. 635
45. TPL, 400, vol 3, p. 204; Pidgeon, Lynda, *Brought Up of Nought*, p. 140
46. TPL, 400, vol 3, p. 204
47. Salter, Elisabeth, *Popular Reading in English, c.1400-1600*, p. 123

48. Royle, Trevor, *The Wars of the Roses: England's First Civil War*, p. 281
49. Ibid, p. 281.
50. Higginbotham, Susan, *The Woodvilles*, p. 24.
51. TPL, 450, vol 3, p. 267; 'Venice: 1461-1470', in *Calendar of State Papers Relating to English Affairs in the Archives of Venice, Volume 1, 1202-1509*, No. 374, 14 April, p. 92-126
52. Royle, Trevor, *The Wars of the Roses*, p. 282
53. Ibid
54. 'Venice: 1461-1470', in *Calendar of State Papers Relating Tto English Affairs in the Archives of Venice, Volume 1, 1202-1509*, No. 365, 30 August, p. 92-126
55. 'Milan: 1461', in *Calendar of State Papers and Manuscripts in the Archives and Collections of Milan 1385-1618*, no. 117, p. 100
56. Higginbotham, Susan, *The Woodvilles*, p. 24
57. *CPR 1461-1467*, 8 June 1463- Westminster, p. 279; 25 January 1464- Northampton, p. 303; 8 and 18 February 1464- Westminster, p. 304; 15 December 1464- Westminster, p. 390
58. *CPR 1461-1467*, 27 May 1462- Leicester, p. 188
59. TPL, 533, vol 4, p. 60; Higginbotham, Susan, *The Woodvilles*, p. 24

2 *After the Royal Wedding*

1. Higginbotham, Susan, *The Woodvilles*, p. 78
2. Ibid, p. 79
3. Hubbard, B., *Kings and Queens of the Middle Ages*, p. 198
4. Pronay, Nicholas and Cox, John (eds), *The Crowland Chronicle Continuations: 1459-1486*, p. 115
5. Ibid
6. Hubbard, B., *Kings and Queens of the Middle Ages*, p. 198.
7. MacFarlane, Alan, *Marriage and Love in England: Modes of Reproduction, 1300-1840*, p. 254, cited in J. L. Laynesmith, *The Last Medieval Queens*, p. 54

8. Thomson, John A. F., *The Transformation of Medieval England, 1370-1529*, p. 129, cited in J. L. Laynesmith, *The Last Medieval Queens*, p. 54
9. Laynesmith, J. L., *The Last Medieval Queens*, p. 54
10. Kettle, Andrew, 'Parvenus in Politics', *The Ricardian*, p. 5
11. Hicks, M. A., 'The Changing Role of the Wydevilles', p. 60
12. Lander, J. R., 'Family, Friends and Politics in Fifteenth-Century England', in Griffiths Ralph A. and Sherborne, James (eds), *Kings and Nobles in the Later Middle Ages*, p. 34
13. Lander, J. R., 'Family, Friends and Politics', p. 34
14. Lander, J. R., *Crown and Nobility 1450-1509*, pp. 110-112
15. CChR, 28 June- Westminster, p. 204
16. Carson, Annette, *Richard III: A Small Guide to the Great Debate*, p. 40
17. Kettle, Andrew, 'Parvenus in Politics', p. 9
18. Ibid, pp. 16-17
19. MacCracken, H. N., 'The Flower of Souvenance: A Moment in the Twilight of Chivalry', *The Sewanee Review*, 20.3 (1912), p. 368
20. Uden, Grant, *A Dictionary of Chivalry*, p. 92
21. Santiuste, David, *Edward IV and the Wars of the Roses*, p. 85
22. Alexander, Michael, *Medievalism: The Middle Ages in Modern England*, p. 25
23. Salter, Elisabeth, *Popular Reading in English*, p. 179
24. MacCracken, H. N., 'The Flower of Souvenance: A Moment in the Twilight of Chivalry', p. 368
25. Ibid, pp. 369-370
26. Hicks, M. A., 'The Changing Role of the Wydevilles', p. 60
27. Higginbotham, Susan, *The Woodvilles*, pp. 55-56; Hollman, Gemma, *Royal Witches*, p. 224
28. Hammond, P. W., *The Battles of Barnet and Tewkesbury*, p. 5
29. Ibid
30. *Ingulph's Chronicle of the Abbey of Croyland, with the Continuations by Peter of Blois and Anonymous Writers*, trans. Riley, Henry T, p. 445
31. Hammond, P. W., *The Battles of Barnet and Tewkesbury*, p. 5

32. Ibid, p. 7. Richard Woodville had been elevated to the title of Earl Rivers in 1466.
33. Ibid
34. TPL, 716, vol 5, pp. 30-32
35. Hammond, P. W., *The Battles of Barnet and Tewkesbury*, p. 7
36. Ibid. Others named included Humphrey Strafford, Earl of Devon, Lord Audley and Sir John Fogge. *Warkworth's Chronicle*, p. 6; Goodman, Anthony, *The Wars of the Roses: Military Activity and English Society, 1452-97*, p. 68
37. Hammond, P. W., *The Battles of Barnet and Tewkesbury*, p. 7
38. *Warkworth's Chronicle*, p. 6; Goodman, Anthony, *The Wars of the Roses: Military Activity and English Society*, p. 68
39. *Halls Chronicle* cited in Hammond, P. W., *The Battles of Barnet and Tewkesbury*, p. 9
40. *Warkworth's Chronicle*, pp. 6-7 and 44-45
41. Pidgeon, Lynda, 'Antony Wydevile, Lord Scales and Earl Rivers', Part 1, p. 17
42. Hammond, P. W., *The Battles of Barnet and Tewkesbury*, p. 11
43. Higginbotham, Susan, *The Woodvilles*, p. 61; Hollman, Gemma, *Royal Witches*, pp. 227-228
44. Hammond, P. W., *The Battles of Barnet and Tewkesbury*, p. 18
45. CPR, *1467-1477*, 11 March 1475-Westminster, p. 553
46. *Rotuli Parliamentorum,* Volume 6, Appendix, p. 232
47. Hollman, Gemma, *Royal Witches*, p. 229
48. Thomas, A. H. and Thornley, I. D. (eds), *The Great Chronicle*, p. 194; Hollman, Gemma, *Royal Witches*, p. 229
49. *Rotuli Parliamentorum,* Volume 6, Appendix, p. 232; *CPR 1467-1477*, 21 February 1470- Westminster, p. 190
50. Hollman, Gemma, *Royal Witches*, p. 229
51. *Rotuli Parliamentorum,* Volume 6, Appendix, p. 232
52. Ibid; *CPR 1467-1477*, 21 February 1470- Westminster, p. 190
53. Griffiths, Ralph A., 'The Crown and the Royal Family in Later Medieval England', in Griffiths Ralph A. and Sherborne, James (eds), *Kings and Nobles in the Later Middle Ages*, p. 18
54. TNA, PROB 11/8/579

55. Sutton, Anne F., Visser-Fuchs, Livia and Hammond, P. W., *The Reburial of Richard Duke of York, 21-30 July 1476*, p. 1
56. For most of what follows, please see *The Reburial of Richard Duke of York*
57. Wakefield Historical Society, 'The Exhumation of Richard Duke of York'
58. *Crowland Chronicle*, p. 139
59. Higginbotham, Susan, *The Woodvilles*, p. 91; Sutton, Anne F., Visser-Fuchs, Livia and Hammond, P. W., *The Reburial of Richard Duke of York*, p. 7
60. Higginbotham, Susan, *The Woodvilles*, p. 91; Sutton, Anne F., Visser-Fuchs, Livia and Hammond, P. W., *The Reburial of Richard Duke of York*, p. 9
61. Edward offered seven pieces of cloth of gold, with Elizabeth offering five.
62. Sutton, Anne F., Visser-Fuchs, Livia and Hammond, P. W., *The Reburial of Richard Duke of York*, p. 37
63. Carson, Annette, *Richard III: A Small Guide to the Great Debate*, p. 40; Griffiths, Ralph A., 'The Crown and the Royal Family in Later Medieval England', p. 18
64. Thomas, D. H., *The Herberts of Raglan and the Battle of Edgecote 1469*, p. 104-106
65. *The Chronicles of the White Rose of York*, p. LXXII.
66. CPR, *1467-1477*, 11 February 1473- Westminster, pp. 421-422; 5 June 1474- Westminster, p. 423; 10 Oct 1474- Westminster, p. 475
67. When on certain business given to him by the king, Anthony was known to delegate this role to others. CPR, *1467-1477*, 17 May 1473- Westminster, p. 415; 25 June 1473- Westminster, p. 393; 29 June 1473- Westminster, p. 393; 1 July 1473- Westminster, p. 393; 1 Aug 1473, p. 412; 13 July 1474- Westminster, p. 443; 10 October 1474- Westminster, p. 475; 16 and 22 November 1475- Westminster, p. 548; 11 February 1476, p. 565
68. Hollman, Gemma, *Royal Witches*, p. 230

3 Marriages and an Illegitimate Child

1. The only source that suggests a time for Anthony's marriage is *The Chronicles of the White Rose of* York, p. 16
2. Maskelyne and H. C. Maxwell Lyte, 'Inquisitions Post Mortem, Henry VII, Entries 1-50', in *Calendar of Inquisitions Post Mortem: Series 2, Volume 1, Henry VII*, p. 16
3. Cockayne, George E., *Complete Peerage*, vol. 11, p. 507
4. *The Great Chronicle*, p. 194; Hollman, Gemma, *Royal Witches*, p. 199
5. *An English Chronicle*, p. 109
6. Her name has also been spelled as Ismania. Scofield, Cora L., *Edward IV*, p. 145
7. MacCracken, H. N., 'The Flower of Souvenance: A Moment in the Twilight of Chivalry', p. 78
8. Pidgeon, Lynda, 'Antony Wydevile, Lord Scales and Earl Rivers: Family, Friends and Affinity, Part 2.', p. 16
9. Ibid, p. 27
10. *CPR 1467-1477*, 27 May 1462- Leicester, p. 188
11. Parker, Kate, 'A Little Local Difficulty: Lynn and the Lancastrian Usurpation', in Harper-Bill, Christopher (ed), *Medieval East Anglia*, p. 120
12. Phillips, Matthew, 'Urban Conflict and Legal Strategy in Medieval England: The Case of Bishop's Lynn, 1346-1350', *Urban History*, 42.3 (2015), p. 366
13. Steane, John, *The Archaeology of Medieval England and Wales*, p. 25
14. Schofield, John and Vince, Alan, *Medieval Towns: The Archaeology of British Towns in Their European Setting*, Second Edition, p. 65
15. Ibid
16. 200,000 bricks were ordered for the South Gate. The room above was also meant to include a chamber for staff and an indoor toilet. Ramirez, Janina, *Femina: A New History of the Middle Ages, Through the Women Written Out of It*, pp. 283-284; Society for the Protection of Ancient Buildings,

'National Treasure: The South Gate, King's Lynn, Norfolk', 11 December 2017

17. Society for the Protection of Ancient Buildings, 'National Treasure: The South Gate, King's Lynn, Norfolk'
18. Pidgeon, Lynda, 'Antony Wydevile, Lord Scales and Earl Rivers', Part 2, p. 17; Historical Manuscript Commission, *The Manuscripts of the Corporations of Southampton and Kings Lynn Eleventh Report, Appendix: Part III*
19. *CPR 1467-1477*, 4 April 1470- Coventry, p. 206
20. Instead, he was granted an annuity of £33 6s and 8d from Lynn and Yarmouth, as well as the same amount per year from Sandwich. *CPR 1467-1477*, 23 January 1473, p. 375
21. Dyer, Christopher, *Standards of Living in the Later Middle Ages: Social Change in England, c. 1200-1520*, p. 7
22. Crawford, Anne (ed), *The Household Books of John Howard, Duke of Norfolk, 1462-1471, 1481-1483*, p. XX
23. For what follows see the city's petition, letters and other related documents about the dispute with the abbot of St Benet's of Hulme over his water meadows in Heigham and the city mills on the Wensum, Norfolk Record Office, NCR 9e/4
24. Collins, Hugh E. L., *The Order of the Garter, 1348-1461: Chivalry and Politics in Late Medieval England*, p. 1
25. Ibid, p. 123
26. Crawford, Anne (ed), *The Household Books of John Howard, Duke of* Norfolk, p. 481
27. Ibid, p. 482
28. Ibid, pp. 281 and 484
29. Agreement between Sir Anthony Wydevile and Richard Wylde and John Holbroke, bailiffs of Newport, Isle of Wight Record Office, NBC/1/15
30. Court of Chancery, Lord Scales v John Towneshend, C 1/28/77
31. Ibid
32. Pidgeon, Lynda, 'Antony Wydevile, Lord Scales and Earl Rivers', Part 2, p. 35

33. Myers, A. R (ed), 'The Household of Queen Elizabeth Woodville, 1466-7', *Bulletin of the John Rylands Library*, 50 (1968), p. 451
34. Ibid (1967), p. 211
35. Ibid (1968), p. 451
36. Letts, Malcom (trans. and ed), *The Travels of Leo of Romitzal through Germany, Flanders, England, France, Spain, Portugal and Italy*, pp. 45-48
37. Ibid, p. 46
38. Ibid
39. *The Chronicles of the White Rose of* York, p. 147
40. TNA PROB 11/8/579
41. Hollman, Gemma, *Royal Witches*, pp. 248-49
42. Pidgeon, Lynda, 'Antony Wydevile, Lord Scales and Earl Rivers', Part 2, p. 17
43. Stow, John, *The Survey of London*, p. 216
44. *CCR, 1409-1413*, 21 May 1412- Westminster, p. 340
45. Ibid, 15 February- Westminster, p. 377
46. 'Chaucer, Thomas', *The History of Parliament Online*
47. Roskell, J. S., *The Commons and their Speakers in English Parliaments, 1376-1523*, p. 150
48. 'Chaucer, Thomas', *The History of Parliament Online*,
49. Roskell, J. S., *The Commons and their Speakers in English Parliaments*, p. 172
50. Ibid, p. 172
51. Ibid, p. 172
52. Carr, Anthony D., 'Sir Lewis John – A Medieval London Welshman', p. 264
53. Ibid, p. 266
54. *CPR 1429-1436*, 20 May 1436-Westminster, p. 591
55. Carr, Antony D., 'Sir Lewis John – A Medieval London Welshman', p. 260
56. Ibid, p. 263
57. H. L. Gray, 'Incomes from Land in England in 1436', *English Historical Review*, 49.196, p. 633

58. Pidgeon, Lynda, 'Antony Wydevile, Lord Scales and Earl Rivers', Part 2, p. 20
59. Carr, Antony D., 'Sir Lewis John – A Medieval London Welshman', p. 262
60. Pidgeon, Lynda, 'Antony Wydevile, Lord Scales and Earl Rivers', Part 2, p. 22
61. Phillips, Kim M., *Medieval Maidens: Young Women and Gender in England, 1270-1540*), p. 39
62. Pidgeon, Lynda, 'Antony Wydevile, Lord Scales and Earl Rivers', Part 2, p. 22
63. Richardson, Douglas, *Plantagenet Ancestry: A Study in Colonial and Medieval Families,* Volume 1, Second Edition (2011), p. 232
64. Ibid
65. TNA PROB 11/8/579; Higginbotham, Susan, *The Woodvilles*, p. 106
66. Ibid
67. Ibid, p. 103
68. Barnfield, Marie, 'Richard's Great Scottish Campaign', *The Ricardian Bulletin,* June 2022, p. 63
69. Higginbotham, Susan, *The Woodvilles*, p. 97
70. Evans, H. T., *Wales and the Wars of the Roses*, reprint 1995, p. 142
71. Barnwell, Edward Lowry, *Perrot Notes or Some Account of the Various Branches of the Perrot Family* (London: Cambrian Archaeological Association, 1867), p. 31
72. Pidgeon, Lynda, 'Antony Wydevile, Lord Scales and Earl Rivers', Part 2, p. 23
73. *CPR 1467-1477*, 23 June 1467- Westminster, p. 23
74. Pidgeon, Lynda, 'Antony Wydevile, Lord Scales and Earl Rivers', Part 2, p. 41
75. The couple's first child, Anthony (named after his grandfather) was born in 1480, so the marriage must have taken place prior to this date. Barnwell, Edward Lowry, *Perrot Notes,* p. 32; Higginbotham, Susan, *The Woodvilles*, p. 80

76. Barnwell, Edward Lowry, *Perrot Notes*, p. 32; Higginbotham, Susan, *The Woodvilles*, p. 80
77. TNA PROB 11/8/579; Higginbotham, Susan, *The Woodvilles*, p. 81
78. Chitty, Henry and Phillipot, John, *The Visitation of the County of Gloucester, Taken in the Year 1623*, ed. Maclean, John and Heane, M. C. (Harleian Society, 1885), p. 129
79. Pidgeon, Lynda, 'Antony Wydevile, Lord Scales and Earl Rivers', Part 2, p. 41
80. Crawford, Anne (ed), *The Household Books of John Howard, Duke of* Norfolk, p. 481

4 Military Career

1. 'Venice: 1461-1470', in *Calendar of State Papers Relating to English Affairs in the Archives of Venice,* Volume 1, 1202-1509, No. 365, 30 August, pp. 92-126
2. *Warkworth's Chronicle*, p. 2
3. Goodman, Anthony, *The Wars of the Roses: Military Activity and English Society,* p. 60
4. TPL, 533, vol 4, p. 60
5. Ibid, p. 2
6. Edward IV reported these rumours in a letter to his chancellor. Halliwell, James Orchard (ed), *Letters of the Kings of England*, Volume 1, p. 131
7. Major, John, *A History of Greater Britain*, trans. and ed. A. Constable, p. 387
8. *Warkworth's Chronicle*, p. 2
9. Major, John, *A History of Greater Britain*, p. 388
10. Scofield, Cora L., *The Life and Reign of Edward IV*, Volume One, reprint 2016, p. 266
11. Goodman, Anthony, *The Wars of the Roses: Military Activity and English Society*, p. 62
12. Ibid, p. 59
13. Walpole, Horace, *A Catalogue of Royal and Noble Authors*, p. 69

14. CPR, *1467-1477*, 24 August 1467-Westminster, p. 19
15. Lewis, Matt, 'The Will of Anthony Woodville, Earl Rivers', Matt's History Blog 23 June 2014
16. CPR, *1467-1477*, 28 April 1469, 4 May 1469- Westminster, p. 156
17. Crawford, Anne (ed), *The Household Books of John Howard, Duke of* Norfolk, p. XXIII
18. CPR, *1467-1477*, 28 April 1469, 4 May 1469- Westminster, p. 156
19. He was granted the role of Governor of Portsmouth in 1467. CPR, *1467-1477*, 29 January 1474- Westminster, p. 422
20. CPR, *1467-1477*, 7 October 1468- Westminster, p. 422
21. *The Chronicles of the White Rose of* York, p. 28
22. Ibid, p. 28
23. Thornley, Isobel D. (ed), *England Under the Yorkists, 1460-1485*, p. 49
24. Hammond, P. W., *The Battles of Barnet and Tewkesbury*, p. 20
25. Higginbotham, Susan, *The Woodvilles*, p. 70
26. Ibid
27. Hammond, P. W., *The Battles of Barnet and Tewkesbury*, p. 20
28. *Crowland Chronicle*, p. 121
29. CPR, *1467-1477*, 30 June 1474- Westminster, p. 450
30. *Historie of the Arrivall of Edward IV*, *Three Chronicles of the Reign of Edward IV*, pp. 1-2; Goodman, Anthony, *The Wars of the Roses: Military Activity and English Society*, p. 68
31. *The Arrivall*, p. 2; Adair, John, 'The Newsletter of Gerhard von Wesel, 17 April 1471', *Journal of the Society for Army Historical Research*, 46.186 (1968), p. 66
32. *Crowland Chronicle*, p. 123
33. Ibid; *The Arrivall*, p. 3
34. *Crowland Chronicle*, p. 123
35. *The Arrivall*, p. 11
36. Baldwin, David, *Elizabeth Woodville: Mother of the Princes in the Tower*, p. 46
37. Adair, John, 'The Newsletter of Gerhard von Wesel, 17 April 1471', p. 68

38. Ibid
39. *Crowland Chronicle*, p. 125
40. Goodchild, Steven, *Tewkesbury: Eclipse of the House of Lancaster, 1471*, p. 35
41. Ibid, p. 127
42. Ibid, p. 129
43. Ibid
44. For what follows, see *The Arrivall*, pp. 11-39
45. Goodman, Anthony, *The Wars of the Roses: Military Activity and English Society*, p. 188
46. *Crowland Chronicle*, p. 129
47. Ibid
48. Wright, Thomas (ed), *Political Poems and Songs Relating to English History, Composed During the Period from the Accession of Edward III to that of Richard III*, Volume 2, 1861, pp. 278-279
49. Thomas More, *Richard III*, p. 51
50. Hanham, Alison, *Richard III and His Early Historians, 1483-1535*, p. 3
51. CPR, *1467-1477*, 20 June 1472-Westminster, p. 339
52. TPL, 812, vol 5, p. 157
53. *Letters of the Kings of England*, Volume 1, p. 145
54. Higginbotham, Susan, *The Woodvilles*, p. 84
55. 'Milan: 1475', in *Calendar of State Papers and Manuscripts in the Archives and Collections of Milan 1385-1618*, nos 303 and 308, pp. 212-213; Hollman, Gemma, *Royal Witches*, p. 247; Knecht, Robert, *The Valois: Kings of France, 1325-1589*, p. 101
56. Knecht, Robert, *The Valois*, p. 101
57. 'Milan: 1475', in *Calendar of State Papers and Manuscripts in the Archives and Collections of Milan 1385-1618*, no. 316, 22 Oct, pp. 212-213
58. Barnfield, Marie, 'Richard's Great Scottish Campaign', *The Ricardian*, June 2022, p. 60
59. Doyle, James E. (ed), *A Chronicle of England, B.C. 55 - A.D. 1485*, 1864, p. 431

60. Barnfield, Marie, 'Richard's Great Scottish Campaign', p. 61
61. Hicks, Michael, *The Prince in the Tower: The Short Life and Mysterious Disappearance of Edward V*, p. 109
62. Barnfield, Marie, 'Richard's Great Scottish Campaign', p. 63
63. TPL, 778, vol 5, p. 106; Higginbotham, Susan, *The Woodvilles*, p. 76
64. Higginbotham, Susan, *The Woodvilles*, pp. 86-87
65. Ibid, p. 89
66. *Crowland Chronicle*, p. 129
67. Wright, Thomas (ed), *Political Poems and Songs Relating to English History*, Volume II, pp. 278-279

5 Tournament Champion

1. Beswick, James, 'Richard II of England and the Smithfield Tournament of October 1390', in Murray, Alan V. and Watts, Karen (eds), *The Medieval Tournament as Spectacle: Tourneys, Jousts and Pas d'Armes, 100-1600*, p. 63
2. Stroud, Michael, 'Chivalric Terminology in Late Medieval Literature', *Journal of the History of Ideas*, 37.2 (1976), p. 324
3. Uden, Grant, *A Dictionary of Chivalry*, p. 327
4. Goodman, Anthony, *The Wars of the Roses: Military Activity and English Society*, p. 180
5. Ibid, p. 180
6. *CCR, 1435-1441*, 10 November 1441- Westminster, p. 397; Gardiner, James (ed), *The Historical Collections of a Citizen of London in the Fifteenth Century*, 1876, p. 183; TPL, 36, vol 2, p. 47
7. Higginbotham, Susan, *The Woodvilles*, p. 39
8. Kettle, Andrew, 'Parvenus in Politics', p. 17
9. MacCracken, H. N., 'The Flower of Souvenance', p. 368
10. Ibid, p. 371
11. Black, William Henry (ed), *Historical Illustrations of the Reign of Edward IV: Comprising Memoirs of Anthony, Earl Rivers*, extract from *Excerpta Historica, or Illustrations of English History*, 1830, p. 3

12. MacCracken, H. N., 'The Flower of Souvenance', p. 371
13. Ibid, p. 372
14. Ibid
15. Uden, Grant, *A Dictionary of Chivalry*, pp. 37-38
16. Higginbotham, Susan, *The Woodvilles*, p. 54
17. Walpole, Horace, *A Catalogue of Royal and Noble Authors*, p. 71
18. Crouch, David, *Tournament* (London: Hambledon and London, 2005), p. 92
19. MacCracken, H. N., 'The Flower of Souvenance', pp. 370-371
20. Crawford, Anne (ed), *The Household Books of John Howard, Duke of* Norfolk, p. xxv
21. Walpole, Horace, *A Catalogue of Royal and Noble* Authors, p. 71
22. MacCracken, H. N., 'The Flower of Souvenance', p. 372
23. Ibid; Uden, Grant, *A Dictionary of Chivalry*, p. 342
24. MacCracken, H. N., 'The Flower of Souvenance', p. 372; Uden, Grant, *A Dictionary of Chivalry*, p. 342
25. MacCracken, H. N., 'The Flower of Souvenance', p. 372
26. Uden, Grant, *A Dictionary of Chivalry*, p. 342
27. Ibid, p. 342.
28. Higginbotham, Susan, *The Woodvilles*, p. 59
29. Uden, Grant, *A Dictionary of Chivalry*, pp. 21 and 343
30. Ibid, p. 343; MacCracken, H. N., 'The Flower of Souvenance', p. 374
31. MacCracken, H. N., 'The Flower of Souvenance', pp. 370-371; Kettle, Andrew, 'Parvenus in Politics', p. 17
32. Kettle, Andrew, 'Parvenus in Politics', p. 16
33. Crawford, Anne (ed), *The Household Books of John Howard, Duke of* Norfolk, p. xxv
34. This motto survives in a manuscript by Christine de Pizan he once owned, now in the British Library; *Christine de Pizan, Collected works* ('The Book of the Queen')
35. Ashdown-Hill, John, *The Third Plantagenet: George Duke of Clarence, Richard III's Brother*, Appendix 2

36. Crane, Susan, *The Performance of Self: Ritual, Clothing and Identity during the Hundred Years War*, p. 10; Staples, Kate Kelsey, 'Fripperers and the Used Clothing Trade in Late Medieval London', in Netherton, R. and Owen-Crocker, Gale R. (eds), *Medieval Clothing and Textiles*, p. 152
37. Crane, Susan, *The Performance of Self*, p. 10
38. Moffatt, Ralph, *The Medieval Tournament: Chivalry, Heraldry and Reality, An Edition and Analysis of Three Fifteenth-Century Tournament Manuscripts*, p. 183
39. *The Chronicles of the White Rose of* York, p. 19
40. TNA, Will of Thomas Clarell, Gentleman and Grocer of London, PROB 11/10/121
41. Uden, Grant, *A Dictionary of Chivalry*, p. 343
42. TPL, 684, vol 4, p. 298
43. Ibid
44. Ibid
45. Crouch, David, *Tournament*, p. 92
46. TPL, 665, vol 4, p. 275
47. Ibid
48. Ibid
49. Richmond, Colin, 'Thomas Malory and the Pastons', in Meale, Carol M. (ed), *Readings in Medieval English Romance*, p. 203
50. Pidgeon, Lynda, 'Antony Wydevile, Lord Scales and Earl Rivers', Part 2, p. 28
51. Higginbotham, Susan, *The Woodvilles*, p. 94
52. Ibid
53. MacCracken, H. N., 'The Flower of Souvenance', pp. 370-371

6 Connections with Burgundy

1. Higginbotham, Susan, *The Woodvilles*, p. 53; Kettle, Andrew, 'Parvenus in Politics', p. 16
2. Higginbotham, Susan, *The Woodvilles*, p. 56
3. *The Chronicles of the White Rose of* York, p. 20
4. TPL, 684, vol 4, p. 297

5. Ibid
6. Ibid, p. 298
7. Dunleavy, Brian, *The Woodville Chronicle*, pp. 141-142
8. Vale, Malcom, 'An Anglo-Burgundian Nobleman and Art Patron: Louis de Bruges, Lord of la Gruuthuse and Earl of Winchester', in Barron, Caroline and Saul, Nigel (eds), *England and the Low Countries in the Late Middle Ages*, p. 116
9. Hollman, Gemma, *Royal Witches*, p. 225
10. Higginbotham, Susan, *The Woodvilles*, p. 53
11. Louis was given the book by Anthony at some later date.
12. Dunleavy, Brian, *The Woodville Chronicle*, p. 139
13. Ibid,
14. British Library, *The Beginnings of the Royal Library*
15. Ibid
16. Ibid; Vale, Malcom, 'An Anglo-Burgundian Nobleman and Art Patron', pp. 119-120
17. Dunleavy, Brian, *The Woodville Chronicle*, p. 134
18. Hellinga, Lotte, *William Caxton and Early Printing in England*, p. 61; Higginbotham, Susan, *The Woodvilles*, p. 82-83
19. Hellinga, Lotte, *William Caxton and Early Printing in England*, p. 66
20. Kern, Darcy, 'Parliament in Print: William Caxton and the History of Political Government in the Fifteenth Century', *Journal of Medieval History*, 40.2 (2014), p. 223
21. Higginbotham, Susan, *The Woodvilles*, p. 53
22. Kettle, Andrew, 'Parvenus in Politics', p. 17
23. Ibid, p. 16
24. Ohler, Norbert, *The Medieval Traveller*, p. 56.
25. Dunleavy, Brian, *The Woodville Chronicle*, pp. 141-142
26. Hammond, P. W., *The Battles of Barnet and Tewkesbury*, p. 36
27. Higginbotham, Susan, *The Woodvilles*, p. 71; Hammond, P. W., *The Battles of Barnet and Tewkesbury*, p. 38
28. Visser-Fuchs, Livia, 'Richard in Holland, 1470-1', *The Ricardian*, 6, 1983, p. 222

29. Vale, Malcom, 'An Anglo-Burgundian Nobleman and Art Patron: Louis de Bruges, Lord of la Gruuthuse and Earl of Winchester', p. 128
30. Hammond, P. W., *The Battles of Barnet and Tewkesbury*, p. 39
31. Visser-Fuchs, Livia, 'Richard in Holland, 1470-1', p. 223
32. Hammond, P. W., *The Battles of Barnet and Tewkesbury*, p. 49
33. Ibid, pp. 54 and 56
34. Vale, Malcom, 'An Anglo-Burgundian Nobleman and Art Patron: Louis de Bruges, Lord of la Gruuthuse and Earl of Winchester', pp. 116 and 120
35. British Library, *Christine de Pizan, Collected works* ('The Book of the Queen')
36. Hollman, Gemma, *Royal Witches*, p. 237
37. *The Chronicles of the White Rose of York*, p. 147
38. Ibid
39. Ibid
40. Ibid
41. Higginbotham, Susan, *The Woodvilles*, p. 89
42. *The Chronicles of the White Rose of York*, p. 147
43. Scholz, Bernhard W., 'Edward the Confessor: "Anglorum Decas"', *Traditio*, 18, 1962, p. 379
44. Meale, Carol, 'Patrons, Buyers and Owners: Book Production and Social Status', in Griffiths, Jeremy and Pearsall, Derek (eds), *Book Production and Publishing in Britain, 1375-1475*, p. 207
45. Harris, Kate, 'Patrons, Buyers and Owners: The Evidence for Ownership, and the Role of Book Owners in Book Production and the Book Trade', in Griffiths, Jeremy and Pearsall, Derek (eds), *Book Production and Publishing in Britain, 1375-1475*, p. 181
46. Barron, Caroline, 'Introduction: England and the Low Countries, 1327-1477', in Barron, Caroline and Saul, Nigel (eds), *England and the Low Countries in the Late Middle Ages*, p. 8
47. Ibid, p. 19
48. Higginbotham, Susan, *The Woodvilles*, p. 53

7 Man of Letters and Patron of William Caxton

1. Meale, Carol, 'Patrons, Buyers and Owners: Book Production and Social Status', p. 201
2. Ibid, p. 217
3. British Library, *The Beginnings of the Royal Library*
4. Ibid
5. Meale, Carol, 'Patrons, Buyers and Owners: Book Production and Social Status', p. 205
6. Ibid, pp. 204-205
7. Ibid, p. 205
8. Edwards, Edward, *Memoirs of Libraries,* Volume 1, p. 389
9. Meale, Carol, 'Patrons, Buyers and Owners: Book Production and Social Status', p. 204
10. Ibid, p. 205
11. Sutton, Anne F. and Visser-Fuchs, Livia, 'Choosing a Book in Late Fifteenth-Century England and Burgundy', in Barron, Caroline and Saul, Nigel (eds), *England and the Low Countries in the Late Middle Ages*, p. 61
12. Cobb, H. S. (ed), *The Overseas Trade of London: Exchequer Customs Accounts, 1480-1*, p. xxxvi
13. Hellinga, Lotte, 'Importation of Books Printed on the Continent into England or Scotland Before c.1520', in Hindman, Sandra (ed), *Printing the Written Word: The Social History of Books, circa 1451-1520*, p. 207
14. Duff, Edward Gordon, *A Century of the English Book Trade*, p. xi
15. Ibid, p. xiv
16. Hubbard, B., *Kings and Queens of the Middle Ages*, p. 202
17. Labarge, Margaret Wade, *Medieval Travellers: The Rich and the Restless*, p. xvii
18. Gill, Louise, 'William Caxton and the Rebellion of 1483', *English Historical Review*, 112.445, 1997, p. 105
19. Duff, Edward Gordon, *Printers, Stationers and Bookbinders of London and Westminster in the Fifteenth Century*, reprint 2011, p. 3

20. Duff, Edward Gordon, *Printers, Stationers and Bookbinders*, p. 3; Whitehead, Stephen, 'The Codex Files: William Caxton and Margaret of York', *Renaissance Magazine*, 21.5, 2017, p. 22
21. Duff, Edward Gordon, *Printers, Stationers and Bookbinders*, p. 3
22. Ibid, p. 4
23. Dunleavy, Brian, *The Woodville Chronicle*, p. 139; Whitehead, Stephen, 'The Codex Files: William Caxton and Margaret of York', p. 22
24. British Library, *The Beginnings of the Royal Library*; Vale, Malcom, 'An Anglo-Burgundian Nobleman and Art Patron', pp. 119-120
25. British Library, *Christine de Pizan, Collected works* ('The Book of the Queen')
26. Ibid
27. Ibid
28. Hollman, Gemma, *Royal Witches*, p. 165
29. Jacquetta's motto of 'sur tous autres' translates as 'above all others'. Anthony's motto of 'nulle la vault' translates as 'nothing is worth it'.
30. Louis' motto is Plus est en vous, 'there is more in you'.
31. British Library, *Christine de Pizan, Collected works* ('The Book of the Queen')
32. Meale, Carol, 'Patrons, Buyers and Owners: Book Production and Social Status', p. 208
33. MS. Bodl. 264, fol. 274r, Oxford, The Bodleian Library
34. Harris, Kate, 'Patrons, Buyers and Owners: The Evidence for Ownership, and the Role of Book Owners in Book Production and the Book Trade', p. 175
35. Ibid; MS. Bodl. 264, fol. 274r, Oxford, The Bodleian Library
36. Khalaf, Omar, 'An Unedited Fragmentary Poem by Anthony Woodville, Earl Rivers in Oxford, Bodleian Library, MS Bodley 264, *Notes and Queries*, 58.4 (2011), p. 487
37. Ibid, p. 488

38. Ibid, p. 487
39. Ibid, p. 489
40. Ibid
41. Ibid
42. Caxton mentions the seven deadly sins poem in his epilogue to Anthony's translation of *The Cordyale*, p. 151
43. It is also a given that Woodville would have owned French or Latin versions of the other two texts he translated for Caxton, the *Cordyale* and Christine de Pizan's *Moral Proverbs*. He also possibly translated another Christine de Pizan text called *Livre du corps de policie.*
44. Gill, Louise, 'William Caxton and the Rebellion of 1483', *The English Historical Review*, Volume CXII, Issue 445, February 1997, Pages 105–118, p. 114
45. Ibid, p. 111; Higginbotham, Susan, *The Woodvilles*, p. 82-83
46. Higginbotham, Susan, *The Woodvilles*, p. 53; Kettle, Andrew, 'Parvenus in Politics', p. 9
47. Clanchy, Michael, 'Parchment and Paper: Manuscript Culture 1100-1500', in Eliot, S. and Rose, J. (eds) *A Companion to the History of the Book*, p. 204
48. Baker, Anita, *The Medieval World*, p. 155
49. Kuskin, William, 'Caxton's Worthies Series: The Production of Literary Culture', p. 51; Labarge, Margaret Wade, *Medieval Travellers: The Rich and the Restless*, p. xvii
50. Hellinga, Lotte, *William Caxton and Early Printing in England,* p. 61
51. Hellinga, Lotte, 'The Guttenberg Revolutions', in Eliot, S. and Rose, J. (eds) *A Companion to the History of the Book*, p. 210; Kern, Darcy, 'Parliament in Print', p. 211
52. Christianson, C. Paul, 'Evidence for the Study of London's Late Medieval Manuscript-Book Trade', in Griffiths, Jeremy and Pearsall, Derek (eds), *Book Production and Publishing in Britain, 1375-1475*, p. 91
53. Doyle, James E. (ed), *A Chronicle of England, B.C. 55 - A.D. 1485*, 1864, p. 432

54. Dunleavy, Brian, *The Woodville Chronicle*, p. 134
55. Hellinga, Lotte, *William Caxton and Early Printing in England*, p. 61; Higginbotham, Susan, *The Woodvilles*, p. 82-83
56. Kuskin, William, 'Caxton's Worthies Series', p. 540
57. Davies, C. S. L., *Peace, Print and Protestantism, 1450-1558*, p. 132
58. Ibid, p. 133; Kuskin, William, 'Caxton's Worthies Series', p. 51
59. Salter, Elisabeth, *Popular Reading in English*, p. 123
60. Thirteen copies of the *Dictes and Sayings* survive. Tokunaga, Satoko, 'Rubrication in Caxton's Early English Books', c. 1476-1478', *Transactions of the Cambridge Bibliographical Society*, 15.1, 2012, p. 68
61. Blake, N. F., 'Manuscript to Print', in Griffiths, Jeremy and Pearsall, Derek (eds), *Book Production and Publishing in Britain, 1375-1475*, p. 414
62. MS 265, *Dictes and Sayings of the Philosophers* (1477)
63. Blake, N. F., 'Manuscript to Print', p. 414
64. Buhler, Curt F., 'The Dictes and Sayings of the Philosophers', The Library, 1934, s4-XV, Issue 3, pp. 316-329, p. 318
65. Pidgeon, Lynda, 'Antony Wydevile, Lord Scales and Earl Rivers', Part 2, p. 15
66. MacCracken, H. N., 'The Flower of Souvenance: A Moment in the Twilight of Chivalry', p. 367
67. Saul, Nigel, *Chivalry in Medieval England*, p. 335
68. Higginbotham, Susan, *The Woodvilles*, pp. 91-92
69. Davies, C. S. L., *Peace, Print and Protestantism*, p. 132
70. Sutton, Anne F. and Visser-Fuchs, Livia, 'Choosing a Book in Late Fifteenth-Century England and Burgundy', p. 68
71. *The Cordyale*, p. 151
72. Weinburg, S. C., 'Caxton, Anthony Woodville and the Prologue to the "Morte D'Arthur"', *Studies in Philology*, 102.1 (2005), p. 52
73. *The Cordyale*, p. XXXV
74. William Caxton explains this is a motivation for Anthony in his epilogue to *The Cordyale*, p. 150

75. Blake, N. F., 'Manuscript to Print', pp. 414-415
76. Ibid, p. 415
77. Ibid, p. 418
78. Barron, W. R. J., 'Knighthood on Trial: The Acid Test of Irony', in Jackson, W. H. (ed), *Knighthood in Medieval Literature*, p. 89
79. Ibid
80. Weinburg, S. C., 'Caxton, Anthony Woodville and the Prologue to the "Morte D'Arthur"', p. 60
81. Ibid, p. 61
82. Ibid
83. Hellinga, Lotte, *William Caxton and Early Printing in England*, pp. 2 and 61
84. Santiuste, David, *Edward IV and the Wars of the Roses*, p. 85
85. Harris, Kate, 'Patrons, Buyers and Owners: The Evidence for Ownership, and the Role of Book Owners in Book Production and the Book Trade', p. 180
86. Davies, C. S. L., *Peace, Print and Protestantism,* pp. 132-133; Dunleavy, Brian, *The Woodville Chronicle*, p. 134; Salter, Elisabeth, *Popular Reading in English,* pp. 96-97
87. Weinburg, S. C., 'Caxton, Anthony Woodville and the Prologue to the "Morte D'Arthur"', p. 47
88. Gill, Louise, 'William Caxton and the Rebellion of 1483', p. 114
89. Ibid, p. 110
90. Ibid, p. 114
91. Kern, Darcy, 'Parliament in Print', p. 211
92. Duff, Edward Gordon, *A Century of the English Book Trade*, p. 24
93. Ibid
94. The Sarum Missal was a liturgy that Caxton commissioned Maynyal to produce in Paris. The printing of English liturgy in France was common at this time. There were around ninety-five editions produced by Caxton at Westminster. Duff, Edward Gordon, *A Century of the English Book Trade*, p. 24; Tokunaga, Satoko, 'Rubrication in Caxton's Early English Books', p. 63

95. Whitehead, Stephen, 'The Codex Files: William Caxton and Margaret of York', p. 23
96. Ibid
97. Duff, Edward Gordon, *A Century of the English Book Trade*, p. xv
98. Ibid, Whitehead, Stephen, 'The Codex Files: William Caxton and Margaret of York', p. 23
99. Stroud, Michael, 'Chivalric Terminology in Late Medieval Literature', p. 329
100. Santiuste, David, *Edward IV and the Wars of the Roses*, p. 85
101. *The Chronicles of the White Rose of York*, p. 146; Harris, Kate, 'Patrons, Buyers and Owners: The Evidence for Ownership, and the Role of Book Owners in Book Production and the Book Trade', p. 180

8 Governor of the Household of Edward, Prince of Wales

1. *Crowland Chronicle*, p. 123
2. CPR, *1467-1477*, 12 January 1473-Westminster, p. 414
3. Hicks, Michael, *The Prince in the Tower,* p. 72
4. CPR, *1467-1477*, 8 July 1471- Westminster, p. 283
5. Ibid
6. Hicks, M. A., 'The Changing Role of the Wydevilles', pp. 76 and 94
7. Ibid, p. 75
8. CPR, *1467-1477*, 20 November 1472- Westminster, p. 361; 10 December 1472- Westminster, p. 365; 6 July- Westminster, p. 449
9. CCR, 1468-1476, no. 858; Hicks, Michael, *The Prince in the Tower*, p. 58
10. Hicks, Michael, *The Prince in the Tower*, p. 59
11. Hicks, M. A., 'The Changing Role of the Wydevilles', p. 76
12. Hicks, Michael, *The Prince in the Tower*, p. 95
13. Ibid, p. 109
14. Ibid

15. CPR, 1467-1477, 12 July 1474-Westminster, p. 455
16. Ibid
17. Emery, Anthony, 'Late-Medieval Houses as an Expression of Social Status', *Historical Research*, 78 (2005), p. 145; Dyer, Christopher, *Standards of Living in the Later Middle Ages*, p. 35
18. Dyer, Christopher, *Standards of Living in the Later Middle Ages*, p. 53
19. Hicks, Michael, *The Prince in the Tower*, p. 71
20. Lander, J. R., *Conflict and Stability in Fifteenth-Century England*, p. 91
21. *The Chronicles of the White Rose of* York, pp. 153-154; *Letters of the Kings of England*, Volume 1, pp. 136-134
22. CPR, *1467-1477*, 10 November 1473-Westminster, p. 417
23. *Letters of the Kings of England*, Volume 1, p. 144
24. Ashdown-Hill, John, *The Mythology of Richard III*, p. 47
25. CPR, *1467-1477*, 10 November 1473-Westminster, p. 417
26. 'John Alcock', *Encyclopedia Britannica*
27. Kekewich, Margaret Lucille, *Books of Advice for Princes in Fifteenth-Century England with Particular Reference to the Period 1450-1485*, p. 340
28. Ibid, p. 341
29. Ibid, p. 349
30. 'Sir John Fortescue', *Encyclopedia Britannica*
31. Kekewich, *Margaret Lucille, Books of Advice for Princes in Fifteenth-Century England*, pp. 229 and 234
32. Ibid, p. 234
33. Kern, Darcy, 'Parliament in Print', p. 209
34. Dunleavy, Brian, *The Woodville Chronicle*, p. 134
35. Mancini, Dominic, p. 85
36. Hicks, Michael, *The Prince in the Tower*, p. 78
37. Ibid, p. 118
38. Ibid, pp. 68-69
39. Ibid, p. 69; CPR, *1467-1477*, 8 July 1475- Westminster, p. 499; 20 June 1475- Sandwich, pp. 534-535
40. Hicks, Michael, *The Prince in the Tower*, p. 118

41. Ibid
42. Ibid, p. 120
43. Ibid, p. 141

9 *Piety*

1. Hicks, Michael, 'Piety and Lineage in the Wars of the Roses: the Hungerford Experience', in Griffiths Ralph A. and Sherborne, James (eds), *Kings and Nobles in the Later Middle Ages*, p. 92
2. CPR, *1467-1477*, 11 March 1475-Westminster, p. 553
3. Higginbotham, Susan, *The Woodvilles*, p. 60
4. Isle of Wight Record Office, NBC/1/15
5. TNA, PROB 11/8/579
6. Goodman, Anthony, *The Wars of the Roses: Military Activity and English Society*, p. 211
7. TNA, PROB 11/8/579
8. Labarge, Margaret Wade, *Medieval Travellers: The Rich and the Restless*, p. 83
9. Pidgeon, Lynda, 'Antony Wydevile, Lord Scales and Earl Rivers', Part 2, p. 5
10. Behrendt, A., 'Pilgrimages of Princes in the 15th Century – Two Holy Land Journeys of German Princes via Rome: A Distinction to the Lower Nobility Class Journeys', *Almatourism*, 6, 2017, p. 91
11. Ibid, p. 99
12. *Warkworth's Chronicle*, p. 6; Goodman, Anthony, *The Wars of the Roses: Military Activity and English Society*, p. 68
13. Ashdown-Hill, John, 'Walsingham in 1469: The Pilgrimage of Edward IV and Richard, Duke of Gloucester', *The Ricardian*, 11.136 (1997), p. 2
14. Ibid, p. 7
15. There is no documented birth. It is also possible that the couple may have suffered miscarriages.
16. TNA, PROB 11/8/579
17. Uden, Grant, *A Dictionary of Chivalry*, p. 139
18. *The Cordyale*, p. 150

19. TPL, 889, vol 5, p. 258
20. 'Venice: 1461-1470', in *Calendar of State Papers Relating to English Affairs in the Archives of Venice, Volume 1, 1202-1509*, No. 454, 10 May; Buhler, Curt F., 'A Letter from Edward IV to Galeazzo Maria Sforza', *Speculum*, 30.2 (1955), p. 239
21. 'Venice: 1461-1470', in *Calendar of State Papers Relating to English Affairs in the Archives of Venice, Volume 1, 1202-1509*, No. 455, 13 May
22. Buhler, Curt F., 'A Letter from Edward IV', pp. 239-240
23. 'Venice: 1461-1470', in *Calendar of State Papers Relating to English Affairs in the Archives of Venice, Volume 1, 1202-1509*, No. 455, 13 May
24. *The Cordyale*, p. 150
25. Veil, Anne, *Shrines of Our Lady in England*, p. 212
26. TNA, PROB 11/8/579
27. Veil, Anne, *Shrines of Our Lady in England*, p. 212; Stow, John, *Survey of London*, p. 420
28. 5 May (27 April) 1476, St Peter's Rome, *Calendar of Papal Registers Relating to Great Britain and Ireland*, Volume 13, 1471-1484, British History Online; *The Cordyale*, p. 150; Pidgeon, Lynda, 'Antony Wydevile, Lord Scales and Earl Rivers', Part 2, p. 24
29. He first asked that if he died beyond the River Trent that he be buried there, but this was later changed to a request to be buried before an image of the Virgin; TNA, PROB 11/8/579
30. TPL, 793, vol 5, p. 128
31. CPR, *1461-1467*, 12 October 1471- London, p. 292
32. TPL, 778, vol 5, p. 106; Higginbotham, Susan, *The Woodvilles*, p. 76
33. TPL, 795, vol 5, p. 131
34. TNA, PROB 11/8/579
35. Ibid
36. *The Cordyale*, p. 151
37. Mancini, Dominic, p. 83

10 Stony Stratford and Execution

1. *Crowland Chronicle*, p. 151
2. Mancini was a foreign visitor who had only been in England since late summer of 1482 and who left after 6 July 1483. He does not give the names of his sources. He was writing for a French audience, particularly his patron, Angelo Cato, who was the Archbishop of Vienne. At the time the French were only too willing to stir up anti-English sentiments. For this reason, we must be wary of some of the events recounted by Mancini.
3. Carson, Annette, *Richard III: A Small Guide to the Great Debate*, p. 43
4. Mancini, Dominic, p. 87
5. Ibid
6. Carson, Annette, *Richard III: A Small Guide to the Great Debate*, p. 42
7. Bicheno, Hugh, *Blood Royal: The Wars of Lancaster and York, 1462-1485*, p. 276
8. Ibid, p. 275
9. Hanham, Alison, *Richard III and His Early Historians*, pp. 2-3; Higginbotham, Susan, *The Woodvilles*, p. 76
10. Higginbotham, Susan, *The Woodvilles*, pp. 116-117
11. Mancini, Dominic, p. 87; Bicheno, Hugh, *Blood Royal: The Wars of Lancaster and York*, p. 276
12. Mancini, Dominic, p. 89
13. Ibid, p. 87
14. Ibid, p. 276
15. Hanham, Alison, *Richard III and His Early Historians*, p. 9
16. *Crowland Chronicle*, p. 155
17. Carson, Annette, *Richard III: A Small Guide to the Great Debate*, p. 42; Hubbard, B., *Kings and Queens of the Middle Ages*, p. 203.
18. Pidgeon, Lynda, *Brought Up of Nought*, p. 206
19. Kingsford, Cecil Lethbridge (ed), *Chronicles of London*, pp. 189-190
20. Ibid, p. 190

21. Ibid, p. ix
22. Walpole, Horace, *Historic Doubts on the Reign of King Richard the Third*, reprint, 1974, pp. 23 and 27
23. Ashdown-Hill, John, *The Mythology of Richard III*, p. 48
24. Ibid, p. 49
25. Ibid, p. 48; Higginbotham, Susan, *The Woodvilles*, p. 121
26. *Crowland Chronicle*, p. 155
27. Mancini, Dominic, p. 93
28. Thomas More, *Richard III*, p. 17
29. Ibid, p. 18
30. Ibid, p. 19
31. Carson, Annette, *Richard III: A Small Guide to the Great Debate*, p. 42
32. Thomas More, *Richard III*, p. 20
33. Ibid
34. Hanham, Alison, *Richard III and His Early Historians*, p. 7
35. Carson, Annette, *Richard III: The Maligned King*, updated edition, 2013, p. 51
36. Mancini, Dominic, p. 91
37. Lander, J. R., *Conflict and Stability in Fifteenth-Century England*, p. 146
38. Hanham, Alison, *Richard III and His Early Historians*, p. 5
39. Bicheno, Hugh, *Blood Royal: The Wars of Lancaster and York*, p. 278
40. Ibid, p. 277
41. According to Thomas More, Anthony had been arrested at Northampton prior to Gloucester and Buckingham moving on to Stony Stratford.
42. Hicks, Michael, *The Prince in the Tower*, p. 72
43. Ibid, p. 118
44. *Crowland Chronicle*, p. 157; Mancini, Dominic, p. 93; Thomas More, *Richard III*, p. 19
45. Thomas More, *Richard III*, p. 14
46. Ibid, p. 16
47. Ibid, pp. LXVI and LXVIII

48. Ibid, p. 19
49. Walpole, Horace, *Historic Doubts on the Reign of King Richard the Third*, p. 25
50. Mancini, Dominic, p. 97 and 99.
51. Davies, C. S. L., *Peace, Print and Protestantism*, p. 93
52. Ibid; Mancini, Dominic, p. 103
53. Hicks, Michael, *The Prince in the Tower*, p. 149
54. Carson, Annette, *Richard III: A Small Guide to the Great Debate*, p. 43
55. Lander, J. R., *Conflict and Stability in Fifteenth-Century England*, p. 98
56. *Crowland Chronicle*, p. 157
57. Carson, Annette, *Richard III: A Small Guide to the Great Debate*, p. 44
58. Ibid
59. Including Lord Hastings, who was also executed on the orders of Richard, Duke of Gloucester, in the same month as those at Pontefract Castle. Walpole, Horace, *Historic Doubts on the Reign of King Richard the Third*, p. 30
60. Ibid, p. 31
61. Mancini, Dominic, p. 113
62. *Crowland Chronicle*, p. 161
63. Thomas More, *Richard III*, p. 57
64. Ibid
65. Thomas More, *Richard III*, p. 20
66. Shakespeare, William, *Richard III*, Act III, Scene III
67. Ashdown-Hill, John, *The Mythology of Richard III*, p. 50
68. Horrox, Rosemary and Hammond, P. W. (eds), *The Harleian Manuscript 433*, Volume II Richard III Society, 1980, p. 119
69. Richardson, Douglas, *Plantagenet Ancestry: A Study in Colonial and Medieval Families*, Volume 1, second edition, 2011, p. 232
70. John Rous cited in Hanham, Alison, *Richard III and His Early Historians*, p. 119
71. Ibid, p. 120
72. Ashdown-Hill, John, *The Mythology of Richard* III, p. 50

73. For full poem, see Appendix 2
74. Nuttall, Jenni, 'The Vanishing Virelai: French "Complainte" in English in the Fifteenth Century', *Medium Ævum*, 85.1 (2016), p. 64
75. Bicheno, Hugh, *Blood Royal: The Wars of Lancaster and York*, p. 287
76. Hanham, Alison, *Richard III and His Early Historians*, pp. 119-120
77. Pidgeon, Lynda, 'Antony Wydevile, Lord Scales and Earl Rivers', Part 2, p. 28
78. Cavell, Emma (ed), *The Herald's Memoir 1486-1490*, Richard III and Yorkist History Trust, 2009, p. 71
79. Ibid, p. 72
80. TNA, PROB 11/8/579
81. Horrox, Rosemary and Hammond, P. W. (eds), *The Harleian Manuscript 433*, Volume II, p. 25
82. Westminster Abbey, 'Sir Thomas Vaughan'
83. Ibid
84. Holmes, Richard, *A Few Sketches of Pontefract Topography*, 1873, pp. 20-21
85. Ibid, p. 58
86. Ibid, p. 60
87. Carson, Annette, *Richard III: A Small Guide to the Great Debate*, p. 43
88. *Crowland Chronicle*, p. 155
89. Bicheno, Hugh, *Blood Royal: The Wars of Lancaster and York*, p. 278
90. Hanham, Alison, *Richard III and His Early Historians*, pp. 2-3; Higginbotham, Susan, *The Woodvilles*, p. 76
91. Mancini, Dominic, p. 103

11 Legacy

1. Hanham, Alison, *Richard III and His Early Historians*, p. 119; Thomas More, *Richard III*, p. 19; *Crowland Chronicle*, p. 161
2. Walpole, Horace, *A Catalogue of Royal and Noble Authors*, p. 68
3. Dunleavy, Brian, *The Woodville Chronicle*, p. 134

4. Higginbotham, Susan, *The Woodvilles*, p. 83
5. Hicks, Michael, *The Prince in the Tower*, p. 75; Hicks, M. A., 'The Changing Role of the Wydevilles', pp. 74-75
6. Higginbotham, Susan, *The Woodvilles*, p. 93
7. Thomas More, *Richard III*, p. 18
8. NCR 9e/4
9. TPL, 707-707, vol 5, pp. 18-19 and 716, vol 5, pp. 30-32
10. *The Chronicles of the White Rose of* York, pp. 153-154; *Letters of the Kings of England*, Volume 1, pp. 136-134
11. Ashdown-Hill, John, *The Mythology of Richard III*, p. 48
12. *Historia Regum Angliae*, cited in Ashdown-Hill, John, *The Mythology of Richard III*, p. 48
13. Bicheno, Hugh, *Blood Royal: The Wars of Lancaster and York*, p. 287
14. Shakespeare, William, *Richard III*, Act I, Scene III
15. Ibid, Act III, Scene III, p. 98
16. Lander, J. R., 'Marriage and Politics in the Fifteenth Century: The Nevilles and the Wydvilles', *Bulletin of the Institute of Historical Research*, 36.94, p. 119

BIBLIOGRAPHY

Abbreviations

CChR - Calendar of Charter Rolls
CCR - Calendar of Close Rolls
CPR - Calendar of Patent Rolls
TNA - The National Archives
TPL - The Paston Letters

Unpublished Primary Sources

Bodleian Libraries: MS. Bodl. 264, fol. 274r, Oxford, The Bodleian Library

Isle of Wight Record Office: Agreement between Sir Anthony Wydevile and Richard Wylde and John Holbroke, bailiffs of Newport, NBC/1/15

Lambeth Palace Library: MS 265, *Dictes and Sayings of the Philosophers* (1477)

Norfolk Record Office: Copies of the city's petition, letters and other related documents about the dispute with the abbot of St Benet's of Hulme over his water meadows in Heigham and the city' mills on the Wensum, NCR 9e/4

The British Library: Christine de Pizan, *Collected Works* (c. 1410-1414), Harley MS 4431

The National Archives:
Court of Chancery, Lord Scales v John Towneshend, C 1/28/77
Postmortem Inquisition of Anthony Woodville: Cambridgeshire, C 142/1/36
Postmortem Inquisition of Anthony Woodville: Hertfordshire, C 142/1/37
Postmortem Inquisition of Elizabeth Scales, C 140/46/45
Will of Anthony Woodville, PROB 11/8/579
Will of Thomas Clarell, Gentleman and Grocer of London, PROB 11/10/121

Published Primary Sources

Black, William Henry (ed), *Historical Illustrations of the Reign of Edward IV: Comprising Memoirs of Anthony, Earl Rivers*, extract from *Excerpta Historica, or Illustrations of English History* (1830)
Calendar of Papal Registers Relating to Great Britain and Ireland, Volume 13, 1471-1484 (London: 1955), British History Online
Calendar of State Papers and Manuscripts in the Archives and collections of Milan, 1385-1618 (London, 1912), British History Online
Calendar of State Papers Relating to English Affairs in the Archives of Venice, Volume 1, 1202-1509 (London, 1864), British History Online
Calendars of Patent Rolls, preserved in the Public Record Office, Edward II to Henry VII (London: 1844-1916)
Calendars of the Close Roll, preserved in the Public Record Office, Edward II to Henry VII (London: 1891-1916)
Calendar of the Charter Roll, preserved in the Public Record Office, Henry VI to Henry VIII (London: 1927)
Cavell, Emma (ed), *The Herald's Memoir 1486-1490* (Donington, Richard III and Yorkist History Trust, 2009)
Christine de Pizan, *The Selected Writings* (New York: W. W. Norton, 1997)
The Chronicles of Enguerrand de Monstrelet, ed., and trans. Johnes, Thomas, two vols. (London: William Smith, 1840)

Cobb, H. S. (ed), *The Overseas Trade of London: Exchequer Customs Accounts, 1480-1* (London: London Record Society, 1990)

The Cordyale, reproduction (Nijmegen: 1914)

Crawford, Anne (ed), *The Household Books of John Howard, Duke of Norfolk, 1462-1471, 1481-1483* (Stroud: Alan Sutton Publishing, 1992)

Davies, John Slyvester (ed), *An English Chronicle of the Reigns of Richard II, Henry IV, Henry V and Henry VI* (London: Camden Society, 1856)

Doyle, James E. (ed), *A Chronicle of England, B.C. 55 - A.D. 1485* (London: Longman, Green, Longman, Roberts & Green, 1864)

Ellis, Henry (ed), *Three Books of Polydore Vergil's English History* (London: John Bowyer Nichols and Son, 1844)

Fabyan, Robert, *The New Chronicles of England and France*, ed. Ellis, Henry (London, 1811)

Gardiner, James (ed), *The Historical Collections of a Citizen of London in the Fifteenth Century* (London: Camden Society, 1876)

Gardiner, James (ed), *The Paston Letters*, reprint (Gloucester: Alan Sutton Publishing, 1983)

Hall's Chronicle (London: 1809)

Halliwell, James Orchard (ed), *Letters of the Kings of England*, Volume 1 (London: Henry Colburn, 1848)

Horrox, Rosemary and Hammond, P. W. (eds), *The Harleian Manuscript* 433, Volume II (Richard III Society, 1980)

Hunter Blair, C. H. (ed), *Visitations to the North, Part III: A Visitation of the North of England Circa 1480-1500* (Durham and London, 1930)

Ingulph's Chronicle of the Abbey of Croyland, with the Continuations by Peter of Blois and Anonymous Writers, trans. Riley, Henry T. (London: George Bells and Sons, 1905)

Kingsford, Cecil Lethbridge (ed), *Chronicles of London* (Oxford: Clarendon Press, 1905)

Letts, Malcom (trans. and ed.), *The Travels of Leo of Romitzal through Germany, Flanders, England, France, Spain, Portugal and Italy* (Cambridge: Hakluyt Society, 1957)

Major, John, *A History of Greater Britain*, trans. and ed. Constable, A. (Edinburgh: Scottish History Society, 1892)

Mancini, Dominic, *The Usurpation of Richard the Third*, trans. and ed. Armstrong, C. A. J. (London: Oxford University Press, 1936)

Munro, Cecil (ed), *Letters of Queen Margaret of Anjou and Bishop Beckington and Others* (London: Camden Society, 1863)

Myers, A. R. (ed), 'The Household of Queen Elizabeth Woodville, 1466-7', *Bulletin of the John Rylands Library*, 50 (1967-1968), pp. 207-235, 443-481

Myers, A. R. (ed), 'The Household of Queen Margaret of Anjou, 1452-3', *Bulletin of the John Rylands Library*, 40.1 (1958), pp. 79-113

Nichols, John (ed), *A Collection of All The Wills Now Known to be Extant Of the Kings and Queens of England* (London: Society of Antiquaries, 1780)

Nicolas, Nicholas Harris and Tyrell, Edward (eds), *A Chronicle of London, from 1089 to 1483* (London: 1827)

Pronay, Nicholas and Cox, John (eds), *The Crowland Chronicle Continuations: 1459-1486* (London: Alan Sutton Publishing, 1986)

Rotuli Parliamentorum, Volume 4 (1783)

Rotuli Parliamentorum, Volume 6 (1767)

Stow, John, *The Survey of London* (London: J M Dent & Sons Ltd), Project Guttenberg (Accessed 02/12/2021)

Stowe, John, *Three Fifteenth-Century Chronicles with Historical Memoranda*, ed. Gardiner, James (London: Camden Society, 1880)

Sylvester, Richard S. (ed), *The Complete Works of St. Thomas More*, Volume 2, *Richard III* (New Haven and London: Yale University Press, 1963)

The Chronicles of the White Rose of York (London: James Bohn, 1845)

The Dictes and Sayings of the Philosophers, reproduction (London: 1877)

Thomas, A. H. and Thornley, Isobel D. (eds), *The Great Chronicle* (London: 1936)

Thornley, Isobel D. (ed), *England Under the Yorkists, 1460-1485* (London: Longmans, Green and Co., 1920)

Three Chronicles of the Reign of Edward IV (Gloucester: Alan Sutton Publishing, 1988)

Wright, Thomas (ed), *Political Poems and Songs Relating to English History, Composed During the Period from the Accession of Edward III to that of Richard III*, Volume 2 (London: Longman, Green, Longman, and Roberts, 1861)

Secondary Sources

Books

A Few Sketches of Pontefract Topography (Pontefract: Richard Holmes, 1873)

Ailes, Adrian, 'Heraldry in Medieval England: Symbols of Politics and Propaganda', in Coss, Peter and Keen, Maurice H. (eds), *Heraldry, Pageantry and Social Display in Medieval England* (Woodbridge, 2002)

Alexander, Michael, *Medievalism: The Middle Ages in Modern England* (New Haven: Yale University, 2017)

Allan, Alison, 'Yorkist Propaganda: Pedigree, prophecy and the 'British History' in the Reign of Edward IV, in Ross, Charles (ed), *Patronage, Pedigree and Power in Later Medieval England* (Gloucester: Alan Sutton Publishing Ltd, 1979)

Almazan, Vincente, 'The Pilgrim-Shell in Denmark', in Dunn, Maryjane and Davidson, Linda Kay (eds), *The Pilgrimage to Compostela in the Middle Ages* (London: Routledge, 2000)

Ashdown-Hill, John, *Elizabeth Widville, Lady Grey* (Barnsley: Pen & Sword, 2019)

Ashdown-Hill, John, *The Mythology of Richard III* (Stroud: Amberley Publishing, 2015)

Ashdown-Hill, John, *The Third Plantagenet: George Duke of Clarence, Richard III's Brother* (Stoud: The History Press, 2013)

Baker, Anita, *The Medieval World* (London: Andre Deutsch, 2018)

Baker, George, *History and Antiquities of the County of Northampton*, Volume 2 (1844)

Baldwin, David, *Elizabeth Woodville: Mother of the Princes in the Tower* (Stroud: The History Press, 2002)

Baring-Gould, Sabine, *The Lives of the Saints*, Second Edition (London: John Hodges, 1874)

Barnwell, Edward Lowry, *Perrot Notes or Some Account of the of the Various Branches of the Perrot Family* (London: Cambrian Archaeological Association, 1867)

Barron, Caroline, 'Introduction: England and the Low Countries, 1327-1477', in Barron, Caroline and Saul, Nigel (eds), *England and the Low Countries in the Late Middle Ages* (Stroud: Alan Sutton Publishing Ltd, 1995)

Barron, W. R. J., 'Knighthood on Trial: The Acid Test of Irony', in Jackson, W. H. (ed), *Knighthood in Medieval Literature* (Woodbridge: D. S. Brewer, 1981)

Bedford, Kristina, *Eltham Through Time* (Stroud: Amberley Publishing, 2013)

Beswick, James, 'Richard II of England and the Smithfield Tournament of October 1390', in Murray, Alan V. and Watts, Karen (eds), *The Medieval Tournament as Spectacle: Tourneys, Jousts and Pas d'Armes, 100-1600* (Woodbridge: Boydell Press, 2020)

Bicheno, Hugh, *Blood Royal: The Wars of Lancaster and York, 1462-1485* (London: Head of Zeus Ltd, 2016)

Biggs, Elizabeth, *St Stephen's College, Westminster: A Royal Chapel and English Kingship, 1348-1548* (Woodbridge: The Boydell Press, 2020)

Blades, William, *The Biography and Topography of William Caxton, England's First Printer* (London and Strasbourg, 1877)

Blake, N. F., 'Manuscript to Print', in Griffiths, Jeremy and Pearsall, Derek (eds), *Book Production and Publishing in Britain, 1375-1475* (Cambridge: Cambridge University Press, 1989)

Blake, N. F., *William Caxton and English Literary Culture* (London: The Hambledon Press, 1991)

Britnell, Richard, 'The Proliferation of Markets Revisited', in Davies, Matthew and Galloway, James A. (eds), *London and Beyond:*

Essays in Honour of Derek Keene (London: University of London Press, 2012)

Caird, Rosalind, Cherry, John, Hume, Philip and Wood, Hugh, *The Ludlow Castle Heraldic Roll* (Eardisley: Logaston Press, 2019)

Carson, Annette, *Richard III: A Small Guide to the Great Debate* (Horstead: Imprimis Imprimatur, 2013)

Carson, Annette, *Richard III: The Maligned King*, Updated Edition (Stroud: The History Press, 2013)

Chitty, Henry and Phillipot, John, *The Visitation of the County of Gloucester, Taken in the Year 1623*, ed. Maclean, John and Heane, M. C. (Harleian Society, 1885)

Chrimes, S. B. *Lancastrians, Yorkists & Henry VII*, Second Edition (London, Melbourne and Toronto: Macmillan, 1966)

Christianson, C. Paul, 'Evidence for the Study of London's Late Medieval Manuscript-Book Trade', in Griffiths, Jeremy and Pearsall, Derek (eds), *Book Production and Publishing in Britain, 1375-1475* (Cambridge: Cambridge University Press, 1989)

Clanchy, Michael, 'Parchment and Paper: Manuscript Culture 1100-1500', in Eliot, Simon and Rose, Jonathan (eds), *A Companion to the History of the Book* (Chichester: Wiley-Blackwell, 2009)

Cockayne, George E., *Complete Peerage*, vol. 11 (London, 1959)

Collins, Hugh E. L., *The Order of the Garter, 1348-1461: Chivalry and Politics in Late Medieval England* (Oxford: Clarendon Press, 2000)

Connolly, Margaret and Mooney, Linne R. R., eds, *Design and Distribution of Late Medieval Manuscripts in England* (York: York Medieval Press, 2008)

Cooper, Stephen, *The Real Falstaff: Sir John Fastolf and the Hundred Years War* (Bradford: Pen & Sword, 2010)

Cooper-Davis, Charlotte, *Christine de Pizan: Life, Work, Legacy* (London: Reaktion Books Ltd, 2021)

Crane, Susan, *The Performance of Self: Ritual, Clothing and Identity during the Hundred Years War* (Philadelphia: University of Pennsylvania Press, 2002)

Crouch, David, *Tournament* (London: Hambledon and London, 2005)

Davies, C. S. L., *Peace, Print and Protestantism, 1450-1558* (London: Hart-Davies MacGibbon Ltd, 1976)

Dingman, Paul, 'Sword-made Men: Mystical Armament and Earthly Authority in Malory's *Le Morte Darthur*' in in Nakashian, Craig M. and Franke, Daniel P. (eds), *Prowess, Piety and Public Order in Medieval Society, Studies in Honour of Richard W. Kaeuper* (Leiden and Boston: Brill, 2017)

Duff, Edward Gordon, *A Century of the English Book Trade* (Bibliographical Society: London: 1905)

Duff, Edward Gordon, *Printers, Stationers and Bookbinders of London and Westminster in the Fifteenth Century*, reprint (Cambridge: Cambridge University Press, 2011)

Dunleavy, Brian, *The Woodville Chronicle* (Southampton: Magic Flute Publications, 2017)

Dunn, Maryjane and Davidson, Linda Kay, eds, *The Pilgrimage to Compostela in the Middle Ages* (London: Routledge, 2000)

Dyer, Christopher, *Standards of Living in the Later Middle Ages: Social Change in England, c. 1200-1520* (Cambridge: Cambridge University Press, 1989)

Easter Smith, Anne, *Daughter of York* (New York and London: Simon and Schuster, 2011)

Edwards, Edward, *Memoirs of Libraries,* Volume 1, (New York: Burt Franklin, 1859)

Evans, H. T., *Wales and the Wars of the Roses*, reprint (Stroud: Alan Sutton Publishing Ltd, 1995)

Gillespie, Vincent, 'Vernacular Books of Religion', in Griffiths, Jeremy and Pearsall, Derek, eds, *Book Production and Publishing in Britain, 1375-1475* (Cambridge: Cambridge University Press, 1989)

Girouard, Mark, *Life in the English Country House* (London: Yale University Press, 1978)

Goodchild, Steven, *Tewkesbury: Eclipse of the House of Lancaster, 1471* (Barnsley: Pen & Sword, 2005)

Goodman, Anthony, *The Wars of the Roses: Military Activity and English Society, 1452-97* (London: Routledge, 1981)

Griffiths, Ralph A., 'The Crown and the Royal Family in Later Medieval England', in Griffiths Ralph A. and Sherborne, James (eds), *Kings and Nobles in the Later Middle Ages* (Gloucester: Alan Sutton Publishing, 1986)

Griffiths, Ralph A., *King and Country: England and Wales in the Fifteenth Century* (London: The Hambledon Press, 1991)

Hammond, P. W., *The Battles of Barnet and Tewkesbury* (Gloucester: Alan Sutton Publishing Ltd, 1990)

Hanham, Alison, *Richard III and His Early Historians, 1483-1535* (Oxford: Oxford University Press, 1975)

Harding, Vanessa, 'Cross-Channel Trade and Cultural Contacts: London and the Low Countries in the Later Fourteenth Century', in Barron, Caroline and Saul, Nigel, eds, *England and the Low Countries in the Late Middle Ages* (Stroud: Alan Sutton Publishing Ltd, 1995)

Harris, Kate, 'Patrons, Buyers and Owners: The Evidence for Ownership, and the Role of Book Owners in Book Production and the Book Trade', in Griffiths, Jeremy and Pearsall, Derek, eds, *Book Production and Publishing in Britain, 1375-1475* (Cambridge: Cambridge University Press, 1989)

Harrison, Kathryn, *Joan of Arc: A Life Transfigured* (New York: Doubleday, 2014)

Harvey, I. M. W., *Jack Cade's Rebellion of 1450* (Oxford: Clarendon Press, 1991)

Hellinga, Lotte, 'Importation of Books Printed on the Continent into England or Scotland Before c.1520', in Hindman, Sandra, ed., *Printing the Written Word: the Social History of Books, circa 1451-1520* (Ithaca and London: Cornell University Press, 1991)

Hellinga, Lotte, 'The Guttenberg Revolutions', in Eliot, Simon and Rose, Jonathan, eds, *A Companion to the History of the Book* (Chichester: Wiley-Blackwell, 2009)

Hellinga, Lotte, *William Caxton and Early Printing in England* (London: British Library, 2010)

Hicks, Michael, 'Piety and Lineage in the Wars of the Roses: the Hungerford Experience', in Griffiths Ralph A. and Sherborne, James, eds, *Kings and Nobles in the Later Middle Ages* (Gloucester: Alan Sutton Publishing, 1986)

Hicks, Michael, 'The Changing Role of the Wydevilles in Yorkist Politics to 1483', in Ross, Charles, ed., *Patronage, Pedigree and Power in Later Medieval England* (Gloucester: Alan Sutton Publishing Ltd, 1979)

Hicks, Michael, *The Prince in the Tower: The Short Life & Mysterious Disappearance of Edward V* (Stroud: Tempus Publishing Limited, 2007)

Higginbotham, Susan, *The Woodvilles: The Wars of the Roses and England's most Infamous Family* (Stroud: The History Press, 2013)

Hollman, Gemma, *Royal Witches: From Joan of Navarre to Elizabeth Woodville* (Cheltenham: The History Press, 2019)

Howard, Donald R., *Writers and Pilgrims: Medieval Pilgrimage Narratives and Their Posterity* (Berkeley and Los Angeles: University of California Press, 1980)

Hubbard, B., *Kings and Queens of the Middle Ages* (London: Amber Books Ltd, 2018)

Iggulden, Conn, *Ravenspur*, reprint (London: Penguin, 2017)

Johnson, Lauren, *Shadow King: The Life and Death of Henry VI* (London: Head of Zeus Ltd, 2019)

Keen, Maurice H., *England in the Later Middle Ages*, reprint (London and New York: Routledge, 1995)

Keen, Maurice, *Chivalry* (New Haven: Yale University Press, 1984)

Kerr, Neil R., *Medieval Libraries of Great Britain: A List of Surviving Books*, Second Edition (London: Royal Historical Society, 1987)

Knecht, Robert, *The Valois: Kings of France, 1325-1589* (London and New York: Hambledon Continuum, 2004)

Krochalis, Jeanne E., '1494: Herionymus Munzer, Compostela and the *Codex Calixtinus*', in Dunn, Maryjane and Davidson, Linda

Kay, eds, *The Pilgrimage to Compostela in the Middle Ages* (London: Routledge, 2000)

Labarge, Margaret Wade, *Medieval Travellers: The Rich and the Restless* (London: Phoenix, 2005)

Lander, J. R., 'Family, Friends and Politics in Fifteenth-Century England', in Griffiths, Ralph A. and Sherborne, James, eds, *Kings and Nobles in the Later Middle Ages* (Gloucester: Alan Sutton Publishing, 1986)

Lander, J. R., *Conflict and Stability in Fifteenth-Century England* (London: Hutchinson & Co Ltd, 1969)

Lander, J. R., *Crown and Nobility 1450-1509* (London: Edward Arnold Publishers Ltd, 1976)

Laynesmith, J. L., *The Last Medieval Queens: English Queenship, 1445-1503* (Oxford: Oxford University Press, 2004)

Levitt, Emma, 'Tiltyard Friendships and Bonds of Loyalty in the Reign of Edward IV, 1461-1483', in Ward, Matthew and Hefferan, Matthew, eds, *Loyalty to the Monarchy in Late Medieval and Early Modern Britain, c. 1400-1688* (London: Palgrave Macmillan, 2020)

Lewis, Katherine J., *Kingship and Masculinity in Late Medieval England* (Oxen: Routledge, 2013)

Leyser, Henrietta, *Medieval Women: A Social History of Women in England, 450-1500* (London: Weidenfeld & Nicolson, 1995)

Licence, Amy, *The York King* (London: Lume Books, 2022)

Lyall, R. J., 'Books and Book Owners in Fifteenth-Century Scotland', in Griffiths, Jeremy and Pearsall, Derek (eds), *Book Production and Publishing in Britain, 1375-1475* (Cambridge: Cambridge University Press, 1989)

McKim, Anne M., 'James Douglas and Barbour's Ideal of Knighthood', in Jackson, W. H., ed., *Knighthood in Medieval Literature* (Woodbridge: D. S. Brewer, 1981)

McSheffrey, Shannon, *Marriage, Sex and Civic Culture in Late Medieval London* (Philadelphia: University of Pennsylvania Press (2006)

Meale, Carol, 'Patrons, Buyers and Owners: Book Production and Social Status', in Griffiths, Jeremy and Pearsall, Derek, eds, *Book*

Production and Publishing in Britain, 1375-1475 (Cambridge: Cambridge University Press, 1989)

Mortimer, Ian, *The Time Traveller's Guide to Medieval England* (New York: Simon & Schuter, 2011)

Ohler, Norbert, *The Medieval Traveller*, translated by Caroline Hillier (Woodbridge: The Boydell Press, 1989)

Ormrod, W. Mark, 'Pardon, Parliament and Political Performance in Later Medieval England', in Nakashian, Craig M. and Franke, Daniel P., eds, *Prowess, Piety and Public Order in Medieval Society, Studies in Honour of Richard W. Kaeuper* (Leiden and Boston: Brill, 2017)

Page, William (ed), *A History of the County of York, North Riding*, Volume 2 (London: Victoria County History, 1923)

Parker, Kate, 'A Little Local Difficulty: Lynn and the Lancastrian Usurpation', in Harper-Bill, Christopher, ed., *Medieval East Anglia* (Woodbridge: The Boydell Press, 2005)

Pelner Cosman, Madelaine, *The Education of the Hero in Arthurian Romance* (Chapel Hill: University of North Carolina Press, 1966)

Phillips, Kim M., *Medieval Maidens: Young Women and Gender in England, 1270-1540* (Manchester: Manchester University Press, 2003)

Pidgeon, Lynda, *Brought Up of Nought: A History of the Woodville Family* (Fonthill Media, 2019)

Pollard, Anthony J., 'English Chivalry and the Decline of Strenuous Knighthood in the Late Fifteenth Century', in Nakashian, Craig M. and Franke, Daniel P. (eds), *Prowess, Piety and Public Order in Medieval Society, Studies in Honour of Richard W. Kaeuper* (Leiden and Boston: Brill, 2017)

Ramirez, Janina, *Femina: A New History of the Middle Ages, Through the Women Written Out of It* (London: WH Allen, 2022)

Rawcliffe, Carole, *The Staffords, Earls of Stafford and Dukes of Buckingham, 1394-1521* (Cambridge: Cambridge University Press, 1978)

Richards, Paul, *King's Lynn Through Time* (Stroud: Amberley Publishing, 2014)

Richardson, Douglas, *Plantagenet Ancestry: A Study in Colonial and Medieval Families,* Volume 1, Second Edition (2011)

Richmond, Colin, 'Thomas Malory and the Pastons', in Meale, Carol M., ed., *Readings in Medieval English Romance* (Woodbridge: Boydell & Brewer, 1994)

Roskell, J. S., *The Commons and their Speakers in English Parliaments, 1376-1523* (Manchester: Manchester University Press, 1965)

Ross, Charles, *Edward IV* (London: Yale University Press, 1997)

Royle, Trevor, *The Wars of the Roses: England's First Civil War* (London: Abacus, 2010)

Salter, Elisabeth, *Popular Reading in English, c.1400-1600* (Manchester: Manchester University Press, 2012)

Santiuste, David, *Edward IV and the Wars of the Roses* (Barnsley, Pen & Sword, 2011)

Saul, Nigel, *Chivalry in Medieval England* (Harvard: Harvard University Press, 2011)

Schofield, John and Vince, Alan, *Medieval Towns: The Archaeology of British Towns in their European Setting*, Second Edition (London and New York: Continuum, 2003)

Scofield, Cora L., *The Life and Reign of Edward IV*, Volume One, reprint (Stroud: Fonthill Media, 2016)

Serdiville, Rosie and Sadler, John, *Knights: Chivalry and Violence* (Oxford: Casemate Publishers, 2017)

Staples, Kate Kelsey, 'Fripperers and the Used Clothing Trade in Late Medieval London', in Netherton, R. and Owen-Crocker, Gale R. (eds), *Medieval Clothing and Textiles* (Woodbridge: The Boydell Press, 2010)

Steane, John, *The Archaeology of Medieval England and Wales* (London and New York: Routledge, 2015)

Stevens, John, *Music and Poetry in the Early Tudor Court* (Cambridge: Cambridge University Press, 1979)

Sutton, Anne F. and Visser-Fuchs, Livia, 'Choosing a Book in Late Fifteenth-Century England and Burgundy', in Barron, Caroline and Saul, Nigel, eds, *England and the Low Countries in the Late Middle Ages* (Stroud: Alan Sutton Publishing Ltd, 1995)

Sutton, Anne F., Visser-Fuchs, Livia and Griffiths, R. A., *The Royal Funerals of the House of York at Windsor* (London: Richard III Society, 2005)

Sutton, Anne F., Visser-Fuchs, Livia and Hammond, P. W., *The Reburial of Richard Duke of York, 21-30 July 1476* (London: Richard III Society, 1996)

Thomas, D. H., *The Herberts of Raglan and the Battle of Edgecote 1469* (Enfield: Freezywater Publications, 1994)

Thompson, Michael, *The Medieval Hall: Te Basis of Secular Domestic Life, 600-1600 AD* (Aldershot: Scholar Press, 1995)

Thomson, John A. F., *The Transformation of Medieval England, 1370-1529* (Longman: London and New York, 1983)

Uden, Grant, *A Dictionary of Chivalry* (London: Longmans, 1968)

Vale, Malcom, 'An Anglo-Burgundian Nobleman and Art Patron: Louis de Bruges, Lord of la Gruuthuse and Earl of Winchester', in Barron, Caroline and Saul, Nigel, eds, *England and the Low Countries in the Late Middle Ages* (Stroud: Alan Sutton Publishing Ltd, 1995)

Veil, Anne, *Shrines of Our Lady in England* (Leominster: Gracewing, 2004)

Walpole, Horace, *Historic Doubts on the Reign of King Richard the Third*, reprint (Wakefield: EP Publishing Limited, 1974)

Walpole, Horace, *A Catalogue of Royal and Noble Authors of England with Lists of Their Works* (Edinburgh: J Mundell & Co., 1796)

Weightman, Christine, *Margaret of York: The Diabolical Duchess* (Stroud: Amberley, 2012)

Wood, Margaret, *The English Medieval House* (London: Ferndale Editions, 1981)

Wright, Laura, 'Trade between England and the Low Countries: Evidence from Historical Linguistics', in Barron, Caroline and Saul, Nigel, eds, *England and the Low Countries in the Late Middle Ages* (Stroud: Alan Sutton Publishing Ltd, 1995)

Articles

Adair, John, 'The Newsletter of Gerhard von Wesel, 17 April 1471', *Journal of the Society for Army Historical Research*, 46.186 (1968), pp. 65-69

Ashdown-Hill, John, 'Walsingham in 1469: The Pilgrimage of Edward IV and Richard, Duke of Gloucester' *The Ricardian*, 11.136 (1997), pp. 2-16

Barnfield, Marie, 'Richard's Great Scottish Campaign', *The Ricardian Bulletin*, June 2022, pp. 54-63

Baugh, Albert C., 'Kirk's Life Records of Thomas Chaucer', *PMLA*, 47.2 (1932), pp. 461-515

Behrendt, A., 'Pilgrimages of Princes in the 15th Century - Two Holy Land Journeys of German Princes via Rome: A Distinction to the Lower Nobility Class Journeys', *Almatourism*, 6 (2017), pp. 89-100

Broekhoff, Jan, 'Chivalric Education in the Middle Ages', *Quest*, 11.1 (1968), pp. 24-31

Brondarbit, Alex, '"Into Our Defense and Saveguarde": Eton College and the Good Lordship of Edward, Duke of York', *Royal Studies* Journal, 4.1 (2017), pp. 1-14

Buhler, Curt F., 'A Letter from Edward IV to Galeazzo Maria Sforza', *Speculum*, 30.2 (1955), pp. 316-329

Buhler, Curt F., 'The Dictes and Sayings of the Philosophers' (The Library 1934, s4-XV issue 3: 316-329), pp. 239-240

Burr, K. E., 'Diplomacy and the Expedition of 1475', *The Ricardian*, 3 (1975), pp. 23-24

Carr, Antony D., 'Sir Lewis John – A Medieval London Welshman', *Bulletin of Celtic Studies*, 22.3 (1967), pp. 260-270

Cline, Ruth Huff, 'The Influence of Romances on Tournaments of the Middle Ages', *Speculum*, 20.2 (1945), pp. 204-211

Donohue, Carolyn Anne, *Public Display and the Construction of Monarchy in Yorkist England 1461-85*, PhD University of York Department of History (2013)

Dunham, William Huse and Wood, Charles T., 'The Right to Rule in England: Depositions and the Kingdom's Authority, 1327-1485', *The American Historical Review*, 81.4 (1976), pp. 738-761

Emery, Anthony, 'Late-Medieval Houses as an Expression of Social Status', *Historical Research*, 78 (2005), pp. 140-161

Fisher, J. L., 'The Petre Documents', *Transactions of the Essex Archaeological Society*, 13.1, p. 66-97

Gill, Louise, 'William Caxton and the Rebellion of 1483', *English Historical Review*, 112.445 (1997), pp. 105-118

Gray, H. L., 'Incomes from Land in England in 1436', *English Historical Review*, 49.196, pp. 607-639

Grummitt, David, 'William, Lord Hastings, the Calais Garrison and the Politics of Yorkist England', *The Ricardian*, 12 (2001), pp. 262-274

Harris, Graham, 'The Dictes and Sayings of the Philosophers', *The Ricardian*, 3 (1975), pp. 15-16

Hicks, Michael, 'Unweaving the Web: The Plot of July 1483 against Richard III and its Wider Significance', *The Ricardian*, 9 (1991), pp. 106-109

Kern, Darcy, 'Parliament in Print: William Caxton and the History of Political Government in the Fifteenth Century', *Journal of Medieval History*, 40.2 (2014), pp. 209-224

Kettle, Andrew, 'Parvenus in Politics: The Woodvilles, Edward IV and the Baronage 1464-1469', *The Ricardian*, 15 (2005), pp. 1-20

Khalaf, Omar, 'An Unedited Fragmentary Poem by Anthony Woodville, Earl Rivers in Oxford, Bodleian Library', MS Bodley 264, *Notes and Queries*, 58.4 (2011), pp. 487-490

Kingsford, Charles Lethbridge, 'Our Lady of the Pew, The King's Oratory or Closet in the Palace of Westminster', *Archaeologia*, 68 (1917), pp. 1-20

Kleineke, Hannes, 'A Note on the Early Career of Sir Edward Woodville', *The Ricardian*, 24 (2014), pp. 87-91

Kuskin, William, 'Caxton's Worthies Series: The Production of Literary Culture', *ELH*, 66.3 (1999), pp. 511-551

Lander, J. R., 'Marriage and Politics in the Fifteenth Century: The Nevilles and the Wydvilles', *Bulletin of the Institute of Historical Research*, 36.94 (1963), pp. 119-152

MacCracken, H. N., 'The Flower of Souvenance: A Moment in the Twilight of Chivalry', *The Sewanee Review*, 20.3 (1912), pp. 366-376

Madden, Frederic, 'Narratives of the Arrival of Louis de Bruges, Seigneur de la Gruthuyse, in England, and of His Creation as Earl of Winchester, in 1472: Communicated in a Letter from Sir Frederic Madden, K.H. F.R.S., &c. to Hudson Gurney, Esq. Vice President', in *Archaeologia*, 26 (1836), pp 265-286

Mareel, Samuel, 'Urban Literary Patronage in the Early Modern Low Countries: Public Festival Culture and Individual Authorship', *Renaissance Quarterly*, 64.1 (2011), pp. 50-78

Moorhen, Wendy, 'Sir John Bromley and Martha, the Wydeville Who Never Was?', *The Ricardian*, 32 (2022), pp. 147-167

Moreton, C. E., 'A Local Dispute and the Politics of 1483: Roger Townshend, Earl Rivers and the Duke of Gloucester', *The Ricardian*, 8 (1989), pp. 305-308

Munro, J. H., 'Bruges and the Abortive Staple in English Cloth: An Incident in the Shift of Commerce from Bruges to Antwerp in the Late Fifteenth Century', Revue belge de philologie et d'histoire, 44.4 (1966), pp. 1137-1159

Nuttall, Jenni, 'The Vanishing Virelai: French "Complainte" in English in the Fifteenth Century', *Medium Ævum*, 85.1 (2016), pp. 59-76

O'Regan, Mary, 'Mediaeval Liturgical and Pious Books', *The Ricardian*, 4 (1977), pp. 23-26

Pascual, Lucia Diaz, 'Jacquetta of Luxembourg, Duchess of Bedford and Lady Rivers (c.1416-1472)', *The Ricardian*, 21 (2011), pp. 67-91

Phillips, Matthew, 'Urban Conflict and Legal Strategy in Medieval England: The Case of Bishop's Lynn, 1346-1350', *Urban History*, 42.3 (2015), pp. 365-380

Pidgeon, Lynda, 'Antony Wydevile, Lord Scales and Earl Rivers: Family, Friends and Affinity, Part 1.', *The Ricardian*, 15 (2005), pp. 1-19

Pidgeon, Lynda, 'Antony Wydevile, Lord Scales and Earl Rivers: Family, Friends and Affinity, Part 2.', *The Ricardian*, 16 (2006), pp. 15-45

Saul, A., 'Great Yarmouth and the Hundred Years War in the Fourteenth Century', *Bulletin of the Institute of Historical Research*, 52.126, pp. 105-115

Scholz, Bernhard W., 'Edward the Confessor: 'Anglorum Decas', *Traditio,* 18 (1962), pp. 379-382

Scofield, Cora L., 'The Capture of Lord Rivers and Sir Anthony Woodville, 19 January 1460', *The English Historical Review*, 37.146 (1922), pp. 253-254

Stroud, Michael, 'Chivalric Terminology in Late Medieval Literature', *Journal of the History of Ideas*, 37.2 (1976), pp. 323-334

Sutton, Anne F. and Visser-Fuchs, Livia, 'A "Most Benevolent Queen": Queen Elizabeth Woodville's Reputation, Her Piety and Her Books', *The Ricardian*, 10 (1995), pp. 214-245

Sutton, Anne F. and Visser-Fuchs, Livia, 'Laments for the Death of Edward IV: "It Was a World to See Him Ride About"', *The Ricardian*, 11 (1999), pp. 525-530

Sutton, Anne F. and Visser-Fuchs, Livia, 'Richard III's Books XIII: Chivalric Ideals and Reality', *The Ricardian*, 9 (1992), pp. 190-205

Sutton, Anne F., 'Lynn Episcopi, a Yorkist Port and Borough, with Particular Reference to the 1480s and the Reign of Richard III', *The Ricardian*, 25 (2015), pp. 19-53

Tokunaga, Satoko, 'Rubrication in Caxton's Early English Books, c. 1476-1478', *Transactions of the Cambridge Bibliographical Society*, 15.1 (2012), pp. 59-78

Visser-Fuchs, Livia, 'English Events in Caper Weinreich's Danzig Chronicle, 1461-1495', *The Ricardian*, 7 (1986), pp. 310-320

Visser-Fuchs, Livia, 'Richard in Holland, 1470-1', *The Ricardian,* 6 (1983), pp. 220-228

Visser-Fuchs, Livia, 'Richard was Late', *The Ricardian*, 11 (1997), pp. 616-619

Visser-Fuchs, Livia, 'The Garters and the Garter Achievements of Charles the Bold, Duke of Burgundy', *The Ricardian*, 23 (2013), pp. 1-19

Watson, Peter J., '"May God Have Pity at this Wretched Spectacle": a Review of the Sources for the Battle of Barnet, 14 April 1471', *The Ricardian*, 12 (2000), pp. 50-70

Waugh, Scott, 'The Lives of Edward the Confessor and the Meaning of History in the Middle Ages', *The Medieval Chronicle*, 3 (2004), pp. 200-218

Weeks, Marjorie, 'The Personality of Richard III', *The Ricardian*, 4 (1977), pp. 5-9

Weinburg, S. C., 'Caxton, Anthony Woodville and the Prologue to the "Morte D'Arthur"', *Studies in Philology*, 102.1 (2005), pp. 45-65

Whitehead, Stephen, 'The Codex Files: William Caxton and Margaret of York', *Renaissance Magazine*, 21.5 (2017), pp. 22-23

Williams, Barrie, 'Richard III and Pontefract', *The Ricardian*, 6 (1984), pp. 366-370

Unpublished Dissertations

Kekewich, Margaret Lucille, *Books of Advice for Princes in Fifteenth Century England with Particular Reference to the Period 1450-1485*, The Open University (1987)

Moffatt, Ralph, *The Medieval Tournament: Chivalry, Heraldry and Reality, An Edition and Analysis of Three Fifteenth-Century Tournament Manuscripts*, University of Leeds (2010)

Whitbread, Rachael E., *Tournaments, Jousts and Duels: Formal Combats in England and France, circa 1380–1440*, University of York (2013)

Whittle, Andrew, *The Historical Reputation of Edward IV 1461-1725*, University of East Anglia (2017)

Online

'Jack Cade', *Encyclopedia Britannica*, 8 Jul. 2022 (accessed 14 October 2022)

'John Alcock', *Encyclopedia Britannica*, 27 Sep. 2022 (accessed 12 February 2023)

'Sir John Fortescue', *Encyclopedia Britannica*, 13 Feb. 2012 (accessed 14 October 2022)

British Library, *Christine de Pizan, Collected works* ('The Book of the Queen')

British Library, *The Beginnings of the Royal Library* (Accessed 04/12/2021)

Caxton, W., *Dictes and Sayings of the Philosophers* (1477), Lambeth Palace, (accessed 22/09/2022)

'Cleley Hundred', in *A History of the County of Northampton: Volume 5, the Hundred of Cleley*, ed. Philip Riden and Charles Insley (London, 2002), pp. 1-18, British History Online (accessed 11 December 2021)

English Heritage, 'Eltham Palace and Gardens' (accessed 23/10/2021)

English Heritage, 'Old Wardour Castle' (accessed 14/01/2023)

Exploring London, 'Treasures of London – The Great Hall at Eltham Palace' (accessed 21/10/2021)

Higginbotham, Susan, 'Richard Woodville, Third Earl Rivers', (accessed 03/11/2022)

Historical Manuscript Commission, *The Manuscripts of the Corporations of Southampton and Kings Lynn Eleventh Report, Appendix: Part III* (London: Her Majesty's Stationery Office, 1887), British History Online (accessed 16/12/2021)

'Houses of Cluniac monks: Priory of Pontefract', in *A History of the County of York: Volume 3*, ed. William Page (London, 1974), pp. 184-186, British History Online

Lewis, Matthew, 'The Will of Anthony Woodville, Earl Rivers', 23 June 2014 (accessed 18/10/2019)

Luminarium: Encyclopaedia Project, 'Thomas de Scales, 7th Baron Scales' (accessed 20/09/19)

Maskelyne and H. C. Maxwell Lyte, 'Inquisitions Post Mortem, Henry VII, Entries 1-50', in *Calendar of Inquisitions Post Mortem: Series 2, Volume 1, Henry VII* (London, 1898), pp. 1-22, British History Online (accessed 18 January 2022)

Rickard, J., 'Siege of London, 12-15 May 1471', *History of War*, 27 February 2014, (accessed 16/02/2022)

Royal Palaces, 'Eltham Palace' (accessed 21/10/2021)
Society for the Protection of Ancient Buildings, 'National Treasure: The South Gate, King's Lynn, Norfolk', 11 December 2017 (accessed 08/11/2022)
The History of Parliament, 'Thomas Chaucer' (accessed 11/02/2022)
The History of Parliament, 'William Allington of Horseheath, Cambridgeshire', (accessed 24/01/2023)
Visit West Norfolk, 'Hanseatic King's Lynn' (accessed 20/01/2022)
Wakefield Historical Society, 'The Exhumation of Richard Duke of York' (accessed 24/02/2023)
Westminster Abbey, 'Sir Thomas Vaughan' (accessed 25/04/2023)
Wilkinson-Keys, Eleanor, 'The Smithfield Tournament of 1467', in *Martial Culture in Medieval Town*, 19/08/2021 (accessed 28/10/2022)

INDEX

Alexander Stewart, Duke of Albany, 70, 89, 90
Alnwick, Northumberland, 34, 74, 75, 76, 77
Anne of Burgundy, 23
Antoine, Count de la Roche, Bastard of Burgundy, 15, 40, 41, 94, 95, 97, 98, 99, 102
Aristotle, 136, 137

Bamburgh, Northumberland, 74, 75, 77
Banbury, Oxfordshire, 44, 45, 82
Battle of Barnet, 18, 82, 83, 84, 85, 154
Battle of Edgecote, 45, 47, 77, 79, 142
Battle of Northampton, 29
Battle of Stoke, 14
Battle of Tewkesbury, 84, 85
Battle of Towton, 18, 29, 31, 32, 33, 55, 75, 90, 136
Battle of Wakefield, 49, 52
Berwick on Tweed, 70, 89, 90
Bishop's Lynn, Norfolk, now known as King's Lynn, 34, 57, 58, 59, 105
Book of the Queen by Christine de Pizan, 107, 116, 117, 119
Brittany, 78, 87, 88, 90, 91, 139, 146
Bruges, Burgundy, 93, 99, 102, 103, 106, 107, 111, 113, 115, 116, 124, 127

Calais, 21, 18, 30, 31, 64, 66, 67, 80, 85, 87, 97, 108, 150, 167
Carmarthen, Wales, 138
Camelot, 41, 126
Canterbury, Kent, 86, 143
Cardinal John Morton, 158
Cardinal Wolsey, 58
Carisbrooke Castle, 78
Cecily Neville, Duchess of York, 69, 162
Cecily of York, daughter of Edward IV, 70, 89, 144
Chancery Court, 62
Charles V of France, 113
Charles VI of France, 116, 117
Charles the Bold, Duke of Burgundy, 36, 40, 64, 70, 81, 88, 90, 91, 93, 97, 99, 101, 102, 103, 104, 106, 107, 110, 111, 115, 140, 172
Chepstow, Wales, 44, 45
Chester, 57, 131, 132, 138
Christine de Pizan, 102, 107, 116, 117, 123
Cologne, Germany, 103, 116
Cordyale, translated by Anthony Woodville, 16, 124, 125, 143
Coventry, 45, 46, 82, 132
Crowland Chronicle, 36, 42, 45, 81, 84, 160, 161
Crusade, 18, 33, 90, 91, 146
Denbigh, North Wales, 132
Dictes and Sayings of the Philosophers, translated by Anthony Woodville, 17, 118, 119, 121, 122, 123, 137, 143, 144
Dominic Mancini, 15, 16, 147, 148, 150, 153, 155, 159, 161
Doncaster, 18, 50, 163, 164, 165
Dunstanburgh, Northumberland, 74, 75, 77
Durham, 75, 77

Edmund, Earl of Rutland, 49, 166
Edward II, 44
Edward III, 28, 60, 118
Edward the Confessor, 109, 110
Edward Woodville, Lord Scales, 23, 70, 139, 159, 160
Edward, Prince of Wales, later Edward V, 15, 16, 19, 42, 52, 54, 69, 89, 90, 104, 108, 119, 121, 129-141, 149, 150, 156, 158, 160, 169, 170, 174, 175
Elizabeth of York, 51, 63, 89, 100
Elizabeth Scales, 29, 31, 38, 54, 60-64, 71-73, 102, 109, 142, 144, 173
Eltham Palace, 61, 99, 103, 113

Enguerrand de Monstrelet, 25, 26
Eton College, 46, 142

First Battle of St Albans, 14, 29
Fotheringhay, Northamptonshire, 44, 49-51
Francis II, Duke of Brittany, 87-88, 146

Gabriel Tezel of Nuremburg, 63
Geoffrey Chaucer, 65, 163
George Douglas, Earl of Angus, 76
George Neville, Bishop of Exeter, later Archbishop of York, 32-33, 44
George Neville, second husband of Mary Fitzlewis, 69, 162
George, Duke of Clarence, 36, 39-40, 43, 44, 46, 51, 64, 70, 78, 79-80, 82, 88, 95, 109, 130, 131, 132
Gerhard von Wesel, 83
Ghent, Burgundy, 107, 115
Grafton Regis, Northamptonshire, 20, 39, 155
Great Yarmouth, Norfolk, 59
Guilliaume de Tignonville, 122, 144
Gwenllian, daughter of William Stradling of Glamorgan, 71

Hanseatic League, 57, 83
Henry Beaufort, Bishop of Winchester, 65-66
Henry Cavendish, second Duke of Newcastle, 117
Henry FitzHugh, 43
Henry Stafford, Duke of Buckingham, 38, 95, 131, 150, 152, 154-157, 159, 167
Henry II, 92, 96
Henry IV, 66, 81, 113
Henry V, 21, 23, 65, 66
Henry VI, 21, 23, 24, 25-26, 27, 28, 32, 33, 35, 37, 44, 57, 59, 74, 81, 82, 84, 85, 101, 105, 107-108, 116, 129, 130, 136-137, 142, 149, 157, 168,
Henry VII, 69, 84, 104, 113, 158, 164
Heraldry, 104, 113
Holborn, London, 95, 96
Holderness coast, 42, 81
Horace Walpole, 17-18, 152, 159, 169-170
Hundred Years War, 21, 27

Isle of Wight, 61, 78, 142

Jack Cade's Rebellion, 28
Jacquetta of Luxemburg, 17, 20, 23-27, 30-31, 37, 39-40, 46-48, 53, 56, 68, 101, 107, 116-117, 144
James I of Scotland, 67

James III of Scotland, 70, 89, 90, 135
Joan of Arc, 27
Johannes Guttenburg, 122
John Alcock, Bishop of Rochester, 70, 132, 135, 138
John Bourchier, Earl of Essex, 29, 86
John Daunger, 46-47
John de Mowbray, Duke of Norfolk, 39, 60, 77, 87, 96, 97
John de Vere, Earl of Oxford, 59, 60, 82, 83
John Dynham, 30
John Easteney, abbot of Westminster, 120
John FitzLewis, 21, 64, 65, 66
John Fortescue, 136
John Grey of Groby, 15, 23, 29
John Rous, 163
John Stow's *Survey of London*, 65
John Sutton, 43
John Talbot, Earl of Shrewsbury, 28
John Tiptoft, Earl of Worcester, 66, 79
John Towneshend, 62
John Woodville, 23, 38, 44, 45, 53, 99
John, Duke of Bedford, 17, 21-22, 23-26, 27, 117
John, Lord Audley, 78-79
John, Lord Howard, 61, 78, 96, 97
Jousting, 15, 92, 94, 98, 99, 102, 137, 169, 172, 174

King Arthur, 41,93, 95-96, 99, 117, 125-126
Kingston-Upon-Hull, 135

L'Historie de Jason, 104
London Bridge, 85
Louis XI, 75, 80, 89
Louis, Lord of Gruuthuse, 63, 103-104, 106-109, 110, 111, 113, 116
Ludlow, 15, 42, 69, 89, 131-132, 133, 138, 139, 141, 149, 150, 151, 152, 156, 157, 160, 167, 169, 174, 175

Margaret of Anjou, 27, 56, 63, 75, 84, 126
Margaret of York, Duchess of Burgundy, 40, 64, 72, 97, 99, 101, 103, 104, 110, 115, 172
Mary Fitzlewis, 64, 68, 70, 71, 73, 162
Mary of Burgundy, 70
Mary Woodville, 23, 53
Maud Stanhope, Lady Willoughby, 48, 170

Metamorphoses by Ovid, 124-25
Middleham, Yorkshire, 151, 164
Middleton, Norfolk, 57, 144
Morte D'Arthur by Thomas Malory, 125-126

Newport, Isle of Wight, 61, 142
Normandy, 21, 25, 30
Northampton, 29, 44, 45, 154, 155, 156, 157, 167
Norwich, 43-44, 57, 60, 170
Nottingham, 44, 46, 70

Our Lady of Pew, Westminster, 145, 146

Palace of Westminster, 120, 130
Paris, 23, 127
Paston family, 30, 32, 44, 99, 146, 170
Paston Letters, 30
Perkin Warbeck, 69, 173
Philip, Duke of Burgundy, 94, 97, 98
Pilgrimage, 16, 18, 43, 64, 122, 143-145, 157, 164, 166, 171, 174
Pontefract, 18, 49, 73, 152, 161-162, 165-166, 169, 174
Porchester Castle, 78
Portsmouth, 78
Portugal, 107, 146
Princess Margaret of Scotland, 70, 135
Printing Press, 15, 103, 111, 112, 114, 115, 116, 126

Ravenspur, Holderness Coast, 81, 173
Reading, Berkshire, 61, 73
Richard Bokeland, treasurer of Calais, 21-22, 67
Richard Grey, 100, 139, 152-154, 155, 156-157, 158, 159, 160, 164, 174
Richard II, 44, 81
Richard Haute, 152, 157-158, 164
Richard Ratcliffe, 161-162
Richard Woodville, first Earl Rivers, 17, 20, 23, 25-27, 28, 30, 33, 39, 43, 60, 77, 117, 118
Richard Woodville, third Earl Rivers, 118
Richard, Duke of York, 28, 35, 49-51
Robert Hertanger, 58
Robert Poyntz, 19, 71, 72
Robert Stillington, Bishop of Bath and Wells, 131
Robin of Redesdale rebellion, 42, 44, 143
Rome, 143, 145

Samuel Pepys, 124
Sandwich, Kent, 30, 86

Santiago de Compostela, Spain, 64, 122, 143, 144
Scotland, 67, 69, 70, 74, 89-90, 135, 136
Second Battle of St Albans, 46, 56
Shrewsbury, 132
Siege of Orleans, 27
Sixtus IV, 145
Smithfield, 15, 40, 93, 94, 96, 97, 98, 99
Smithfield tournament, 94-98
Socrates, 121, 122
South Gate, Bishop's Lynn, 58
Southampton, 79
St Benet's Abbey, Norfolk, 60, 170
St Mary Overy, Southwark, 30
Stony Stratford, Northamptonshire, 152, 153, 154, 155, 156, 159, 162

The Arrivall, 82, 86
The Chronicles of the White Rose of York, 53, 109
The Great Chronicle, 56
The Hague, 105, 106,
Thomas of Lancaster, 166
Thomas Chaucer, 65-66, 68
Thomas Clarell, 98
Thomas Grey, Marquess of Dorset, 15, 38, 39-40, 51, 52, 54, 88, 100, 131, 139, 141, 151, 152, 154, 159-160, 167, 171
Thomas Hansard, 100
Thomas Herbert, 53, 71
Thomas Malory, 93, 125-126
Thomas More, 16, 153, 154, 158, 161, 162, 170
Thomas Neville, Bastard of Fauconberg, 16, 80, 84-85, 86, 87
Thomas Smythe, 118
Thomas Vaughan, 108, 109, 129-130, 133, 139, 140, 152, 154, 157, 158, 160-162, 165, 166, 168
Thomas Wake, 46-47
Thomas, Lord Scales, 27, 35, 55, 60, 62
Thomas, Lord Dacre of the South, 51, 130
Tower of London, 29, 33, 85-86, 91
Trinity Guildhall, Bishop's Lynn, 58

Ulrich von Liechtenstein, 95

Venice, 33, 145
Virgin Mary, 43, 50, 142, 143, 144, 146, 164

Wakefield, 49, 52
Walsingham, Norfolk, 43, 143, 144, 179
Walter Devereaux, Lord Ferrers, 53

Wardour Castle, 78-79
Warkworth, Northumberland, 74
Warkworth's Chronicle, 74-6
Warwick Castle, 46
Westminster Abbey, 109, 120, 122, 129, 133, 165
Westminster, 15, 100, 103, 108, 109, 112, 114, 116, 120, 122, 127, 129, 130, 131, 133, 136, 145, 165
Wigmore Castle, 132
William Allington, Speaker of the Commons, 109
William Conyers of Marske, 42, 43
William de la Pole, Earl of Suffolk, 28
William Herbert, Earl of Pembroke, 44, 53, 54, 71
William Marshal, 96
William Neville, Earl of Kent, 75
William Shakespeare, 162, 172
William, Lord Hastings, 17, 38, 39, 44, 46, 51, 53, 54, 81, 82, 83, 87, 99, 105, 109, 141, 149, 150-151, 152, 167
Windsor, 63, 109, 151
Witchcraft, 46-48
Worcester, 132
Wynkyn de Worde, 128